Interfaith Afterlives of Jesus

Westar Studies

The Westar Studies series offers distinctive scholarly publications on topics related to the field of Religious Studies. The studies seek to be multi-dimensional both in terms of the subject matter addressed and the perspective of the author. Westar Studies are not related to Westar seminars but offer scholars a deliberate space of free inquiry to engage both scholarly peers and the public.

Interfaith Afterlives of Jesus

Jesus in Global Perspective 2

GREGORY C. JENKS

EDITOR

Introduction by Arthur J. Dewey

CASCADE *Books* · Eugene, Oregon

INTERFAITH AFTERLIVES OF JESUS
Jesus in Global Perspective 2

Westar Studies

Cascade Books
An Imprint of Wipf and Stock Publishers
199 W. 8th Ave., Suite 3
Eugene, OR 97401

www.wipfandstock.com

PAPERBACK ISBN: 978-1-6667-5246-5
HARDCOVER ISBN: 978-1-6667-5247-2
EBOOK ISBN: 978-1-6667-5248-9

Cataloguing-in-Publication data:

Names: Jenks, Gregory C., editor.

Title: Interfaith afterlives of Jesus : Jesus in global perspective 2 / edited by Gregory C. Jenks.

Description: Eugene, OR: Cascade Books, 2023. | Westar Studies. | Includes bibliographical references.

Identifiers: ISBN 978-1-6667-5246-5 (paperback). | ISBN 978-1-6667-5247-2 (hardcover). | ISBN 978-1-6667-5248-9 (ebook).

Subjects: LCSH: Jesus Christ—Influence. | Jesus Christ—Islamic interpretations. | Jews—Conversion to Christianity. | Jesus Christ—Jewishness. | Jesus Christ—Oriental interpretations. | Jesus Christ—Mormon interpretations. | Naturalism—Religious aspects.

Classification: BT83.85 I59 2023 (print). | BT83.85 (ebook).

04/07/23

Unless otherwise indicated, all Scripture quotations are from the New Revised Standard Version Bible, copyright © 1989 National Council of the Churches of Christ in the United States of America. Used by permission. All rights reserved worldwide.

Robert M. Price, "Contextualization as Incarnation" first appeared in *Journal of Unification Studies* 1 (1997) 43–54. It is published here with their permission.

The poem "Bethlehem 1970" by Richard E. Sherwin was originally published in *The Jerusalem Post* (December 24, 1970) and is used here with their permission.

Jay Harold Ellens
1932–2018

John Tracy Greene
1944–2021

Richard A. Freund
1955–2022

Colleagues, mentors, friends

Contents

Preface to *Afterlives of Jesus* | ix
 —GREGORY C. JENKS

Contributors | xv

Introduction | 1
 —ARTHUR J. DEWEY

1 Contextualization as Incarnation | 11
 —ROBERT M. PRICE

2 Jesus Christ in the Holy Qur'an and the Prophetic
 Traditions | 25
 —MUSTAFA ABU SWAY

3 Writing the Afterlives: From Jesus to the Vilna Gaon | 52
 —RICHARD A. FREUND †

4 The "Disappeared" Jesus and the Emancipation of European
 Jewry | 68
 —LORRAINE J. PARKINSON

5 Jesus and Contemporary Jewish Identity | 79
 —RICHARD E. SHERWIN

6 Jesus as a Yogi in Hinduism | 109
 —VISHAL SHARMA

7 Ruist (Confucian) Receptions of Jesus in Late Imperial
 China | 124
 —RYAN PINO & BIN SONG

8   The Christology of Joseph Smith | 140
    —A. KEITH THOMPSON

9   Engaging Jesus in Secular Australia | 158
    —DAVID MERRITT

10 Jesus and the Transforming Influence of Friendship | 174
    —JOHN H. W. SMITH

11 In Celebration of a "Wild" Faith: Jesus in the Australian
    Landscape | 189
    —REX A. E. HUNT

Preface to *Afterlives of Jesus*

Gregory C. Jenks

Jesus of Nazareth has been a focus for immense reflection, scholarship and spirituality over the twenty centuries which have passed since his death in Jerusalem during the administration of the Roman Prefect of Judaea, Pontius Pilate. While Christianity is in decline, interest in Jesus shows no sign of abating. Across time and around the world even today, there is a rich and diverse repertoire of theological writings, devotional works, liturgies, art of various kinds, historical research, and charitable projects which constitute the "afterlives" of Jesus.

Contrary to the confidence expressed in the Epistle to the Hebrews—"Jesus Christ is the same yesterday, today, and forever" (Heb 13:8)—there is immense diversity and variation in the ways that Jesus has been understood in the past, is understood currently, and will be understood in the future.. In his classic 1985 study,[1] Jaroslav Pelikan traced some of the variations through which Jesus has been imagined and reimagined by Christians during almost two thousand years. Even within the constraints of *Christian* reinterpretations of Jesus, Pelikan found considerable diversity as the character of Jesus was appropriated for the cultural needs of successive periods of western history. As Keith Harper observed in a very positive review of the work when it was reissued in a special edition for its twenty-fifth anniversary in 1999, Pelikan offered an "eclectic and diversified" set of historical, theological and cultural interpretations of Jesus, but "addressed

1. Pelikan, *Jesus through the Centuries.*

this difficulty by choosing 'The Beautiful, The True and The Good,' as a framework to keep his differing, often conflicting, images of Christ from becoming too divergent."[2]

However, it was only in his final chapter that Pelikan turned to consider the significance of Jesus beyond Christianity. That chapter was titled "The Man Who Belongs to the World."[3] Despite the promise of that title, Pelikan did not consider how Jesus has been appropriated by people of various faiths or even no faith. Instead, he crafted his final chapter around the theme of Christian missionary efforts during the eighteenth and nineteenth centuries, while noting the significant cultural reassignment of Jesus which was taking place, "although Jesus himself had lived in the Near East, it was as a religion of Europe that his message came to the nations of the world and the islands of the sea—a religion of Europe both in the sense of a religion *from* Europe and, often, a religion *about* Europe as well."[4]

Only after several pages describing this missionary effort, and its precursors in the very different missions of Cyril and Methodius to the Slavs and Augustine to the British, does Pelikan address the attempts by Christian missionaries to present their Jesus in local cultural terms. Even so, we are a long way from people of other cultures and other faiths finding something about Jesus which they wished to claim for themselves on their own terms. All the same, in his final paragraph, Pelikan dares to imagine a Jesus who is more diverse than the manifold Christian interpretations of him over the centuries:

> By a curious blend of these currents of religious faith and scholarship with the no less powerful influences of skepticism and religious relativism, the universality-with-particularity of Jesus has thus become an issue not only for Christians in the twentieth century, but for humanity. The later chapters of this book show that as respect for the organized church has declined, reverence for Jesus has grown. For the unity and variety of the portraits of "Jesus through the centuries" has demonstrated that there is more in him than is dreamt of in the philosophy and Christology of the theologians. Within the church, but also beyond its walls, his person and message are, in the phrase of Augustine, a "beauty ever ancient, ever new," and now he belongs to the world.[5]

2. Harper, "Review."

3. Pelikan, *Jesus through the Centuries*, 220–33.

4. Pelikan, *Jesus through the Centuries*, 221–22.

5. Pelikan, *Jesus through the Centuries*, 232–33.

GLOBAL PERSPECTIVES ON JESUS

Even within the first three centuries of the Common Era (from Jesus to Constantine, from Nazareth to Nicaea) we see both a proliferation of understandings and immense variation in the assessments of Jesus. We are fortunate to have two recent and comprehensive studies that trace the patterns of reception (and criticism) during the first three hundred years after Jesus.[6]

Reception history studies have taught us to look beyond the historical origins of a text or a figure, and to delve more deeply than simply tracing the ideas captured in a particular text (whether canonical or otherwise).[7] To understand an idea more deeply and to appreciate its significance over time we need to pay attention to the history of its reception: what is retained, what is rejected, how is it reshaped, what new meanings have been attached to the idea?

While the New Testament Gospels and the creeds of the church are part of the early reception history process, they do not define the meaning of Jesus, nor do they exclude the generation of further afterlives as people in different contexts reflect on the significance of Jesus *for them*. While religious communities can (and do) define orthodoxy and set the limits of belief and practice for their members, this does not have any remit beyond their own spiritual jurisdiction. In particular, as the churches are now discovering, official Christianity no longer has exclusive intellectual property rights to the "Jesus brand."

This has actually been an issue for leaders in the various Jesus movements since at least the first century, as has been documented in the recent groundbreaking report from the Westar Institute.[8] We see the sharpness of this issue in Paul's Letter to the Galatians (one of his earliest surviving letters), where he asserts his own apostolic authority and denounces anyone promoting a different gospel from his own interpretation of Jesus.

> I am astonished that you are so quickly deserting the one who called you in the grace of Christ and are turning to a different gospel—not that there is another gospel, but there are some who are confusing you and want to pervert the gospel of Christ. But even if we or an angel from heaven should proclaim to you a gospel

6. Keith et al., eds., *Reception of Jesus*; and Vearncombe et al., *After Jesus*.

7. Other recent "afterlives" studies include Morse, *Encountering Eve's Afterlives*; and Levine and Brettler, *Bible with and without Jesus*.

8. Vearncombe et al., *After Jesus*.

contrary to what we proclaimed to you, let that one be accursed!
As we have said before, so now I repeat, if anyone proclaims to you
a gospel contrary to what you received, let that one be accursed!
(Gal 1:6–9)

A similar dynamic is seen the Johannine Epistles where the freshly
minted label "antichrist" is attached not only to the anticipated eschato-
logical opponent of Jesus but also to dissident church members who refuse
the spiritual authority of the Elder. There are also traces of these tensions
within the Gospel traditions, particularly the Gospel of John.

This loss of control over the "Jesus brand" may be an inconvenient
truth for many Christian leaders, but it also part of the explanation for the
many different afterlives of Jesus that are to be found in the community today. Where such deviant views might have been denounced in the past, or
suppressed with coercive force when the church has exercised the authority to do so, there are very few places in the world today where someone
can suffer real-world negative consequences for holding views about Jesus
which differ from those of their Christian leaders. Sadly, in some jurisdic-
tions religious communities can still persecute people on the basis of their
beliefs by denying them education, employment and health care.

AFTERLIVES OF JESUS

This three-volume set explores several of the historical and contemporary
afterlives of Jesus. *Afterlife* in this context is not a synonym for "life after
death." This is not a study of resurrection or a theological exploration of
what kind of post-death existence might be enjoyed by Jesus of Nazareth or
any other human being. Rather, we are exploring the continuing impact of
Jesus across time, distance and culture, including within different religious
traditions.

As this series will demonstrate, the afterlives of Jesus have taken many
forms and not all of them are healthy. Some have clearly been toxic, although the criteria for determining in real time which versions of Jesus
are deviant mutations and which are simply original developments are not
always obvious. Some people will appeal to the historical Jesus as a bench-
mark for validating these afterlives, but that is problematic on so many
levels. Others will appeal to religious authority to determine the matter,
but the status of such determinations already begs so many questions that
many people will not find that a plausible solution to the dilemma. While

the Aryan Jesus is now easily recognized as a toxic mutation rather than an authentic afterlife, many other examples are contested or ambivalent. For myself, the criteria are not strictly historical or doctrinal, but more concerned with outcomes; for the participants, for the wider society, and for the planet. I regard as toxic deviants any afterlives of Jesus which exploit vulnerable persons, entrench injustice or threaten the long-term wellbeing of the ecosystem, regardless of their historical or religious pedigree.

The current global context provides some particular lenses through which to consider the historical and emerging afterlives of Jesus. These include the collapse of liberal social democracy as the preferred social model in many countries, the concurrent resurgence of authoritarian societies and power structures, the impact of pervasive social technologies, a retreat from the myth of perpetual progress, the reality of climate change, and the possible extinction of humanity within the next seven generations. When taking these considerations into account, we may well wonder what significance Jesus may have for our grandchildren and their grandchildren. Several of the essays in this volume will address such questions, while others will explore what the sage from Nazareth has meant to various people in earlier times.

The essays in these three volumes have been contributed by a diverse set of people. Most of us have never met each other, and several of the contributors are people I have never met in person. For me that makes the opportunity to collaborate in this way and on this topic all the more rewarding. Many of the contributors are scholars with formal qualifications in some academic field or another, while others are religious practitioners who contribute from their expert knowledge of their own tradition and of the significance of Jesus within their own cultural and religious communities. Many of the contributors are faculty from the School of Theology at Charles Sturt University in Australia. Several are Fellows of the Westar Institute. I am grateful to each of them for the gift they have brought to this gathering of people who appreciate the afterlives of Jesus in all their diversity and complexity.

The global COVID-19 pandemic has impacted this project and delayed its completion. A number of potential contributors found their work was either delayed or derailed by the pandemic. I am especially sad to note that Michael Kelly died after a long struggle with illness before he was able to complete his chapter. His legacy continues as some contributors became involved in the project on his recommendation. His wit and wisdom is greatly missed, and his courage is immensely admired.

I wish to record my special thanks to Barry Davis and Allie Leitzel, who volunteered to proofread a large number of essays by contributors from outside North America, myself included. They gently guided us into forms of expression that would communicate more effectively in that context. They have also been a great source of encouragement and support.

This collection of essays is dedicated to the memory of J. Harold Ellens, John T. Greene, and Richard Freund, each of whom was a mentor for me in my own research and publishing. I know they were also valued colleagues and mentors for several other contributors to this set of essays, and in a way the book serves as yet another literary afterlife for each of them. They were great souls and generous friends. We treasure our memories of them all.

Grafton, Australia
June 30, 2021

BIBLIOGRAPHY

Harper, Keith. Review of *Jesus through the Centuries: His Place in the History of Culture*. H-Net Reviews in the Humanities & Social Sciences. Published on H-AmRel in March 2000. http://www.h-net.org/reviews/showpdf.php?id=3925/.

Keith, Chris et al., eds. *The Reception of Jesus in the First Three Centuries*. 3 vols. London: T. & T. Clark, 2020.

Levine, Amy-Jill, and Marc Zvi Brettler. *The Bible With and Without Jesus: How Jews and Christians Read the Same Stories Differently*. San Francisco: HarperOne, 2020.

Morse, Holly. *Encountering Eve's Afterlives: A New Reception Critical Approach to Genesis 2–4*. Oxford Theology and Religion Monographs. Oxford: Oxford University Press, 2020.

Pelikan, Jaroslav. *Jesus through the Centuries: His Place in the History of Culture*. New Haven: Yale University Press, 1985.

Vearncombe, Erin K., et al. *After Jesus before Christianity: A Historical Exploration of the First Two Centuries of Jesus Movements*. San Francisco: HarperOne, 2021.

Contributors

Mustafa Abu Sway is Professor of Philosophy and Islamic Studies at Al-Quds University, Jerusalem.

Arthur J. Dewey is Professor of Theology at Xavier University in Cincinnati, Ohio.

Richard A. Freund was the late Bertram and Gladys Aaron Professor of Jewish Studies at Christopher Newport University, Newport News, Virginia.

Rex A. E. Hunt is a religious naturalist, progressive liturgist, and social ecologist who lives on the Central Coast in New South Wales, Australia.

David Merritt is a retired minister of the Uniting Church in Australia and former director of Christian Education for the Uniting Church in Australia.

Lorraine J. Parkinson is an author and teacher in the field of Christian-Jewish relations, in Brisbane, Australia.

Robert M. Price is editor of the *Journal of Higher Criticism*, host of *The Bible Geek* podcast, and the author of numerous books and articles.

Ryan Pino is a PhD student at Harvard University in comparative theology, theology of religions, and the historical development of Confucian-Christian dialogue.

Vishal Sharma is a former Hindu monk now based at Grafton, on the north coast of New South Wales, Australia.

Richad E. Sherwin is emeritus professor of Western Literature at Bar Ilan University in Israel.

John H. W. Smith is a retired Uniting Church in Australia minister and a founding member of the Progressive Christian Network of Victoria.

Bin Song is assistant professor of philosophy and religion, Washington College, Chestertown, Maryland.

A. Keith Thompson is professor of law in the School of Law (Sydney campus), at Notre Dame University Australia.

Introduction

Arthur J. Dewey

Each of the following essays is a journey to the outback. The authors invite readers to accompany them on a variety of treks into the interior. They ask readers to leave behind the traditional take on Jesus and to explore with them the possibilities of seeing Jesus in a variety of afterlives.

It takes courage to reimagine what many take for granted. This is the case, not only in considering the Galilean sage, but perhaps more so when engaging non-Christian traditions. Non-Christian traditions have been invariably read according to Christian assumptions. But what would happen if one took a non-Christian tradition on its own terms while introducing the question of the relevance of Jesus?

Readers will see that each of these essays is quite unique. The ways in which Jesus surfaces in these conversations will be provocative and surprising.

But have we not realized by now that Jesus is no longer under ecclesial control or embalmed in doctrinal winding sheets? Have we not realized that Jesus has leaked out and belongs to the earth?

Our initial essay by Robert Price places the question of contextualization of the gospel within the historical orbit of the development of early Christianity. He endeavors to move beyond the usual conservative/liberal standoff. One side claims that the essence of major doctrines and mythemes must be maintained despite the use of new analogies lest revelation lose itself into some hybrid syncretism, while the other side argues that the gospel must be redrawn by the needs and questions of each age. Barth versus Tillich plays out again and again. How can one responsibly engage with new and developing communities? Is it always the dilemma between heretical mutation or orthodox suffocation?

Price proposes a creative understanding of incarnation to move beyond this impasse. He takes what many would regard as a fundamental concept that remains essentially unchanged and explores what happens when it is employed in new situations. Incarnation for Price is not a one-time event but an ongoing development. Beginning with the insights of von Allmen's picture of the theological diversity, evolution, and adaptation of early Christianity, Price adds the sketch of Schmithal's gnostic apostles, where each apostle bears not the tidings of the recently incarnated savior but the inner dwelling of the Christ spirit. These missionaries bring the insight that every gnostic might and does incarnate Christ. The leaders who deliver this electric message are not antichrists but vicars or icons, that point beyond themselves to true life. In effect, if incarnation is not embodied in a new framework, remaining a stranger to the distinctions of a culture, then it falls short and unrealized in a kind of docetism. For Price incarnation occurs when the Logos becomes realized anew in developing cultural contexts. This means that recent and surprising versions of Christian communities may be new and genuine instances of incarnation.

In "Jesus in the Holy Qur'an and the Prophetic Traditions" Mustafa Abu Sway presents the distinctive Muslim take on Jesus. To appreciate this different interpretation of Jesus may well be an opening for an ecumenical breakthrough among the Abrahamic peoples. Recognizing that Jesus is part of the larger prophetic tradition beginning with Abraham could be seen as a rehearsal of the ancient spirit of the *convivencia* of Umayyad Spain, as these Abrahamic traditions celebrate together the right to be different within this threefold conversation. Abu Sway offers what he terms "an Islamic theology of soft-otherness" where believers from each faith are never totally different from each other.

Abu Sway further argues that the Muslim apprehension of Jesus may well present theological and historical positions that differ both from what would be later christological formulations in the developing Christian tradition and from the rabbinical understanding regarding Jesus. In the Qur'an Jesus' existence testifies to the One God, not to a Trinitarian configuration. Jesus is bound with Muhammad in the brotherhood of the prophets, born of Mary through the omnipotence of Allah, a Messiah, and Messenger of

Allah. His miraculous birth, the signs and wonders he performed, the *Injil* (gospel) he delivered, do not render Jesus more than a mortal with limited knowledge, a servant who recognizes the Omniscient One. Such an understanding of Jesus strikingly resembles the argument of Hans Küng, who contended that the original statements about Father, Son, and Spirit differed from the later dogmatic formulations. Jesus being "chosen and authorized by God" did not mean that he was seen as a divine person. Does the Qur'an witness to that earlier layer of understanding Jesus?

We find another instance of an early differing interpretation regarding the death of Jesus. In the Qur'an Jesus was not crucified. While it appeared to unbelievers that Jesus underwent crucifixion, Allah actually raised him to Himself. Both the Acts of John and the Gospel of Peter can be cited as evidence of such positions. Even the second coming of Jesus can be understood within a Muslim framework. A variety of traditions suggest that Jesus will have a vital role in the final times.

Richard A. Freund places the theme of the "afterlife of Jesus" within a larger ongoing historical movement, as he explores the afterlives of the teachings of some of the greatest sages of the rabbinic tradition. He finds that the afterlife of rabbinic teachings entails a multigenerational process of oral performance, study, reflection, writing, editing, and publishing.

The earliest stage of the tradition—the oral level—is awash in multiple oral performances and variations, as flexibility and attention to different audiences are part and parcel of oral performance. But complications abound when the oral traditions are put into writing. Using the example of Socrates, Freund points out that each of the written traditions (Plato, Xenophon, and Aristophanes) cannot be read critically without recognizing the assumptions and limits of each writer. A synoptic reading of these writings leads one to realize that the Socrates we know today is a composite figure. To get to the historical Socrates may well be an almost impossible task. What is easier to see is that a well-known individual's sayings and ideas have been problematically handed down through the lenses of his students.

Freund then contends that the original oral material from Jesus suffers a similar fate. Recent critical scholarship has shown that the Gospels are not verbatim accounts; rather, each reflects the concerns and biases of the writer and community. What we can hope to find regarding the historical Jesus may be at best a gist of his teaching, detected after strenuous analysis.

Freund then goes further to see that the ever-growing rabbinic tradition needs to be understood along these dialectical and developmental lines. He carefully notes that the pedagogical enterprise of the Jewish oral tradition, even when set in writing, is still noticeable through an attentive reading of the text. In fact, the written rabbinic texts amalgamate the variety of earlier voices to urge the reader to see the possibilities of a developing tradition. The growing talmudic material fosters this approach. Freund then provides more modern examples by investigating the afterlives of four rabbis (Isaac Luria, Hayim Vital, Israel Ben Eliezer, and Gaon of Vilna) and their students. The oral/written dialectic becomes increasingly complicated due to the emergence of the printing press. Luria's lecture notes, the students' notes of Hayim, and the stories and perhaps a letter of Baal Shem Tov, are published upon the deaths of the esteemed rabbis. Many of the unpublished writings of Gaon of Vilna were in print shortly after his death. The afterlife influence and normative effect of each of these teachers was compounded and increased as the printed editions came out.

Lorraine J. Parkinson uses the main character of Aharon Appelfeld's 1998 novel *The Conversion* as a focal point for her contention that the Jesus who disappeared from Christianity and surfaced briefly in emergence of the Enlightenment, Jesus the Jew, whose works and message transcended tribal bounds, a witness for justice, compassion, and peacemaking, may well be achieving a new afterlife in this tumultuous present. The character Karl Hübner represents many early twentieth-century Jews who recognized that social position, economic mobility, and respectability had a price. Despite the original dream of the Enlightenment envisioning a fundamental human equality, society demanded the conversion of Jews. Yet even this did not prevent the residual anti-Semitism and the chilling indications of the coming Holocaust.

Hubner eventually sees through the encircling lies, finds happiness with a woman who brings back remembrance of his Jewish past, and resigns his longed-for position to seek integrity in the mountains of his ancestors. He and Gloria, refusing to forget their Jewishness, decide to stay where they are, only to be engulfed in the flames of hatred. Parkinson points out that this story carries a most uncomfortable truth: conversion of the Jews is a form of extinction. Indeed, the church has historically anticipated the Holocaust by the shameful use of the sacrament of baptism.

It is time to return to the promising note of the Enlightenment, to call people to stand on their own two feet and take Jesus the Jew on his own terms. The Holocaust has given people the opportunity to see through the lingering anti-Semitism of church and society and, at the same time, to see that Jesus no longer belongs to the churches. Now critical scholarship and the calls for social justice can give Jesus a most significant afterlife. Jesus in the twenty-first century has leaked out beyond the dogmatism and control of the churches. It is time to recognize Jesus as a key to recognizing the oneness of humanity, connected through universal principles of justice, peace, equality, and compassion. The short-lived dream of the Enlightenment returns in the reappearance of Jesus of Nazareth, a beacon for the planet.

In "the troublesome legacy of Jesus for contemporary Jews," the poet Richard E. Sherwin poignantly delivers a meditation concentrated on seventeen of his poems. He has found that, while for many of his Israeli contemporaries Jesus has no afterlife, it is hardly the same for him, whose complicated, diasporic life cannot deny how Jesus has affected his own search for meaning.

Sherwin quite rightly underscores how Christianity and Western culture have attempted to bleach Jesus of his Jewishness. But what the *Sho'ah* has laid bare is that Jesus has been "pulled down from churches and shipped . . . to the gas, the furnaces." In fact, Jesus has been burnt out of Christian theology and can be found "as a jew . . . just a man." It is this existential recognition of Jesus as a Jewish eccentric, helping the helpless, feeding the poor, that haunts the poems of Sherwin. Jesus the Jew allows Sherwin to touch and maintain the deep veins of his Jewish tradition, despite the incongruities of his diasporic life and cultural mélange.

This focus on Jesus provides Sherwin with a touchstone by which he can detect the pretensions and bankruptcy of Christian traditions. Without being a scholar searching for the historical Jesus, Sherwin touches the third rail of critical scholarship. He unmasks the "fake news" of the churches, while revealing how that Nazarene speaks to his own eccentric trek into the interior. Each poem startles the reader with expressions of "freedom out of chaos."

Vishal Sharma explores an afterlife of Jesus that is not as well-known in the West. "Jesus as a Yogi in Hinduism" relates how the Yogi-saint Paramahansa Yogananda's life's work entailed the demonstration that the teachings of Jesus can be integrated within Hindu belief and practice. Yogananda's mission was reverse of the usual Western missionary direction. Instead of bringing Christ to India, Yogananda taught the spiritual potential of Christ consciousness to those uninitiated in the West. In his practice and writings Yogananda offered to reach what Jesus spoke as the kingdom of God by disclosing an underlying unity of the world's great religions and universal methods for attaining the direct personal experience of God.

Sharma details how Yogananda got inside the sayings of Jesus. In his *Second Coming* Yogananda concentrated not on a literal interpretation but on the realization of "Christ consciousness" that could be achieved by everyone through meditation. Indeed, this path to God through meditation can also be found in Sufism, the Kabbalah, Zen Buddhism, and contemplative Christianity. Yogananda can read the various gospels in nonexclusive ways. By moving beyond the shell of the tradition, he opens texts for intuitive breakthroughs. Sharma even includes visionary conversations Yogananda had with Jesus, who gave him the task of bringing this wisdom to the West.

Sharma points out that within the spiritual Hindu traditions Jesus is easily understood as a true yogi of extraordinary powers. Yoga can bring to the communities of the West the ability of enlightenment, of incarnating the Christ consciousness. Indeed, precisely at this time when the planet is roiled in wars, famine, and the assaults of climate change, such a vision of this afterlife of Jesus may well prove to be an essential spiritual asset for peoples around the globe.

The article by Ryan Pino and Bin Song brings the question of the afterlife of Jesus into relatively unchartered territory. "Ruist (Confucian) receptions of Jesus in Late Imperial China" goes beyond the usual historical scholarship regarding the various Christian missions into China. Little has been considered about the Ruist reception of Christianity. By concentrating so much on the Christian foreground, historians have neglected the Ruist perspective. As a result, significant historical events, intellectual trends and socioeconomic realities of the broader Chinese context have gone unnoticed.

Pino and Song offer their article as an early attempt at righting the historical record. They do not see their work as the final word but a spur to deeper and more articulated historical investigation. After a quick survey of the various Ruist receptions of Jesus in the history of the Ru-Christian encounter, they focus their discussion on the late imperial period (from the seventeenth to the twentieth century), noting that they are scratching the surface in describing the ways that Ruist reception of Jesus occurred.

What is crucial in their observations is that one needs to see how the Ruist response ranged widely from perplexity (over such Christian notions as incarnation and trinity) to a sense of incongruity (how could a sage be executed as a criminal?). Others thought Jesus' teaching to be shallow, his miracles suspect magical performances. Confucian skepticism, cosmology, concubinage, and ethnocentrism became points of contention. Indeed, the *foreignness* of Jesus proved a major stumbling block.

Nevertheless, the story does not end there. Some Ru scholars who engaged Matteo Ricci were encouraged to reread Ru classics and to take notions from their tradition (sagehood, an impersonal understanding of heaven [*Tian*], and an idea of the Lord on High [*Shangdi*]) in order to come to some understanding of Jesus. Such Ruist thinkers resisted an exclusivist form of orthodoxy and attempted to harmonize diverse teachings such as Buddhism, Daoism, and Christianity. In very creative ways some Ruist thinkers revised their sense of their tradition to incorporate Jesus within their intellectual lineage.

The introduction of Protestant missionaries in the nineteenth century complicated the Ruist response. Some of these missionaries built upon Ricci's foundation and continued to dialogue with Ruism. However, most converts did not come from the literati. By focusing on this last point Western writers unfortunately have overlooked the continued response by Ruist thinkers. In fact, several Chinese sources reveal the ongoing Ruist-Christian engagement. Further, in the twilight of the imperial period, a new twist was added. Ruist reformer Kang Youwei used Christian notions of monotheism and a religious founder to reimagine a national reform movement within China. Kongzi for the Chinese now took on the status of Jesus in Christianity. There also emerged during this last period, as the empire was collapsing and Western powers were intruding, a wholesale replacement of Ruism by an exclusive Christianity. In this albeit brief resumé Pino and Song provide a stunning sampling of how Ruist thinkers cunningly composed various afterlives of Jesus.

For many people Mormonism appears at best a religious oddity. A. Keith Thompson presents, in contrast, a provocative exploration of Joseph Smith's Christology. Through the prism of Stephen Webb's interpretation of Joseph Smith's theology, Thompson takes seriously foundational insights of Smith to lay out radical entailments of a very different afterlife of Jesus.

Thompson challenges readers to think outside of "established theological boxes" in reconceptualizing the nature of God and matter. He then notes that, while Smith's thinking reflects some earlier theological reflection (such as by Origen), the theological paradigms of following Nicaea have stifled that theological vision. Thompson concludes his article by exploring what happens theologically when Smith's insight into the nature of matter and light receives critical focus.

As Thompson revisits salient portions of Smith's writings, he underscores the following: what the divine power consists in, that the possibility of human transformation is more than a mere metaphor, and that the notion of preexistence does not end with the Christ, that "the light of the world" has deep metaphysical consequences.

Perhaps most exciting is Thompson's reflection on "All spirit is matter." This allowed Smith to reimagine not simply the preexistence of Jesus, but much more: the postmortem appearances of Jesus, the nature of the Pauline "heavenly body," even the notion of forming the world from a material substance not unlike the divine nature. Such thinking raises the very question of what "matter" is. In our post-Einsteinian, quantum universe we are acquainted with the equation of matter and energy, and with how things are hardly in stasis. Thompson contends that Smith's conception of matter is more than meets the eye; it has infinite folds and unbounded depths, continuing to evolve to the form of Christ.

David Merritt's "Engaging Jesus in Secular Australia: Two Educational Approaches" comes out of the reality of religious life in Australia. Merritt begins by noting what has been happening within Australia. As is the case in much of the Western world, there is a widespread lack of religious literacy in a society increasingly secular, while recent critical biblical scholarship has brought significant challenges to the traditional understandings of Jesus. Merritt asks whether a progressive religious educator can overcome such obstacles.

One approach to reaching contemporary audiences has been for the teacher to bridge the two-thousand-year detour by deconstructing the biblical text and then reconstructing the material in light of recent sociohistorical insights. However, such an approach fails to involve the very people the educator wants to reach. Disconnection inevitably occurs as the teachers walk students through what appears to be an endless list of things one needs to know. The existential search for something "directly relevant" in one's life, "something that helps me become a more spiritual person," cannot be overlooked. Is there a way critical biblical scholarship can become genuinely connected to contemporary life without losing either the needs of the audience or the insights of critical work?

Utilizing the findings of the scholars of the Jesus Seminar about the sayings of Jesus and taking seriously the current understanding of the role of the learner's present experience and motivation, Merritt demonstrates through two examples (a parable and an aphorism of the historical Jesus) a method that addresses both sides of the dilemma. First, it is crucial that the educator does the critical homework before engaging the students. By delving into the historical context and literary formats, the educator can begin to see the crucial issues of the text and how current concerns can be aligned. Then upon a reading of the text, the educator can ask questions that come from the experience of the audience that tie into the momentum of the text. The educator also asks basic questions of the text to help situate the conversation. This thoroughgoing engagement with Jesus' words and wisdom not only connects with present experience but can confront and reshape that experience. A surprising afterlife of Jesus is discovered in this genuine engagement.

John W. H. Smith transports the recent scholarly findings about the Galilean sage, Jesus of Nazareth, into the chaos of our present life. His review of the "world without friends" detailed in the devastating reports on Australian health, welfare, homelessness, personal violence, and racism appears to stagger any hope of response. Nevertheless, he finds promise for our culture, bankrupt of value, in exploring the possibilities of friendship and compassion in conversation with the recently investigated Jesus material.

Relying on the recent work of the Jesus Seminar—John Dominic Crossan, Marcus J. Borg, et al.—Smith reviews the words and actions of Jesus and the early communities and detects a Jesus who embodied a compassionate response to the reality of life. Jesus' fundamental vision of God's empire can be understood in the words of Crossan as a "companionship of empowerment." For when people are valued for who they are, living in community where friendship can thrive and sympathy can be expressed, where people discover that transformation occurs through sustained relationships, then they can begin to respond creatively to the shock and awe of our present life.

Indeed, Smith agrees with Karen Armstrong, who considers the deep ramifications of living compassionately. Essential to human relationships in fulfilling our humanity, compassionate living provides the path to justice and peace and the opportunity to discover the social power that underpins healing and harmony, nonviolence and solidarity. Just as Jesus and his early followers experimented with living compassionately, so too today people can courageously transform a desperate planet.

Our final essay delivers a vibrant vision. Rex A. E. Hunt urges readers to a radical sense of attention. His "In Celebration of a 'Wild' Faith: Jesus in the Australian Landscape" begins with the recognition that awe and wonder emerge when humans shift their attention away from themselves and fully engage nature in all its flavors and wildness. He contends that the natural world has the capacity to engender a response we usually call religious or spiritual. Moreover, we have not only lost touch with the vibrant depths of life, but even the ways we voice our wonder have been prefabricated in our outdated religious traditions.

This is especially so in Southern Hemisphere religious responses that have ignored the very landscape of Australians' lives. Both garden and wilderness have been neglected. Indeed, one can range from the amoeba to the galaxies, taking in the sweep of evolution and the great swatches of time and space, and leave this overwhelming experience at the church door. It is time, Hunt declares with Rabbi Heschel that we become "cantors of the universe." To do this entails renewed attention to nature, to the rocks and the wilderness, as we begin to acknowledge the awesome and the overwhelming. But we need to give voice to all of this—not simply in poetry, but in song and liturgy, in new ways of expressing what is right in front of us, by creating a rich tapestry of life's depths. In fact, such an approach allows us to reread the biblical tradition and recognize what is often overlooked in the words and vision of Jesus. We can begin to remember that the three peoples of the Book are desert-born. It is time to rediscover a garden in the outback, to realize how precious our life is together on this blue marble.

Hunt underscores the rich tones that come from that Galilean sage's fragment about the lilies and points out what often is overlooked. Jesus was referring to the lilies' beauty, to that unspoken something that breaks our hearts. But more, through his wit and wisdom Jesus delivered a challenge, daring us to reimagine the world by paying attention to what seems to be insignificant. Hunt asks, Could the afterlife of Jesus today be embodied in a vision and ethic of ecological care? Can our intense noticing become the beginning of devotion—not worshiping an otherworldly god but celebrating the depths of our unimaginable life?

I

Contextualization as Incarnation

Robert M. Price

I have long been fascinated with missiological and theological debates over "contextualization" or "indigenization" because they seemed especially likely to illuminate the long-obscure "black box" of Christian origins.[1] When theologians hold out for the right of Third World Christians to articulate their faith in their own experiential and conceptual terms,[2] they are at least implicitly acknowledging that the earliest Christianity had undergone much the same process. This is the secret subtext of the debate, and the reason for the surprising vehemence of the discussions.[3]

The various syncretistic movements born on the mission fields of Africa,[4] Latin America, and Asia—e.g., the Aladura churches of Africa—are unwitting pawns in a proxy war over volatile issues of demythologizing,

1. This chapter first appeared in *Journal of Unification Studies* 1 (1997) 43–54. It is published here with their permission.

2. Hogg, *Karma and Reincarnation*; Boyd, *India and the Latin Captivity*; Mbiti, *New Testament Eschatology*; Schreiter, *Constructing Local Theologies*.

3. Oosthuizen, *Post-Christianity in Africa*.

4. Oosthuizen and Hexham, eds., *Empirical Studies*; Haliburton, *Prophet Harris*; Martin, *Kimbangu*; Sundkler, *Bantu Prophets*; Jules-Rosette, *African Apostles*.

remythologizing, and propositional revelation. The amount of liberty to be accorded to the indigenous churches is in direct proportion to the freedom one believes the earliest churches exercised. This becomes clear in the unease provoked by Daniel von Allmen's article.[5]

This groundbreaking essay is precisely parallel to Ernst Käsemann's famous 1951 lecture, *Begrundet der neutestamentlische Kanon die Einheit der Kirche?*[6] Käsemann, requested by the World Council of Churches to conjure from the Aladdin's lamp of "biblical theology" a theological platform for ecumenical unity, found instead that it was the New Testament canon itself that was the root of the problem. It was the problem not the solution, the apple of discord rather than the olive branch, the sword not the ploughshare. For within its canonical boundaries could be found a genuine precedent to which any sectarian faction could and did appeal against its rivals. Käsemann painted a scenario in which the New Testament canon was not unlike the Jerusalem temple in the last days before the capitulation to Titus: a holy precinct occupied by warring messianic militias. No wonder the churches could not settle their differences by appealing to the New Testament! It was trying to put out the fire with gasoline!

In the same way, von Allmen looked through the wrong end of the telescope, using the tumultuous mutation of Christianity in the modern day as a lens through which to sharpen our focus on earliest Christianity.[7]

---

5. Von Allmen, "Birth of Theology."

6. Käsemann, "Canon of the New Testament."

7. John G. Gager, *Kingdom and Community* performs a similar maneuver, using the lens of recent studies of millenarian and revitalization movements to reexamine early Christianity. Holmberg (*Sociology and the New Testament*) and Jonathan Z. Smith ("Too Much Kingdom") seem to me to miss the important point when they object that Gager's comparative model is ultimately drawn from Christian-influenced cargo cults, ghost dances, and boxer rebellions, and that Gager thus winds up comparing Christianity to Christianity, not to a non-Christian "control group." So what? Gager might describe what he is doing a bit differently, but the validity of his experiment is by no means affected by this lack of clarity. To raise the question of Christian influence is merely to inject the confusion of the genetic fallacy. Christianity has taken many different social forms. Gager's is an attempt to compare the vestiges of our knowledge of early Christianity with the lineaments of a distinctive type of Christian movement with the goal of seeing how well the two match. A close match might indicate that in these revitalization sects the Christian DNA had bred true, that they are an atavistic throwback, as the birth of a man who looked rather apish might help corroborate our surmises about our anthropoid forbears. Daniel von Allmen's comparison of hypothesized ancient Christianity with modern Aladura Churches is similarly apt and similarly revealing. In fact, von Allmen's and Gager's studies would tend to strengthen each other.

Rudolf Bultmann had already—in agreement with *Religionsgeschich-tlicheschule* (history of religions school) scholars Wilhelm Bousset and Richard Reitzenstein—taken for granted the variegated, cosmopolitan syncretism of the Hellenistic world as the hothouse in which the gospel seed had sprouted into a luxuriant jungle of exotic hybrids combining the myths of Gnosticism, Jewish apocalyptic and the mystery cults. What von Allmen did was to show how the same process was repeating itself today as the gospel seed takes root in all manner of far-flung cultures with their inherited religious backgrounds.

If the earliest missionaries in New Testament times had contextual-ized the gospel, remythologized it in the fantastic trappings of their own cultures' myths, why complain if modern mission churches do the same thing, reinventing Christianity as the Hellenistic apostles did? In one bold stroke, von Allmen was both claiming the Christianity of the New Testament, with its evolving, creative character, as a precedent legitimiz-ing parallel indigenization today;[8] and implicitly invoking the principle of historical analogy to show that present-day tendencies to syncretism in the mission churches corroborate the *Religionsgeschichtlicheschule* picture of (syncretistic) Christian origins.

Conservative churchmen—shocked by syncretistic trends in the churches their missionaries spilled sanctified sweat and blood to estab-lish—find themselves in the position of any parent faced with the unpleas-ant reality that junior suddenly has his own opinions, and that they do not

---

8. Alfred Loisy pursued much the same program, e.g., in *Gospel and the Church*, his rebuttal to the liberal Protestant Adolf von Harnack. Harnack maintained that one ought to strip away the temporary, culturally relative "husk" of apocalyptic Judaism to find the abiding kernel of Jesus' message: the higher righteousness and the infinite value of the human soul. All the rest was dead wood, superfluous husk. Loisy, on the contrary, main-tained that what Harnack took for the kernel was instead a seed, something destined for growth and containing potent germs of future, very different things, including all the oak-like growth of the Catholic and Orthodox churches (whose liturgies and vestments Harnack had dismissed as superstitious mummery). Loisy had more of a traditional Catholic appreciation for the heritage of the church, but he was also much more radical, as a New Testament critic, than Harnack. His historical Jesus was much more like Albert Schweitzer's benign Charles Manson than Harnack's pious Leo Buscaglia. Loisy saw that to canonize theological evolution, instead of drawing some canonical line somewhere, about some particular set of nonnegotiable doctrines and stories, was to make possible Catholic modernism. One need not embrace the liberal biblicism of the modernist Prot-estants, the latest in a series of Protestant "back to the Bible" movements. One might instead freely admit that the truth is a growing organism and look forward to new devel-opments. Von Allmen is much like Loisy in this respect.

match his parents'. Instead, those opinions seem (to the parents) unduly influenced by the young person's peers and by current fads and fashions. What is the parent to do? To preempt the child's choices is to stymie his maturity. To force the child to do what the parent thinks is right—is wrong! Even if you win the particular battle, you lose the war. Either the child, frustrated, will rebel against the parents' authority altogether, or, worse yet, he will meekly acquiesce and never develop mature autonomy. So with the churches. They fear to see the younger, syncretistic movements compromising the faith once and for all delivered to the saints, but should they impose a stifling theological legalism? Which is more to be feared: heretical mutation or orthodox suffocation?

Perhaps parents are so defensive, so overprotective, because they are defending themselves, their own past, more than their children's future. That is, if they agree the younger generation of churches may be entitled to find their own way to a new expression of the gospel, even to a new gospel, will the implication not be that the older generation had made an idol of what had only temporary and local—not universal—significance? If we allow that Obeah metaphysics and ancestor worship may be a legitimate context for remythologizing the gospel, doesn't that mean that traditional Nicene Christianity was no more than historically relative—hence dispensable—clothing for the gospel, rather than the essence of the gospel itself? Richard J. Coleman puts it this way:

> The heart of the matter can be expressed, 'Does God reveal himself in concepts and propositions which are direct and objective?' Or from a different perspective the central issue might be worded, 'Can man formulate statements about God and his nature that are valid for everyone in all places and times?' The evangelical answers an emphatic 'yes' to both questions, the liberal an emphatic 'no.' Both questions are irretrievably bound to the issue of historical relativity.[9]

The issue is that of "propositional revelation." The traditional conservative and the liberal modernist are both saying that revelation comes in time-bound forms, but the liberal is willing to put major theological concepts into this category, while the conservative limits the time bound character only to the specific wording of the biblical text. Do the concepts (e.g., Jesus' Sonship) lie on this or that side of the great divide between the

---

9. Coleman, *Issues of Theological Warfare*, 87.

temporal and the eternal?[10] Are concepts the revelation, or only the time-bound forms of revelation? If the latter, we are saying revelation is non-propositional. Clark H. Pinnock, whom I would judge the only Evangelical theologian now worth reading, puts the matter clearly: "Are theological propositions merely mundane objectifying representations, ideas from within the rim of human genius, set forth in response to an ecstatic revelation experience?"[11] His answer is equally clear: "Revelation . . . is essentially propositional in nature,"[12] i.e., a revelation of normative, divinely provided "didactic thought models."[13]

Another way of putting the central issue in this debate over contextualization and what it implies about the relativism of Christianity per se is the difference between Paul Tillich and Karl Barth, on the left and right extremes of the neo-orthodox spectrum, respectively.[14] Tillich employed the "method of correlation" between gospel and culture, admitting that the blanks which the gospel must fill are redrawn by the needs and questions of every age. Barth, on the other hand, insisted that the questions of an unregenerate humanity are worthless and can only provide a Procrustean Bed to truncate the gospel, as liberalism had always done. No, Barth said, we cannot even see what the right questions are until the gospel force-feeds us the answers! Applied to the missionary issue of syncretism, this conservative position fears the gospel will be gambled away in any hybrid fusion with indigenous, alien mythemes. But from the Tillichian standpoint, where there cannot be said to be any revelation at all if no one receives it, like a tree falling in a forest with no one there to hear it, the gospel will become a dead fetish, a museum relic, unless it is indigenized, contextualized ever anew.

10. Ramm, "Continental Divide."

11. Pinnock, *Biblical Revelation*, 110.

12. Pinnock, *Biblical Revelation*, 66.

13. Pinnock, "Evangelical Theology," 24.

14. What makes Tillich theologically left-wing neo-orthodox rather than just plain liberal? First, his concern to interpret biblical mythology rather than stripping it off (siding with Bultmann against Harnack and Kant). Second, his agenda to "save the appearances" of the whole Christian creed instead of "jettisoning" (Bishop Pike) troublesome articles of faith completely, as Griffin (*Process Christology*, 12) admits he does with the resurrection, which winds up being pretty vestigial in his system. Third, his belief in an encounter with the Truth from outside the human situation, in contrast to "Christ of culture" liberals, who understand revelation simply to "re-present" the best views and insights of human nature and culture (e.g., Ogden, *Reality of God*; Tracy, *Blessed Rage*; and Buri, *Can We Still Speak?*).

The two alternatives might be compared to two images drawn from other religions.[15] If we insist that the major doctrines and mythemes (e.g., a transaction between God and Satan to redeem humanity, or a courtroom scene at the end of the world) must be maintained, at most only conveyed by new analogies (as in the missionary book *Peace Child*), then we are saying something very much like the Islamic claim that the Qur'an exists only in Arabic. If translated into any other language, even in the best translation possible, it no longer counts as the word of God. There is more than a mere analogy between linguistic translation and cross-cultural redescription.[16]

We may take two examples from the theological reconceptualization entailed in translating the Hebrew Tanakh into the Greek Septuagint. As Hans-Joachim Schoeps[17] shows, the Hebrew word *Torah* tempers the implication of "law" with that of "instruction." Viewing it as a sort of "instruction manual," Jews regard the Torah as a gift of grace, hardly as a burden, as anyone will readily understand who has faced the prospect of installing a new computer without benefit of a manual! One bemoans such "freedom from the law"! But then you find there is after all a set of instructions, but it becomes clear that they have been poorly rendered into your language by someone not adept in it! Even so, when the "instruction manual" of the Torah was translated into another language, the very word "Torah" suffered damage in the shipping! It emerged as the Greek *nomos*, which denoted something more like "law" in the sense of an inflexible and punitive traffic code. For Moses to present "the law" to the people of Israel would be like reading them the riot act! And that's pretty much what Luther thought Moses was doing!

Similarly, Heb 10:5–10 cites Ps 40:6–8 to expound the idea that the heavenly Christ assumed a body of flesh to offer it as a sacrifice. While such a notion of an incarnation of a god was quite familiar in the Hellenistic world, it represented a radical departure in terms of biblical theological categories. And the psalm quote abets the incarnational understanding only

15. I believe that in an attempted exercise in cross-cultural, multireligious theology, the form, the method, must reflect the content. That is, it will be inauthentic to proceed in a manner drawn deductively from Christian premises and then to impose the results on the data of diverse religious phenomena. Religious pluralism and inductivity must be woven into our method along the way. Thus, recognizing that the various religions have produced a whole range of answers to a whole range of problems that all of them face, we will be fools to keep our parochial blinders on till we reach the end of our deliberations, just as no scholar would begin his or her research into a major topic without first examining the research and thinking of others on the same topic.

16. I borrow the term from Kelsey, *Uses of Scripture*.

17. Schoeps, *Paul*, 29.

once it, too, has been reincarnated into a Greek form. For the original text was a simple declaration by a worshiper that he stands ready to heed the command of God that he report to the temple to bear witness to answered prayer. It is this which is prescribed for him in the sacred Torah scroll. But the Septuagint has changed the line "Ears thou hast dug for me," i.e., you have given me an attentive ear, into "a body thou hast prepared for me," an interesting suggestion of Apollinarian incarnationism (the Logos took on little more than a human body, not a complete human persona). The Hellenistic religious conceptuality is introduced and facilitated by means of the translation of the Hebrew text into the Greek language.

And this is what Islamic theologians fear. The Word of God may possibly be more a matter of concepts than of individual words, but the concepts are built from certain Arabic words, and they will not survive unscathed in the words of any other language. Buddhists have the same problem trying to identify what it is that is transmitted in the process of reincarnation. There is no *atman*, no unchangeable soul, and yet there is some continuity despite the changing of physical form. Is it the other four *skhandas* (aggregates) of the ego-self that pass on, the same deck of cards but reshuffled? How much change can occur before we are no longer talking about a constant object beneath the changes?

And this brings us to our opposite alternative for understanding theological contextualization. Rather than the Word of God staying put in its original language lest it mutate into something else, we might envision contextualization akin to the Buddhist analogy of soulless reincarnation as each candle lighting the next in the series. Such a "passing of the torch" would be replication of a kind, to be sure, but *what* kind?

The issue here is the same debated by Arians and Athanasians: would the newly recontextualized gospel be *homoousias* (of the same nature) with the original or only *homoiousias* (of like nature) with it? If the latter, Paul would be rather upset: "not that there is another gospel, but there are some who . . . want to pervert the gospel of Christ. But even if we or an angel from heaven should proclaim to you a gospel contrary to what we proclaimed to you, let that one be accursed!" (Gal 1:7–8).

James D. G. Dunn, in his *Unity and Diversity in the New Testament*, deals with much the same issues that are central to Daniel von Allmen's essay, namely, the degree to which the contextualizing of the gospel already in the New Testament represents several layers of substantial reformulation. Dunn asks if it is possible to distill a core of essential gospel behind the variety of forms it has taken in the New Testament documents. The results are meager: all the New Testament writers presuppose that salvation has something to do with Jesus, the man who died but was exalted.

The implication is strangely like, yet also unlike, that arrived at by Harnack. Is there a basic gospel kernel which can be isolated from the husk? It depends whether this analogy is meant to be closer to the analogy of a pearl inside an oyster or to the DNA in a cell. (Here again, please note, the concept itself changes with the terms used to express it!) The pearl may be removed from the oyster and placed in another casing without any loss. But one cannot strip the DNA from a cell. The DNA is a component of a cell. It is nothing by itself, any more than your picture tube would be worth anything without the rest of the TV set.

Harnack saw the gospel of the higher righteousness and the infinite value of the individual soul as a pearl which had been and always would be transferred from casing to casing. Dunn saw the gospel essence as more like DNA, dependent for existence equally on whatever cell matter surrounded it. Dunn would see the gospel as a soul that can be passed on only by reincarnation in a new body—"For we know that if the earthly tent we live in is destroyed, we have a building from God, a house not made with hands, eternal in the heavens. For in this tent we groan, longing to be clothed with our heavenly dwelling—if indeed, when we have taken it off we will not be found naked" (2 Cor 5:1–3). By contrast, Harnack would see the gospel as a body that can be transferred from place to place by any type of vehicle, an oxcart, airplane, spaceship, gondola, or automobile. Harnack's gospel-kernel is both necessary and sufficient unto itself, while Dunn's is necessary but not sufficient: it must always be incarnated.

To borrow yet another set of early theological terms, we might say that the Dunn/von Allmen version of the gospel is strictly anhypostatic. It attains hypostatic instantiation for the first time only in combination with some incarnate form. Historically, the incarnate humanity of Jesus was said to be *enhypostatic*, receiving its personhood, as distinct from its real human quality, from its divine side (Leontius of Byzantium). If not for the project of the incarnation, there would have been no human Jesus. Piet Schooneberg[18] suggested a reversal of the ancient schema, so that the Logos would be understood as *enhypostatic*[19] (without personhood of its own) until it

18. Schooneberg, *Christ*, 85, 87.

19. The term goes back to Cyril of Alexandria who, however, applied it to the human nature of Jesus, not to his Logos-nature.

became *enhypostatic* in its union with the human person Jesus of Nazareth. It is Schooneberg's version that would be parallel to the "reincarnation" of the gospel in new cultural-philosophical contexts.

I have already remarked on the similarity of von Allmen's understanding of the remythologizing of the New Testament gospel and Rudolf Bultmann's. The similarity still holds. Here I think of the remark of Bultmann to the effect that while we know very little about the historical Jesus, all we need to affirm is the fact that there was one. We need to affirm the *das* not the *was* of the incarnation. The *that*, not the *what*. The fact, not the content. Bultmann's disciples threw off his yoke to embark on a "New Quest of the Historical Jesus" (Fuchs, Ebeling, Bornkamm, Käsemann, Robinson, etc.). They feared becoming docetists, emptying the ostensible "incarnation" of any genuine human historicity. Bultmann feared such an endeavor, whether it met with any plausible success or not, would lead to a new liberal Protestant hero worship of Jesus rather than acceptance of the (more abstract) Christ of faith.

Another disciple of Bultmann, Walter Schmithals, did the opposite. As I read him,[20] Schmithals overtakes Bultmann and passes him on the way (John 20:3–10). Schmithals argues that the concept of an authoritative itinerant apostle of Christ was not inherited by Christianity from its Jewish ancestry but rather borrowed from Syrian gnostics, whose apostles did not bear the tidings of a recently incarnated Savior now returned to heaven. Instead, they preached the inner indwelling of a Christ spirit who had become incarnate in all gnostics, paramountly in the gnostic apostle himself, who was fully cognizant of the indwelling of the Christ-Aion in him and sought to awaken his hearers to the mystery of "Christ in you, the hope of glory" (Col 1:27). Thus "when it pleased God to reveal his Son in me," the Galatians received Paul "as an angel of God, as Christ Jesus" (Gal 4:14).

We see the fuller implications of this in the apocryphal Acts of Paul. John, Andrew, Peter, and Thomas. These Acts are docetic, and all of them sooner or later feature a scene in which Christ himself appears in the likeness of the apostle. In accord with Schmithals's theory, these Acts attest the earlier ministry of gnostic apostles who first preached an exclusively interior Spirit-Christ with which one was anointed unto salvation and enlightenment. This Christ was not and had never been a single physical individual. Rather, each and every gnostic might and did incarnate him. I believe that if we broaden out von Allmen's picture of early Christian theological diversity, evolution, and adaptation by adding Schmithals's sketch of

20. Schmithals, *Office of Apostle.*

the gnostic apostles to the mix, we will be able to make sense of even more of the phenomena of syncretism and indigenization.

Schmithals's notion of gnostic apostles of a Christ within is exactly analogous to the shocking Zen Buddhist saying, "If you chance to meet the Buddha on the road—*kill* him!" Because the real Buddha is inside you. Mahayana Buddhism (of which Zen is a subtype) is docetic. The incarnation of the Buddha was a mere appearance. And it follows that both Buddhism and Bultmannism, alike docetic, have embraced the same model of missionary expansion via remythologization (reincarnation). Buddhism and Bultmannism seem to me exactly parallel in that each recognizes a particular self-understanding or understanding of human existence as its gospel. All else is negotiable and inessential. Any cosmological or even theological assumptions will do. Since in neither case does salvation/liberation/authenticity depend upon a particular God-belief or God-concept—that would be to reduce the existential encounter with grace to the mastery of a theological theory, hence a scheme of self-salvation by cognitive works—any belief can be tolerated. The belief in miracles was equally tangential in both Buddhism and Bultmannism. If one prefers theologians less radical than Bultmann, suffice it to note that moderate Reformed and Evangelical theologians like Jack Rogers and G. C. Berkouwer share with Bultmann the basic notion that the abiding and only infallible aspect of the New Testament is its core-proclamation of salvation.

In a recent piece of contextualizing theology, Hee-Sung Keel[21] adopts "the theological method of Claude Geffre, who regards the history of theology as a series of incarnations of the Word."[22] Indeed, we have found it difficult to avoid incarnational analogies. Geffre's insight is crucial, and, when combined with Bengt Sundkler's striking notion of the messianic and prophetic founders of Third World indigenous churches as being living "icons" of Christ,[23] it can be extended even further, enabling us, I think, to solve a very important problem.

Euro-American Protestant and Catholic theologians get mild indigestion hearing of certain social, sexual, and family-structure adaptations taking place in the younger churches. A serious upset stomach begins to churn at attempts to mix traditional Christianity with, e.g., reincarnation or ancestor-veneration. But the migraines start in earnest when leadership

21. Keel, "Jesus the Bodhisattva."

22. Geffre, *Christianisme*.

23. Sundkler, *Zulu Zion*, 193.

emerges in the form of charismatic individuals shouldering the capacious mantle of prophet, apostle, or even messiah. Such indigenous church leaders in past eras have included the Apostle Mani, the Prophet Joseph Smith, and Hong Xiuquan, the Brother of Jesus and Taiping Messiah.[24] Contemporaries include Simon Kimbangu, Andre "Jesus" Matswa, Simon Peter Mpade, the Prophet Harris, and the Reverend Sun Myung Moon.

In the cases of individuals like these, conservatives are quick to hurl accusations of "antichrist" and "false prophet," just as Martin Luther vilified the pope as a usurper of the centrality of Christ. But even liberal, "mainline" churches are minded to rend their garments in outrage and shock when they hear such claims and suddenly discover that the word *heresy*, long since relegated to the ecclesiastical mothballs, may have some continued utility after all! Even secular taxonomists of religion may feel compelled to place such a movement in a new classification simply because another figure is threatening to eclipse Jesus. In this case no value judgment lies at the basis of the judgment, only taxonomic fastidiousness.

If Christianity is defined over against its fellow Semitic monotheisms by virtue of its Christocentricity, any shift of the center of gravity should destabilize the Christian identity of a movement.

In the 1950s the Universalist Church in America adopted as its corporate logo a design featuring a circle with a cross off center, a bit to the left, indicating that Universalism acknowledges its Christian roots but was in the process of transcending them, moving beyond them. But it had not yet reached any new center. Their off-center cross might stand for all these indigenous younger churches which seem to be evolving beyond their Christian roots but have not yet arrived anywhere else.

It would not be fair to brand them non-Christian (or "post-Christian" as does Oosthuizen[25]) since that is to jump the gun and to anticipate a stage not yet reached—and which may never be reached. The Church of Jesus Christ of Latter-day Saints has not yet moved far enough away from Christocentricity as to merit being called the Church of Joseph Smith of Latter-day Saints. It is still quite clearly a Christian movement, though it may be farther removed from the ideal type of Christocentric Christianity. And so it is with the Unification Church.

If the old Universalist symbol of an off-center cross would be an apt icon for such Christian movements with a new prophet, apostle, or messiah, is

24. Spence, *God's Chinese Son*; and Lanternari, *Religions of the Oppressed*.
25. Oosthuizen, *Post-Christianity in Africa*.

there any way of making sense of this off-center character in terms of Christian theological categories? That is, can we explain it in terms which will leave its Christian identity intact, that will make sense of the rising importance of the new guru intelligible *as a Christian development* and not just as a development, implicitly, away from Christianity to something else?

Yes, there is. This is where we may find it useful to synthesize the approaches of Geffre and Sundkler. Suppose that, a la Geffre, each new advance of the Christian gospel into a new cultural system is best understood as a new incarnation of the gospel word. What new light would this throw on Sundkler's suggestion that charismatic apostles and messiahs in these movements be understood not as rivals of Christ, hence as antichrists, but rather as vicars or icons of Christ, symbols that point beyond themselves, as Jesus himself did, pointing on to his Father, claiming for himself the status of the way, not of the destination?

I think the result would be to recognize each such charismatic icon of Christ as, to paraphrase Ritschl, "having the value of Christ for them." Each one might be understood as an appropriate extension of the incarnation into the new cultural framework. Each instance would be a new "scandal of particularity" in order that the members of each culture might recognize in Christ, "'This at last is bone of my bones and flesh of my flesh'" (Gen 2:23). In fact it almost begins to look as if anything short of such radical incarnational contextualism should count as a kind of docetism, since it would impose a barrier between the "incarnate Christ," who is said to have become "in every respect . . . as we are, yet without sin" (Heb 4:15), but who really remains a stranger to the cultural distinctives that define us. A la Schmithals's gnostic Christ, the incarnation would not really have been fulfilled until the proclaimed Christ took on the human flesh of the apostolic proclaimer.

This means that even from the standpoint of a Christian in a more traditional Christian community, someone like the Reverend Moon, self-proclaimed Lord of the Second Advent, could be acknowledged as a true extension of the incarnation of the Word in Christ. And, at least in the case of this movement, such a construal is remarkably close to the movement's own theological self-understanding according to which the Reverend Moon has assumed the continued function of Christ, bearing the mantle of Jesus as Elisha did that of Elijah.[26]

26. This pattern also has the benefit of paralleling naturally the relevant anthropological categories. See Hill, "Local Hero," in which we read of an agelong series of local prophets and miracle-workers whose shadow is cast so long that forever afterward new charismatic individuals of the same type are perceived as the return or reincarnation

BIBLIOGRAPHY

Allmen, Daniel von. "The Birth of Theology: Contextualisation as the Dynamic Element in the Formation of New Testament Theology." *International Review of Missions* 64/253 (January 1975) 37–52.

Boyd, Robin H. S. *India and the Latin Captivity of the Church: The Cultural Context of the Gospel.* Monograph Supplements to the Scottish Journal of Theology. London: Cambridge University Press, 1974.

Buri, Fritz. *How Can We Still Speak Responsibly of God?* Philadelphia: Fortress, 1968.

Coleman, Richard J. *Issues of Theological Warfare: Evangelicals and Liberals.* Grand Rapids: Eerdmans, 1972.

Dunn, James D. G. *Unity and Diversity in the New Testament: An Inquiry into the Character of Earliest Christianity.* Philadelphia: Westminster, 1977.

Gager, John G. *Kingdom and Community: The Social World of Early Christianity.* Prentice-Hall Studies in Religion Series. Englewood Cliffs, NJ: Prentice-Hall, 1975.

Geffre, Claude. *Le Christianisme au risque de l'interpretation.* Cogitatio fidei 120. Paris: Cerf, 1983.

Griffin, David R. *A Process Christology.* Philadelphia: Westminster, 1973.

Haliburton, Gordon MacKay. *The Prophet Harris: A Study of an African Prophet and His Mass-Movement in the Ivory Coast and the Gold Coast 1913–1915.* New York: Oxford University Press, 1973.

Hill, Scott D. "The Local Hero in Palestine in Comparative Perspective." In *Elijah and Elisha in Socioliterary Perspective*, edited by Robert B. Coote, 37–74. Semeia Studies. Atlanta: Scholars, 1992.

Holmberg, Bengt. *Sociology and the New Testament: An Appraisal.* Minneapolis: Fortress, 1990.

Hogg, A. G. *Karma and Reincarnation: An Essay toward the Interpretation of Hinduism and the Re-statement of Christianity.* Madras: Christian Literature Society, 1909.

Jules-Rosette, Bennetta. *African Apostles: Ritual and Conversion in the Church of John Maranke.* Symbol, Myth, and Ritual Series. Ithaca: Cornell University Press, 1975.

Käsemann, Ernst. "The Canon of the New Testament and the Unity of the Church." In *Essays on New Testament Themes*, 95–107. Translated by W. J. Montague. Studies in Biblical Theology 41. London: SCM, 1964.

Keel, Hee-Sung. "Jesus the Bodhisattva: Christology from a Buddhist Perspective." *Buddhist-Christian Studies* 16 (1966) 169–85.

Kelsey, David M. *The Uses of Scripture in Recent Theology.* Philadelphia: Fortress, 1975.

Lanternari, Vittorio. *The Religions of the Oppressed: A Study of Modern Messianic Cults.* New York: Mentor, 1965.

Loisy, Alfred. *The Gospel and the Church.* Translated by Christopher Home. New ed. with prefatory memoir by G. Tyrrell. London: Pitman, 1908.

Martin, Marie-Louise. *Kimbangu: An African Prophet and His Church.* Translated by D. M. Moore. Grand Rapids: Eerdmans, 1976.

Mbiti, John S. *New Testament Eschatology in an African Background: A Study of the Encounter between New Testament Theology and African Traditional Concepts.* 1971. Reprint, London: SPCK, 1978.

---

of their predecessors, just as some perceived Jesus as the return of Elijah or of John the Baptist, or John the Baptist as the returned Elijah.

Ogden, Schubert M. *The Reality of God, and Other Essays*. San Francisco: Harper & Row, 1977.

Oosthuizen, G. C. *Post-Christianity in Africa: A Theological and Anthropological Study*. Grand Rapids: Eerdmans, 1968.

Oosthuizen, G. C., and Irving Hexham, eds. *Empirical Studies of African Independent/ Indigenous Churches*. Lewiston, NY: Mellen, 1992.

Pinnock, Clark H. *Biblical Revelation: The Foundation of Christian Theology*. Chicago: Moody, 1971.

————. "An Evangelical Theology: Conservative and Contemporary." *Christianity Today*, January 5, 1979, 23–29.

Ramm, Bernard, "The Continental Divide in Contemporary Theology," In *A Christianity Today Reader*, edited by Frank E. Gaebelein, 57–72. New York: Pyramid, 1968.

Richardson, Don. *Peace Child*. Glendale, CA: Regal, 2005.

Schoeps, Hans-Joachim. *Paul: The Theology of the Apostle in the Light of Jewish Religious History*. Translated by Harold Knight. Philadelphia: Westminster, 1974.

Schoonenberg, Piet J. A. M. *The Christ*. Translated by Della Couling. New York: Seabury, 1971.

Schreiter, Robert J. *Constructing Local Theologies*. Maryknoll, NY: Orbis, 1986.

Schmithals, Walter. *The Office of Apostle in the Early Church*. Translated by John E. Steely. Nashville: Abingdon, 1969.

Smith, Jonathan Z. "Too Much Kingdom, Too Little Community." *Zygon* 13 (1978) 123–30.

Spence, Jonathan D. *God's Chinese Son: The Taiping Heavenly Kingdom of Hong Xiuquan*. New York: Norton, 1996.

Sundkler, Bengt G. M. *Bantu Prophets in South Africa*. 2nd ed. London: Published for the International African Institute by the Oxford University Press, 1961.

————. *Zulu Zion and Some Swazi Zionists*. Oxford Studies in African Affairs. London: Oxford University Press, 1976.

Tracy, David. *Blessed Rage for Order: The New Pluralism in Theology*. New York: Seabury, 1975.

2

Jesus Christ in the Holy Qur'an and the Prophetic Traditions

MUSTAFA ABU SWAY

When the angels said, 'O Mary, Allah gives you the good news of a *Word* from Him whose name is the Messiah, Jesus son of Mary, eminent in [this] world and the Hereafter, and one of those brought near [to Allah].

He will speak to people in the cradle and in adulthood and will be one of the righteous.'

She said, 'My Lord, how shall I have a child when no human has ever touched me?' He said, 'So it is that Allah creates whatever He wishes. Whenever He decrees on a matter, He just says to it "Be!" *and it is.* (Qur'an, 3:45–47)[1]

---

1. Citations from the Holy Qur'an in English are from Khuttab, *The Clear Qur'an* (https://theclearquran.org) with occasional modification by the author.

Islam is the only non-Christian faith that makes it imperative to believe in Jesus Christ. The Islamic creed, as presented in the Qur'an and the Sunna of the Prophet, is inclusive of all previous original revelations (i.e., the scriptures of Abraham, the *Torah* of Moses, the *Zabur*/Psalms of David, and the *Injil*/Gospel of Jesus) and, therefore, the prophets of the Children of Israel are integral to Islamic faith. The testimony that Muhammad is the Messenger of God, entails belief in all the messengers and prophets, including Jesus Christ.

The Prophet's relationship with his predecessors was to bring the line of prophethood to completion, where every prophet is integral to the linear history of revelation; he said:

> My relationship to the prophets before me is like someone who built a house of bricks, and he made it beautiful and completed it, except that he left the place of one brick in a corner empty. People visited and circled this structure, marveled at its beauty, and exclaimed: Why not put this brick in its place? [Then], the Prophet said: "I am that brick, and I am the Seal of the Prophets." (Narrated by *Al-Bukhari* #3342 and *Muslim* #4361)

Furthermore, the Prophet reflected on the bond between the prophets in a tradition that mentions his relationship to Jesus Christ; he said:

> I am more entitled than all people to Jesus son of Mary, in this life and the hereafter. There is no prophet between me and him. The prophets are brothers coming from the same origin, except that they have different mothers, and their religion is one. (Narrated by *Al-Bukhari* #3443 and *Muslim* #2365)

The original Arabic language of this Hadith referring to the "same origin" above (*ikhwa li'allat*) is more about Jesus and Muhammad being metaphorically half brothers, having one father, with different mothers. In the *Sahih Al-Bukhari* compendia for prophetic traditions the Hadith above is listed under the category "The traditions that say the religion of the prophets is one." Ibn Qayyim Al-Jawziyyah (d. 751 AH/1350 CE) included the same Hadith in his exegesis of the following qur'anic verse:

> He has ordained for you [believers] the Way which He decreed for Noah, and what We have revealed to you [O Prophet] and what We decreed for Abraham, Moses, and Jesus, commanding: "Uphold the faith, and make no divisions in it." What you call the polytheists to is unbearable for them. Allah chooses for Himself

whoever He wills, and guides to Himself whoever turns [to Him].
(Qur'an, 42:13)

His interpretation could be summarized as saying that the one father
is the religion of monotheism (i.e., Islam as the universal religion that was
revealed to all prophets), and the mothers are the respective laws each one
received, entailing differences. An example of a different law is the preser-
vation of the Sabbath requirements during the time of Friday prayers, when
it is also prohibited for Muslims to conduct business transactions during
this time. An example of a law that is kept is the prohibition against creating
graven images and worshiping them.

There are twenty-five prophets who are mentioned in the Qur'an
(peace be upon them all), and others who are not:

> There are messengers whose stories We have told you already and oth-
> ers We have not. And to Moses Allah spoke directly. (Qur'an, 4:164)

In addition to the Qur'an and Prophetic traditions, Islamic scholarly
literature spanning fourteen centuries reflects the utmost respect for Mary
(Peace be upon her). The Qur'an allocates a large space for her story in several chapters, including Sura Maryam (chapter 19), which is named after
her. She is also the only woman to be mentioned by name in the Qur'an
(not the name of Prophet Muhammad's mother!). All Muslim scholars,
without any exception, reflect the qur'anic story that Mary was the most
pious woman, spiritually pure, dedicating herself to the worship of God
in seclusion (there is no Joseph or any other man in her life in the Qur'an;
more details on this story will follow). We find mention in the Book (the
Qur'an) how Mary secluded herself from her people to an eastern place.

> She placed a screen between herself and them; then We sent to her
> Our Spirit (i.e., the archangel Gabriel), and he appeared before
> her in the form of a man in all respects. (Qur'an, 19:16–17)

> And Mary, the daughter of Imran, who guarded her chastity, and
> so We breathed into her of Our Spirit, and she believed in her
> Lord's Words and His Scriptures and was one of the pious.
> (Qur'an, 66:12)

The miraculous creation of Jesus Christ was compared to Adam to
show that God is Omnipotent, and while Jesus had no father, Adam had
neither father nor mother:

> Indeed, the example of Jesus in the sight of Allah is like that of Adam. He created him from dust, then said to him, "Be!" And he was! (Qur'an, 3:59)

His esteemed status was reflected in how he was honored in the descriptions the "word of God" and a "spirit from Him":

> O People of the Book [i.e., the Christians in this context]! Do not exceed the limits in your religion, nor say of God aught but the truth. The Messiah Jesus, son of Mary, was [no more than] a Messenger of Allah and His Word, ("Be!"—and he was) which He bestowed on Mary and a spirit created by Him; so believe in God and His Messengers. Say not: "Three (trinity)!" Cease! (it is) better for you. For Allah is (the only) One Ilâh (God), glory be to Him (Far Exalted is He) above having a son. To Him belongs all that is in the heavens and all that is in the earth. And Allah is All-Sufficient as a Disposer of affairs. (Qur'an 4:171)

Jesus was born through an immaculate birth. His is a miraculous story from the beginning and until he was raised by God, sparing him any harm by the children of Israel, who did transgress against earlier prophets. The Qur'an categorically denies that Jesus was killed or crucified, while it appeared to people as if there was a crucifixion:

> But for their violation of their covenant, and their denial of Allah's signs, and their unjustified killing of the prophets, and their saying, "Our hearts are wrapped" . . . Rather, Allah put a seal upon them on account of their denial, so they do not believe, except for a few. (155) And on account of their denial and their saying against Mary a great slander (156), and their saying, "We have surely killed the Messiah, Jesus, son of Mary, the Messenger of Allah" . . . In fact, they did not kill him, nor did they crucify him, but it appeared to them as if they had. And indeed, those who differed over him are in doubt about it. They have no knowledge of it—just following assumptions. And certainly, they did not kill him (157). Rather, Allah raised him up to Himself, for Allah has always been Almighty, All-Wise (158). (Qur'an, 4:155–58)

Islam is younger than Judaism and Christianity. It brings to completion the line of prophecy both in message and person. Humanity was ready for the universal final revelation and final prophet. Other than the indirect numerous contextual mentions of the prophets in the Qur'an, Prophet Moses (Peace be upon him) is mentioned 136 times, much more than any other prophet or messenger. Jesus Christ is mentioned twenty-five times, and Prophet Muhammad himself is mentioned only five times, with one of these five mentions being "Ahmad" (having the same root as *Muhammad*, i.e., *h-m-d*), which Jesus Christ foretells in the Qur'an:

> And recall when Jesus, son of Mary, said, "O Children of Israel, I am Allah's Messenger to you, confirming what preceded me of the Torah and a bearer of glad tidings of a messenger who comes after me, whose name is Ahmad" ... (Qur'an, 61:6)

These numbers in favor of prophets other than Prophet Muhammad make a strong argument that the Qur'an is not a self-centered book written by the Prophet or his companions!

The names of Jesus Christ in the Qur'an are Jesus (*'Isa*), Christ/Messiah (*Al-Masih*), and Jesus son of Mary (*'Isa ibn Maryam*). He is considered one of the five messengers and prophets who were steadfast (*ulu al-'azm*), in addition to Noah, Abraham, Moses, and Muhammad, though there is an interpretation that all prophets were steadfast:

> Be patient [O Muhammad!] just as those messengers who were steadfast were patient ... (Qur'an, 46:35)

The essential monotheistic theological messages that were revealed in past revelations are included in what a Muslim believes, especially putting all prophets on equal footing:

> Say: "We believe in Allah and what has been revealed to us, and what was revealed to Abraham and Ishmael and Isaac and Jacob and the tribes, and what was given to Moses and Jesus and the prophets from their Lord; we do not make any distinction between any of them and to Him do we submit." (Qur'an, 3:84)[2]

It is no wonder that Paul Schwarzenau, in *Korankunde für Christen*, referred to the Qur'an as an ecumenical revelation.[3] Compatible with Schwarzenau's idea is the Islamic paradigm for *convivencia* among the children of Abraham and beyond. This *convivencia* could be kept while each group consciously celebrates the right to be different. This paradigm could not be found elsewhere; it would be anachronistic to claim that it had existed in a previous time or place. It is for this reason that I advocate

---

2. *Cf.* "The Messenger believes in what has been revealed to him from his Lord, as do men of faith. Each one [of them] believes in Allah, His angels, His books, and His Messengers. [The believers say]: 'We make no distinction between one and another of His Messengers'" (Qur'an, 2:285).

3. Hofmann, *Islam*, 21.

an Islamic theology of soft-otherness, for the Jew or the Christian is not totally other for the Muslim. This is reflected in the Qur'an in the ability for a Muslim to do business with the People of the Book, to eat their food, and for Muslim men to marry from among their women (Qur'an, 5:5). This means the maternal side of the family being Jewish or Christian. There are ample other details.

In practice, to give a concrete example of the beautiful and complex social mosaic, suffice it to say that my mother breastfed the daughter of our Christian neighbors, resulting in Lamis and I becoming a Christian sister and a Muslim brother, according to Islamic law.

The Qur'an speaks about warm amicability between Christians and Muslims:

> . . . and you will find that the nearest of them in *(genuine)* love towards those who have attained faith are those who said, "We are indeed Christians." That is because among them are priests and monks, and because they never act arrogantly. (Qur'an, 5:82)

The Islamic worldview presents theological and historical narratives that are different from the postrevelational position that evolved and became dominant in Christianity, and categorically distinct from the essential rabbinical Jewish position regarding Jesus Christ. While this chapter recognizes the serious theological differences, it does not reflect in any way a less than perfect love on the part of the author towards Jesus Christ himself and Mary. This is a matter of faith.

A FAMILY PROFILE:
AL `IMRAN, MARY AND JESUS

From the beginning of life on earth, divine guidance was bestowed on humanity through the agency of the prophets. The monotheistic message formed the core of revelation; whenever it suffered from the vagaries of transmission, it was reconfirmed through a new prophet and a new revelation. This process continued until humanity was ready for a final, universal revelation in the form of the Qur'an. From an Islamic perspective, all the prophets, from Adam to Muhammad (Peace be upon them), are prophets of Islam. Jesus Christ was one of them and came before Prophet Muhammad, the Seal of the Prophets.[4] Jesus Christ's story in the Qur'an begins with

---

4. "Muhammad is not the father of any of your men, but [he is] the Messenger of Allah,

the positioning of his maternal lineage,[5] the family of `Imran, within the family of prophets:

> Allah did choose Adam and Noah, the family of Abraham, and the family of `Imran above all people . . . Offspring, one of the other; and Allah hears and knows all things. (Qur'an, 3:33–34)

It is as if there was a fourth spiritual stage for humanity. There is a sense of spiritual elation that paves the way for the emergence of Jesus Christ. This impeccable family background begins with his maternal grandmother dedicating her daughter Mary (Peace be upon her) while Mary was still in her womb, thinking that she was a male, to the service of Allah:

> Behold! A woman of `Imran said: "O my Lord! I do dedicate unto Thee what is in my womb for Thy special service: so accept this of me: for Thou hearest and knowest all things." (Qur'an, 3:35)

> When she was delivered, she said: "O my Lord! Behold! I am delivered of a female child!" . . . (Qur'an, 3:36)

Her mother named her Mary (*Mariam*) and asked Allah SWT to protect her and her offspring from Satan: ["and I seek refuge with the outcast"]. Allah SWT accepted her in a unique way:

> Right graciously did her Lord accept her; He made her grow in purity and beauty . . . (Qur'an, 3:37)

PROPHET ZACHARIAH TAKES CARE OF MARY

Mary became an orphan as a child, and many people competed to take care of her. It reached the stage that they had to cast their lots:

> . . . You were not with them when they cast lots with their "pens," as to which of them should be charged with the care of Mary; nor were you with them when they disputed [this issue]. (Qur'an, 3:44)

---

and the *Seal of the Prophets*: And Allah has full knowledge of all things" (Qur'an, 33:40).

5. Needless to say, from an Islamic perspective, Jesus Christ had absolutely no paternal lineage, as will be discussed later on. Even the metaphorical use of "Father" is ruled out in Islamic theological discourse in favor of a pure monotheistic belief system (i.e., Tawhid). This qur'anic position should be contrasted with two conflicting accounts of Jesus Christ's genealogy in the Gospel of Mathew (1:1–16) and the Gospel of Luke (3: 23–38). These two accounts have different names and different numbers of generations.

"To the care of Zachariah was she assigned," but the surprise was that whenever he went to check on her, to take care of her and to bring her provisions, as her guardian, he was surprised to find out that divine intervention took care of her miraculously:

> . . . Every time that he entered the niche [where she worships] to see her, he found her supplied with sustenance. He said: "O Mary! Whence [comes] this to you?" She said: "From Allah: for Allah provides sustenance to whom He pleases, without measure." (Qur'an, 3:37)

Mary's answer made Zachariah conscientious of Allah's omnipotence. He seized that moment, which was full of spirituality, to make a supplication to Allah SWT. Zachariah's wife was barren, and he prayed for offspring! The answer came very quickly with good tidings:

> "O Zachariah! We give you good news of a son: his name shall be Yahya: on none by that name have We conferred distinction before." (Qur'an, 19:7)

Yahya, or John the Baptist as he is known in English, was a prophet, like his father:

> "O Yahya! Take hold of the Book with might": And We gave him Wisdom even as a youth. (Qur'an, 19:12)

Prophet Muhammad referred to Jesus and Yahya, in the story of the Ascension (*Al-Mi`raj*), as the "maternal cousins" (*Ibnayy al-Khalah*).[6] The Qur'an does not say much about Yahya's life. He is described as being "noble, chaste, and a prophet."[7] His vocation as a prophet must have rendered support to Jesus Christ.

MARY AND JESUS: NO DIVINIZATION:

It is no wonder that the Qur'an declares that Mary was chosen over all women of earth. Through divine acceptance, she reached a very high spiritual rank, for she was prepared for a great role that surpasses human imagination:

---

6. Literally, they are the two sons of the maternal aunts. Bukhari, *Sahih*, Hadith # 3598.

7. Qur'an, 3:39.

> Behold! The angels said: "O Mary! Allah hath chosen thee and
> purified thee—chosen thee above the women of all nations.
> O Mary! Worship thy Lord devoutly: prostrate thyself and bow
> down [in prayer] with those who bow down." (Qur'an, 3:42–43)

No other woman is mentioned in the Qur'an by name except Mary, and no woman is praised and distinguished like her. According to Ibn Hazm, Mary was a prophetess, because she received revelation. This position, albeit being in the minority among Muslim scholars, reflects the very high status that Mary was accorded. Nevertheless, like all other human beings, she was ordered to worship her Lord, Allah SWT, for how could one think otherwise? The Qur'an inculcates a deep respect for Mary and her son but never places them above humanity. To the contrary, the Qur'an stresses their very humanity:

> Christ, the son of Mary, was no more than a Messenger; many
> were the Messengers that passed away before him. His mother was
> a woman of truth. They had to eat food [to subsist]. See how Allah
> does make His Signs clear to them; yet see in what ways they are
> deluded away from the truth! (Qur'an, 5:75)

This verse is part of an anti-Trinity qur'anic critique:

> They do blaspheme who say: Allah is one of three in a Trinity:
> for there is no god except One God. If they desist not from their
> word [of blasphemy], verily a grievous punishment will befall the
> blasphemers among them. (Qur'an, 5:73)

Because of the de facto divinization of Mary and the formal divinization of Jesus Christ, Allah SWT asks Jesus a rhetorical question:

> And behold! Allah will say: "O Jesus the son of Mary! Did you say
> unto people, 'Worship me and my mother as gods in derogation of
> Allah?'" He will say: "Glory to You! Never could I say what I had
> no right [to say]. Had I said such a thing, You would indeed have
> known it. You know what is in my heart, though I know not what
> is in Yours. For You know in full all that is hidden.
> Never said I to them aught except what You did command me to
> say, to wit, 'Worship Allah, my Lord and your Lord'. . ." (Qur'an,
> 5:116–17)

The words of Jesus are those of a mortal with limited knowledge and a real servant, who recognizes the Omniscient Lord. He submitted to Allah SWT and conveyed the message to his people. There are additional qur'anic verses that reject all polytheistic theologies. While it is beyond the scope of this chapter to enumerate all of them, a few representative verses will further highlight the tawhidic narrative. The first example is a very short chapter dedicated to the confirmation of the oneness of Allah SWT and the rejection of any organic relationship with his creation:

> Say: "Allah is Unique [in His Oneness]! Allah, the Source [of everything]. He has not fathered anyone nor was He fathered, and there is nothing comparable to Him!" (Qur'an, 112)

This is probably the second-most recited Sura in the Qur'an after the opening chapter (i.e., *Al-Fatiha*), the recitation of which is imperative during the five daily prayers. Also, chapter 112 is featured in *Dhikr*.[8] This is translated in the life of the religious Muslim into hundreds, if not thousands, of recitations every year of verses that have anti-Trinitarian content. The oneness of Allah is deeply inculcated into the psyches of Muslims. While the language of this chapter is general, I have never failed to remember, as a background, the Christian narrative about the Sonship of Jesus.

The end of Sura 19—*Mariam* (Mary)—includes a very critical account of the idea of Jesus' Sonship, which is addressed in general language. Nevertheless, it is understood in this context to be a reference to the claim that Jesus Christ is the Son of God. The qur'anic narrative reflects how grave this claim is:

> They say: "[Allah] Most Gracious has begotten a son!"
> Indeed, you have put forth a thing most monstrous!
> As if the skies are ready to burst, the earth to split asunder, and the mountains to fall down in utter ruin.
> That they should invoke a son for [Allah] Most Gracious.
> For it is not consonant with the majesty of [Allah] Most Gracious that He should beget a son.
> Not one of the beings in the heavens and the earth but must come to [Allah] Most Gracious as a servant. (Qur'an, 19:88–93)

Furthermore, Jesus Christ's humanity is emphasized every time he is called the "son of Mary,"[9] or when he is described as a "servant"[10] who is

---

8. It is the recollection of the name of Allah. It could use supplications taught by Prophet Muhammad or simply reciting the Qur'an.

9. Qur'an, 43:57.

10. Qur'an, 43:59.

a recipient of Allah's favors, and as a prophet whose vocation is to call the people to worship the only Lord that exists:

> . . . fear Allah and obey me. For Allah, He is my Lord and your
> Lord: so, worship ye Him: this is a straight way. (Qur'an, 43:63–64)

The miraculous and fatherless birth of Jesus Christ is not a valid reason to raise him to a status above that of a normal human being. The Qur'an uses the story of Adam, who was created without a father or a mother, to illustrate the humanity of Jesus Christ. Being created without a father reflects the omnipotence of Allah rather than the divinity of the created:

> The similitude of Jesus before Allah is as that of Adam; He created
> him from dust, and then said to him: "Be": and he was. (Qur'an, 3:59)
>> In essence, all creation came into existence through "Be":
>> Verily, when He wills a thing, His Command is, "Be," and it
> is! (Qur'an, 36:82)

Allah SWT is absolutely distinguished from his creation. There are no grey areas; all that which is limited to space-time relationships, all that which is historical, all that which exists here and now is different from him:

> . . . there is nothing whatever like unto Him . . . (Qur'an, 42:11)

Every being, no matter how high this being ranks in the order of the created, remains in a state of *otherness* in relationship to Allah SWT. Yes, Jesus Christ came into existence miraculously, and he ranks high among the prophets and messengers, yet he remains a human being in every respect. The nature of Jesus Christ is summarized in the following verses, which constitute a reminder to the Christians, and everyone else:

> O People of the Book! Commit no excess in your religion: nor
> say of Allah aught but the truth. Christ Jesus the son of Mary was
> [no more than] a Messenger of Allah, and His Word, which He
> bestowed on Mary, and a Spirit proceeding from Him: so, believe
> in Allah and His Messengers. Say not "Trinity": desist—it will be
> better for you: for Allah is One God: Glory be to Him: [Far exalted
> is He] above having a son. To Him belong all things in the heavens
> and on earth. And enough is Allah as a Disposer of affairs.
> Christ does not disdain to serve and worship Allah . . . (Qur'an,
> 4:171–72)

There are numerous other verses that condemn those who say, because of the Trinity, that Jesus is God:

> They do blaspheme who say: "Allah is Christ the son of Mary."
> But said Christ: "O Children of Israel! Worship Allah, my Lord
> and your Lord." Whoever joins other gods with Allah—Allah will
> forbid him the Garden, and the Fire will be for the wrongdoers.
> There will be no one to help.
> They do blaspheme who say Allah is one of three in a Trinity for
> there is no god except One God . . . (Qur'an, 5:72–73)

The last verse rejects the Trinity construct and considers it blasphemous. All three "persons" of the Trinity do exist in the Qur'an independently. Allah SWT is different from both, the Spirit of the Holy[11] (i.e., the Archangel Gabriel) and Jesus Christ. Allah SWT is the Creator, and the other two were creatures, accidentals, who are dependent in their existence on Allah SWT. It is He who strengthened and supported Jesus Christ through the Spirit of the Holy:

> Those Messengers We endowed with gifts, some above others: To
> one of them Allah spoke; others He raised to degrees [of honor];
> to Jesus the son of Mary, We gave clear [Signs], and strengthened
> him with the Spirit of the Holy. (Qur'an, 2:253)

The language of the verse leaves no room for speculation about the inequality of the three; Jesus Christ *needed* help, the Spirit of the Holy (i.e., the Holy Spirit) was *used* to render support to Jesus, and all took place at the Will of Allah SWT.

Today, there is a prominent Christian theological trend represented by Hans Küng (d. 2021). He realized "how great the distance is between the original statements about Father, Son and Spirit and the later dogmatic Church teachings on Trinity." To solve the problem, he came up with a new definition of the Trinity where it becomes "God's revelation in Jesus Christ through the Spirit," and where Jesus is "chosen and authorized by God." Murad Hofmann commented on Küng's theology:

> If the real intention of this Christology is to say that Jesus is neither
> begotten by God nor that he is consubstantial with him, and that
> God's spirit does not represent a divine person, then it is Muslim
> and confirms the statement that 'Muslims are the better Christians'—and, incidentally, the older Christians. Only in the Qur'an
> has the Christology of the Jewish Christians, as rediscovered by
> Küng, remained pure.[12]

11. *Ruh Al-Qudus.* "The Holy Spirit" is not an accurate translation.

12. Hofmann, *Islam*, 25–26.

THE IMMACULATE CONCEPTION

In Sura 19 *Miriam*, the chapter of the Qur'an which is named after her, Mary is portrayed as a very pious woman who dedicated her time to worship Allah SWT. Indeed, she chose to do so in seclusion, and it is there that the Angel revealed to her the news about the Immaculate Conception:

> Relate in the Book [the story of] Mary, when she withdrew from her family to a place in the East.
> She placed a screen [to screen herself] from them; then We sent to her Our angel, and he appeared to her as a man in all respects. (Qur'an, 19:16–17)

The sudden appearance of that "man," the angel, before her was not welcomed! Any woman of her status would have rejected the angel's presence as portending evil. A pious woman, she sought refuge in Allah SWT:

> She said: "I seek refuge in from thee to [Allah] Most Gracious: [come not near] if you do fear Allah." (Qur'an, 19:18)

The mission and nature of this "man" was revealed to her; it was time to tell her about her own mission in carrying the Word of Allah, a Sign and challenge for humanity:

> He said: "Nay, I am only a messenger from thy Lord, to announce to thee the gift of a [spiritually] purified son." (Qur'an, 19:19)

First, Mary has to experience the sudden appearance of the angel in her isolated spot where she worships Allah SWT, and now the news comes to her that she is to conceive a son! The news must have had a tremendous psychological impact on her. One can easily detect the initial rejection:

> She said: "How shall I have a son, seeing that no man has touched me, and I am not unchaste? (Qur'an, 19:20)

Yet, the angel makes clear that it is a divine decree, and that the only way forward is submission to the will of Allah:

> He said: "So [it will be] thy Lord saith, 'That is easy for Me: and [We wish] to appoint him as a Sign unto people and a Mercy from Us': it is a matter [so] decreed." (Qur'an, 19:21)

The essence of this message is repeated in the Qur'an's third chapter, called *Al `Imran*, where the angels give glad tidings of a "Word" from Allah, and that his name will be "Christ Jesus son of Mary." He will be held in honor in both worlds, and he will speak both to people from the crib and as an adult. In addition, Allah SWT will teach him the "Book and Wisdom, the Torah and the Gospel" (Qur'an, 3:45–48). Initially in her encounter with the angel, Mary confirms her piety as a state that contradicts the notion of carrying a son without knowing a man. The answer stresses Allah's omnipotence, which created the laws of nature but is not bound by them:

> . . . Allah creates what He wills: when He has decreed a Plan, He but says to it, 'Be,' and it is! (Qur'an, 3:47)

Mary conceived him, and she went to a remote place where she went through labor. Here she wished the whole story had not happened, for it is one thing to be pregnant, and it is another thing to carry the child home. This happening to a well-known, pious single woman was too much to handle; she wished she were dead:

> So, she conceived him, and she retired with him to a remote place.
> And childbirth drove her to the trunk of a palm tree: she said [in her anguish]: "Ah! Would that I had died before this! Would that I had been a thing forgotten and out of sight!" (Qur'an, 19:22–23)
> Yet there was a voice that tried to console her during these difficult times:
> But he cried to her from beneath her: "Grieve not! For thy Lord had provided a rivulet beneath thee;
> And shake towards yourself the trunk of the palm tree; it will let fall fresh ripe dates upon you.
> So, eat and drink and cool your eye. And if you do see any human being, say: 'I have vowed a fast to [Allah] Most Gracious, and this day will I enter into no talk with any human being.'" (Qur'an, 19:24–26)

Whose voice was it? Muslim scholars differ on source of the voice. Ibn Kathir (d. 774 AH/1372 CE) stated that Ibn Abbas (companion and cousin of Prophet Muhammad) said the voice came from (the archangel) Gabriel, because Jesus did not speak until Mary reached her family. Also, this position was adopted by Sa`eed Ibn Jubair, Al-Dahhak, `Amr Ibn Maimun, Al-Sadi, and Qatadah that it was the angel Gabriel, peace be upon him—meaning that he called her from the bottom of the valley. The other position is reflected by Mujahid, who said that it was Jesus son of Mary who spoke to her.[13]

13. Kathir, *Tafsir*, 3:115.

If it were the angel who spoke to Mary, the narrative would form simply a continuation of the message of support. This, however, poses a different problem; it means that the angel stayed with Mary throughout the pregnancy, for there are no indications of any interruptions of his stay. Some Muslim scholars speak of a miraculous short-term pregnancy, yet there is nothing to substantiate this from the Qur'an. In addition, the Qur'an has already stated that after the conception she retired to a "remote place" (19:22). The remoteness of the place to which Mary retires is relative to the place where the conception took place; her movement to this out-of-the-way spot could be interpreted as signaling the end of this specific mission of Gabriel to Mary, so that from this point Mary is left alone.

At any rate, those scholars who say the voice is the voice of the angel position him at the bottom of the valley. This understanding presumes that the angel's presence is inappropriate since the angel takes the form of a man in the immediate place where Mary delivers her son; to this place, a high place, no name is given:

> And We made the son of Mary and his mother as a sign: We gave them both shelter on high ground, affording rest and security and furnished with springs. (Qur'an, 23:50)

Note in the above verse that Allah SWT is rendering support to Mary and her son, and that the agency of the angel is absent. This understanding provides support to the second position: If the voice is that of the baby Jesus, his speaking to her is simply the beginning of his support for his mother, giving her courage to take him to her family. Once her family exclaims about the baby, he comes to her rescue, for if she had been left on her own, no one would have believed her:

> At length she brought the [babe] to her people, carrying him [in her arms]. They said: "O Mary! Truly an amazing thing you have brought!
> O sister of Aaron![14] Your father was not a man of evil, nor your mother a woman unchaste!

14. Muhammad Asad, in *The Message of the Qur'an*, 460, has the following footnote to explain why Mary was called "Sister of Aaron": "In ancient Semitic usage, a person's name was often linked with that of a renowned ancestor or founder of the tribal line. Thus, for instance, a man of the tribe of Banu Tamim was sometimes addressed as 'son of Tamim' or 'brother of Tamim.' Since Mary belonged to the priestly caste, and hence descended from Aaron, the brother of Moses, she was called a 'sister of Aaron' (in the same way as her cousin Elisabeth, the wife of Zachariah, is spoken of in Luke 1:5, as one 'of the daughters of Aaron'" (MAS).

But she pointed to him. They said: "How can we talk to one who is a child in the cradle?"

He said: "I am indeed a servant of Allah: He [revealed] to me the Book and made me a prophet;

And he made me blessed wheresoever I be, and enjoined on me Prayer and Charity as long as I live:

And [He] made me kind to my mother, and not overbearing or miserable;

So, Peace is on me the day I was born, the day that I die, and the day that I shall be raised up to life [again]." (Qur'an, 19:27–32)

A tradition of Prophet Muhammad adds another attribute of Jesus Christ that attests to his special status:

Abu Hurayrah (May Allah be pleased with him) narrated that the Messenger of Allah (Peace be upon him) said:

"There is no newly born except that [at the moment of birth] Satan disturbs him, so he begins to cry from Satan's disturbance with the exception of the son of Mary and his mother."

Then Abu Hurayrah added: Recite if you will [the supplication of Mary's mother in the Qur'an, 3:37]:

". . . And I commend her and her offspring to Thy protection from Satan, the Accursed one."[15]

The timing of Jesus Christ's birth must have taken place early in autumn, because the "fresh ripe dates" in Palestine are harvested towards the end of September.

The overall picture is summed up in Sura 66 *Al-Tahrim* in a context that considers Mary a spiritual role model. Each of two women—the wife of the Pharaoh and Mary—was presented "as an example for those who believe."

And Mary the daughter of 'Imran, who guarded her chastity; and We breathed into [her body] of Our spirit; and she testified to the truth of the words of her Lord and of his Revelations and was one of the devout [servants]. (Qur'an, 66:12)

One can reflect on the beauty of some fourteen hundred years of Islamic literature that reflect the message of the Qur'an and the Sunnah vis-à-vis Mary. Muslim scholars throughout the ages held Mary in high esteem and never doubted her chastity. The Islamic position reflects the

15. Al-Mundhiri, *Mukhtasar Sahih Muslim.*

truth about her; she was a very pious woman whom Allah SWT accepted. She was chaste and carried Jesus miraculously without a father.

There are two non-Muslim extreme positions regarding Mary. The first group considered her the God-bearing (*theotokos*) Mary, the "Mother of God" and began praying to her. (One wonders, to whom did Mary pray after delivering Jesus?) The second group went to extremes in the opposite direction, accusing Mary of being unchaste, and asserting that Jesus Christ was the fruit of adultery. According to *The Jewish Encyclopedia*,[16] the word *mamzer* (Hebrew for "bastard") was applied to Jesus. This latter group, according to the Qur'an, is from among the "People of the Book" who "worshipped the calf" (Qur'an, 4:153), were commanded to "transgress not in the matter of the Sabbath" (Qur'an, 4:154), "broke their Covenant[, and] . . . slew the Messengers in defiance of right" (Qur'an, 4:155); and:

> That they rejected Faith; that they uttered against Mary a grave false charge. (Qur'an, 4:156)

After the encounter between Mary and her family, and the miraculous speech of baby Jesus Christ in defense of his mother, the Qur'an does not provide other details about his childhood. He reemerges in the qur'anic narrative as an adult prophet preaching the word of Allah SWT and performing miracles in support of his vocation as a Messenger.

THE GOSPEL (AL-INJIL)

Allah SWT, out of his mercy, never left humanity without guidance. This is why He sent one messenger after another, and sometimes there was more than one messenger or prophet. There are four revealed books that are mentioned by name in the Qur'an; other than the latter they include the Torah of Moses, the *Zabur* of David, and the *Injil* of Jesus. After the Qur'an mentions Noah and Abraham, and that there were prophets among their offspring, Jesus Christ appears, continuing the line of prophecy:

> Then, in their wake, We followed them up with [others of] Our messengers: We sent after them Jesus the son of Mary, and bestowed on him the Gospel . . . (Qur'an, 57:27)

---

16. Jacobs et al., "Jesus of Nazareth."

The relationship between the Gospel (*Injil*, which is always mentioned in the singular in the Qur'an)[17] that Jesus received, and the Torah can be illustrated through the following verse, which appears in a context that mentions some of the laws of the Torah, the Jews' relationship to it, and that it is imperative to judge according to revelation:

> And in their footsteps, We sent Jesus the son of Mary, confirming the Law that had come before him: We sent him the Gospel: therein was guidance and light, and confirmation of the Law that had come before him: a guidance and an admonition to those who fear Allah. Let the People of the Gospel judge by what Allah had revealed therein . . . (Qur'an, 5:46–47)

As a messenger to the Children of Israel, Jesus Christ states that besides bringing the Signs to them from their Lord, he came to them in order to confirm the Torah, which was before him. Yet, vis-à-vis the Law, he addressed them by saying,

> And to make lawful to you part of what was [before] forbidden to you . . . (Qur'an, 3:50)

The confirmation of the previous message means a confirmation of the theology of *Tawhid*. It is simply attesting to the oneness of Allah, a message that was brought by every prophet:

> For We assuredly sent amongst every people a messenger, [with the command], "Serve Allah and eschew Evil . . ." (Qur'an, 16:36)

Some of the content of the Gospel, other than the confirmation of *Tawhid* and the relationship to the Torah and the Mosaic law, was revealed in the Qur'an. One of the most remarkable messages was a prophecy about the coming of Prophet Muhammad:

> Those who follow the Messenger, the unlettered (*Ummiyy*) Prophet, whom they find mentioned in their own [Scriptures], in the Torah and the Gospel . . . (Qur'an, 7:157)

The same message was confirmed in another qur'anic narrative:

> And remember, Jesus, the son of Mary, said: "O Children of Israel! I am the messenger of Allah [sent] to you, confirming the Torah

---

17. The Qur'an recognizes the revelation of one Gospel that does not exist anymore in its original form. This is why there is no recognition of the canonical Gospels or those described as apocryphal.

[which came] before me, and giving Glad Tidings of a Messenger
to come after me, whose name shall be Ahmad . . ." (Qur'an, 61:6)

This particular verse inspired many Muslim scholars to explore the
Gospels and the Torah. Numerous books have been written throughout
Islamic history on this subject. As an example, such scholars see verses such
as Deut 18:18 as a reference to Prophet Muhammad rather than to Jesus.

There is a very important correlation between "from their brethren"
(Deut 18:18) and the "unlettered" adjective in Qur'an, 7:157. To begin with
the latter, "unlettered" is a very popular translation, which is indeed an
interpretation, of *'Ummiyy'*, the original word in Arabic. Once it is mentioned, *'Ummiyy'* denotes illiteracy. The Prophet Muhammad was indeed
unlettered, but there is another meaning that was ignored:

> Among the People of the Book are some who, if entrusted with a
> hoard of gold, will [readily] pay it back; others amongst them, who
> if entrusted with a single silver coin, will not repay it unless you
> constantly stood demanding, because they say, "there is no call on
> us [to keep faith] with these Gentiles" (*Ummiyyin*; pl. of *Ummiyy*)
> . . . (Qur'an, 3:75)

The Arabs were mostly illiterate at the time the Qur'an was revealed,
but it cannot be a reference to illiteracy in this verse, for it would include the
illiterate Jew. A prophet was expected, but he was expected to come from
the line of Isaac not Ishmael. Here I invoke the phrase "from their brethren"
(Deut 18:18). If the prophecy were about someone from their brothers, the
Prophet would have been from the line of Isaac, or more precisely, from the
line of Jacob—because Esau was also excluded from the picture through
deception! "From their brethren" would be the descendants of Abraham
through his son Ishmael. Essentially, the People of the Book rejected the
Prophet Muhammad because he was a non-Israelite Prophet.

Considering the etymology of Ahmad, there is a prophecy in Hag-
gai 2:7 that corresponds to Qur'an, 61:6: "And I will shake all nations, and
the *desire* of all nations will come." The original Hebrew word for "desire"
is *himda*. The word "desire" is so general that it could be applied to any
prophet. *Himda* on the other hand has the same three consonants identical
with Ahmad (*h-m-d*). The name Jesus Christ, for example, does not have
any shared consonant with *himda*. Abdul-Ahad Dawud, formerly David
Keldani, a priest of the Uniate-Chaldean sect, has the following to say:

The Gospel of St. John, being written in Greek, uses the name *Par-acletos*, a barbarous form unknown to classical Greek literature. But *Periclytos*, which corresponds exactly with Ahmad in its signification of "illustrious," "glorious" and "praised," in its superlative degree, must have been the translation into Greek of *Himda* or probably *Hemida* of the Aramaic form, as uttered by Jesus Christ. Alas, there is no Gospel extant in the original language spoken by Jesus![18]

THE MIRACLES

The miracles in the Qur'an are out-of-the-ordinary events that take place by means of a prophet's hands, to support him in his vocation. It is Allah SWT who enables the prophet to perform the miracle by his leave, or who directly interferes in history and allows the miracle to take place. The miracle, or rather "sign" (*ayah*) in the language of the Qur'an, points in the direction of Allah, the Omnipotent, and not in the direction of the prophet, who has no control over its course. Jesus Christ was no different; he was allowed several miracles.

In addition to being a Sign himself, being the Word of God, and not God the Word, Jesus Christ had the following miracles:

> Then will Allah say: "O Jesus the son of Mary! Recount my favor to you and to your mother. Behold! I strengthened thee with the spirit of the holy, so that you did speak to the people in infancy and in maturity. Behold! I taught you the Book and Wisdom, the Torah and the Gospel. And behold! You did make out of clay, the figure of a bird, by My leave, and you did breathe into it, and it became a bird by My leave, and you did heal those born blind, and the lepers, by My leave. And behold! You did bring forth the dead by My leave. And behold! I did restrain the Children of Israel from [harming] you when you showed them the Clear Signs, and the unbelievers among them said: 'This is nothing but evident magic.'" (Qur'an, 5:110)

There are other miracles that took place through the hands of Jesus Christ. He informed the Children of Israel about things that they had done or said in the privacy of their homes:

---

18. Abdul-Ahad Dawud, *Muhammad in the Bible*, 24.

... And I declare to you what you eat, and what you store in your houses. Surely, therein is a Sign for you if you did believe. (Qur'an, 3:49)

One other remarkable miracle that took place upon a request from Jesus Christ's Disciples (*Al-Hawariyyun*) was the Table with food that was sent down from heaven. Jesus Christ warned them against making such a demand and asked them to fear Allah. They, on the other hand, wanted this Table as an assurance that Jesus had told them the truth. Jesus, then, made the following supplication:

> Jesus the son of Mary Said: "O Allah our Lord! Send us from heaven a Table set [with viands], that there may be for us—for the first and the last of us—a solemn festival and a Sign from You; and provide for our sustenance, for You are the best Sustainer [of our needs]."
> Allah said: "I will send it down unto you . . ." (Qur'an, 5:114–15)

This last verse came with a warning, for those who witness a miracle like this and eat from it are expected to be true believers through and through. No names are mentioned of those Disciples, but their emergence as a group took place in a context in which Jesus Christ sensed animosity towards his message from the Children of Israel:

> When Jesus found unbelief on their part he said: "Who will be my helpers [to the work of] Allah?" The Disciples said: "We are Allah's helpers: we believe in Allah, and you bear witness that we are Muslims." (Qur'an, 3:52)

THE CRUCIFIXION

Jesus Christ was sent to the children of Israel. Some of them believed in his prophethood and the rest were unbelievers. At one point, they plotted against him (Qur'an, 3:54). They forgot that they were dealing with Allah SWT, who saved his servant miraculously:

> Behold! Allah said: "O Jesus! I will cause you to die (*mutawaffika*)[19] and raise you to Myself and clear you [of the falsehoods] of those who blaspheme . . ." (Qur'an, 3:55)

19. The etymology of the root *w-f-y* (i.e., of *mutawaffika*) invokes the notion of completion and fulfillment. It is different from the root *m-w-t*, which is associated directly with death (cf. Qur'an, 19:33). Therefore, *mutawaffika* created uncertainty about what

Those who plotted against Jesus Christ, the high priest and the San-hedrin, were convinced that their scheme was fulfilled, and that Jesus was crucified. They were not aware of a divine plan that saved him:

> And that they said [in boast], "We killed Christ Jesus the son of Mary, the Messenger of Allah"—but they killed him not, nor cru-cified him, *but so it was made to appear to them*, and those who differ therein are full of doubts, with no certain knowledge, but only conjecture to follow, for a surety they killed him no—Nay, Allah raised him up unto Himself; and Allah is Exalted in Power, Wise. (Qur'an, 4:157)

Several legends emerged in the attempt to interpret this verse. "*But so it was made to appear to them*" sparked human imagination. Muhammad Assad in his commentary on the crucifixion story said that

> the Qur'an categorically denies the story of the crucifixion of Je-sus. There exist, among Muslims, many fanciful legends telling us that at the last moment God substituted for Jesus a person closely resembling him (according to some accounts, that person was Judas), who was subsequently crucified in his place. However, none of these legends finds the slightest support in the Qur'an or authentic Traditions, and the stories produced in this connection by the classical commentators must be summarily rejected. They represent no more than confused attempts at "harmonizing" the Qur'anic statement that Jesus was *not* crucified with the graphic description, in the Gospels, of his crucifixion.[20]

Another aspect associated with the story of the crucifixion in Christi-anity is the idea of salvation. The Islamic worldview allows room for repen-tance throughout the life of the human being. Every human being is born with a clear record; there is no concept of original sin, and Eve is not re-sponsible for the fall in the Qur'an.[21] Every human being is responsible for

---

happened to Jesus Christ right before he was raised in order to avoid the crucifixion. There are Muslim scholars who interpreted it to indicate the death of Jesus, while oth-ers interpreted it in terms of a kind of sleep, since the Qur'an does use the same root for sleeping, for it is presented in the Qur'an as a kind of death. (cf. Qur'an, 39:42). All interpretations speak of a certain completion. Some interpretations could be classified as *Israeliyyat* (i.e., reflecting either Jewish or Christian narratives that either contradict or do not have corresponding Islamic sources in the Qur'an or the authentic compendia of Hadith). Cf. Ibn Kathir, *Tafsir*, 1:346 (MAS).

20. Asad, trans., *Message*, 134.

21. See Qur'an, 2:35–37. The Qur'an uses dual grammatical verbal forms to describe the fact that Adam and Eve were deceived by Satan without their names being mentioned.

her deeds, and repentance is a direct relationship with Allah, the Forgiver (*Al-Tawwab*). That no one is responsible for what others are committing is a recurrent theme in the Qur'an:[22]

> . . . Every soul draws the meed of its acts on none but itself: no bearer of burdens can bear the burden of another . . . (Qur'an, 6:164)

In addition, the Islamic worldview vis-à-vis the original-sin construct is in line with Deut. 24:16; both the Qur'an and Deuteronomy differentiate between the responsibility of parents and children.[23]

The fact that Jesus Christ was not crucified, and that he was raised to Allah SWT does mean that he is not mortal. He was destined, like other human beings, to be born, to die, and to be resurrected:

> "So peace is on me the day I was born, the day that I die, and the Day that I shall be raised up to life [again]." (Qur'an, 19:33)

THE SECOND COMING

It might be helpful at the beginning of this section to affirm that there are no direct references in the Qur'an to the second coming of Jesus Christ. In the best-case scenario, we can discuss the interpretation of some verses in the light of many traditions that do *confirm* the second coming. On the other hand, there are contemporary scholars who do not venture beyond what the Qur'an says and dismiss the traditions relevant to this issue altogether. Belief in the Qur'an does not necessitate a belief in the interpretation of any scholar. Muslims never adopted any book of exegesis, and Muslim scholars have always kept a healthy distance from accepting a single exegetical reading of the Qur'an. In addition, Islamic scholarship is a decentralized activity, whereby anyone can say anything. On the one hand, this decentralization has kept the interpretation of the Qur'an a lively and thriving academic field. On the other, it allowed a plethora of opinions that cannot all be substantiated on the basis of the Islamic sources.

The narrative renders the identification of the first one to succumb to deception mission impossible. The fall ended almost immediately with Adam repenting and Allah SWT accepting his repentance.

22. Cf. Qur'an, 17:15; 35:18; 39:7; 53:38.

23. Deut 24:16: "Parents shall not be put to death for their children, nor shall children be put to death for their parents; only for their own crimes may persons be put to death."

The study of the Hadith is also a very sophisticated field. It is very important, and the Sunnah of the Prophet Muhammad is a manifestation of the Qur'an itself in the life of the Prophet. It also explains and augments the message of the Qur'an. Nevertheless, despite a very deep respect and acceptance of certain compendia of Hadith, such as Sahih Al-Bukhari and Sahih Muslim, there are challenges, and there is no consensus about accepting the compendia in toto. Even if the Hadith is authentic and had limited independent chains of narrators, such as one chain of narrators a (e.g., *Āhād*), there are two different positions regarding the inclusion of such Hadith in Islamic faith. While there are those who would accept the *Āhād* tradition, in matters of faith, there are those who reject it; they would include it in practical matters only. The multiple chains of narrators are described as *Mutawātir*. The latter category could indicate multiple confirmations of the whole text (i.e., the wording) of the Hadith or a confirmation of its message, with the wording being different, or even including other issues or details that are not part of every Hadith. The first is described as *Mutawātir Lafzan*, and the second as *Mutawātir Ma'nan*.

Raising Jesus Christ from among his people brought the first chapter of Jesus Christ's life to its completion. The Qur'an does not provide details about what comes next except for couple of verses such as the following:

> And [Jesus] shall be a Sign [for the coming of] the Hour [of Judgment] . . . (Qur'an, 43:61)

This verse could be interpreted in three ways. The first interpretation depends on transliterating the first Arabic word in the verse. The first word in Arabic is *wainnahu*; it comprises three words: *wa* is "and," *inna* is "verily," and *hu* is a suffixed pronoun. The pronoun in Arabic is the equivalent of "he" in English, and in the absence of "it," this pronoun could refer to Jesus, for the whole context is about him, or, according to Al-Hassan Al-Basri and Sa'eed Ibn Jubayr, the pronoun refers to the Qur'an itself.

The other two interpretations are concerned with Jesus Christ. One of them is the position of Ibn Ishaq, who considers the miracles themselves that Jesus performed to be the Sign for the Hour. Bringing the dead back to life is a reminder of what will be the case on the day of judgment.

The last position speaks directly about a second return of Jesus Christ, and that this return is an indication of the end of time. This is the position of Mujahid. In addition, Ibn Kathir attributed this position, using indirect speech which weakens the report, to Abu Hurayrah, Ibn 'Abbas, Abu

Al-`Aliyah, Abu Malik, `Ikrimah, Al-Hassan, Qatadah, and Ad-Dahhak. Some of them are scholars from among the companions of the Prophet, and the rest are second generation. Ibn Kathir, furthermore, states that there are numerous traditions of the Prophet that speak about Jesus descending before the day of judgment and becoming a just leader and a fair ruler.[24]

These traditions reflect a new role for Jesus Christ that he did not experience before; he will fulfill a role of a community leader who implements Islam:

> Abu Hurarya narrated that Allah's Messenger (Peace be upon him) said: "By Him in Whose Hands my soul is, surely [Jesus,] the son of Mary will soon descend amongst you and will judge mankind justly [as a Just Ruler]; he will break the Cross and kill the pigs and there will be no *Jizya* [i.e., taxation taken from non-Muslims]. Money will be in abundance so that nobody will accept it, and a single prostration to Allah [in prayer] will be better than the whole world and whatever is in it."
>
> Abu Huraira added: "If you wish, you can recite [this verse of the Qur'an]:
>
> "And there is none of the People of the Book [Jews and Christians] but must believe in him [i.e., Jesus as an Apostle of Allah and a human being] before his death. And on the Day of Judgment, he will be a witness against them [if they do not believe]." (Qur'an, 4:159)[25]

Other traditions provide additional details. These include Jesus landing in Damascus, and that he will kill the antichrist, the false messiah (*Al-Massih Al-Dajjal*), near Lydda (Lod, in Palestine), and that Jesus will die before the actual day of judgment.[26]

The prominent scholars who state that the traditions that report Jesus Christ's second coming reached the level of being *Mutawātir* include Mahmoud Al-Alousiyy in his *Ruh Al-Ma`ani*; he states that these traditions could have reached (*la`allaha balaghat*) the *Mutawātir Ma`nan*. Moreover, a prominent scholar of Hadith, Ibn Kathir, says that "the traditions, that report the Messenger of Allah (peace be upon him) telling about Jesus (peace be upon him) descending before the day of judgment as just leader and

---

24. Ibn Kathir, *Tafsir*, 4:135.

25. Bukhari, *Sahih*, vol. 4, book 55, #657.

26. Cf. Muslim, *Sahih Muslim*, 18:63; Dawud, *Muhamamd in the Bible*, 4:117; Al-Tirmidhi, *Sunan at-Tirmidhi*, 9:92; Ibn Majah, *Sunan Ibn Majah*, 2:1356; Deedat, *What the Bible Says*, 4:181.

impartial ruler, are *Mutawātir*." This was the essential position of Ibn Hajar in *Fath Al-Bari Sharh Sahih Al-Bukhari*.[27]

The names of the scholars that confirmed the *Mutawātir* status of these traditions are too many to enumerate here. There are those who dedicated whole books to this issue with the same result. Some of the scholars and titles include Muhammad Zahid Al-Kawthari, *Nazrah `Abirah fi Maza`im man Yunkir Nuzul `Issa `Alayhi Al-Salam Qabla Al-Akhirah* (1362 AH/1943 CE); Abdullah Al-Ghumari, *`Aqidat Ahl Al-Sunnah fi Nuzul `Issa `Alayhi Al-Salam* (1369 AH/1949 CE).[28]

The other school, which does not accept these traditions to be *Mutawātir*, and which holds that they remain within the sphere of *Āhād*, includes some prominent names like Sheikh Muhammad Abdo. He also attempted to interpret these traditions metaphorically. The descent of Jesus means that the spirit of his message, which includes his teachings about mercy, love, and peace, will prevail.[29]

BIBLIOGRAPHY

Al-Albani, Muhammad Nasser Al-Din. *Qissat Al-Massih Al-Dajjal wa Nuzul `Issa `Alayhi Al-Salam wa Qatlihi Iyyah*. Amman: Al-Maktabah Al-Islamiyyah, 2000.

Al-Bukhari, Muhammad ibn Ismail. *Sahih Al-Bukhari: The English Translation of Sahih Al Bukhari with the Arabic Text*, edited by Muhammad Muhsin Khan. Alexandria, VA: al-Saadawi, 1996.

Al-Kashmiri, Muhammad Anwar Shah, and Abdul Fattah Abu Ghuddah, eds. *Al-Tasrih bima Tawatar fi Nuzul Al-Masih*. 5th ed. Beirut: Dar Al-Qalam, 1992.

Al-Mundhiri, Hafiz Zakiuddin Abdul-Azim. *Mukhtasar Sahih Muslim*. Amman: Al-Maktabah Al-Islamiyyeh, 1991.

Al-Tirmidhi, Abu Isa Muhammad. *Sunan at-Tirmidhi: The English Translation of "Jami` at-Tirmidhi."* With Arabic text, translated by Abu Khaliyl, edited by Abu Tahir Zubair Ali Za`i. Riyadh: Maktabah Dar-us-Salam, 2007.

Asad, Muhammad, trans. *The Message of the Qur'an*. Translated and explained by Muhammad Asad. Gibraltar: Dar Al-Andalus, 1980.

Dawud, Abdul-Ahad. *Muhammad in the Bible*. 5th ed. Doha: Ministry of Awqaf and Islamic Affairs, 1994.

Deedat, Ahmed. *What the Bible Says about Muhammad*. Chicago: Kazi, 1991.

Hofmann, Murad. *Islam: The Alternative*. Translated by Christiane Banerji. 1st English ed. Reading, UK: Garnet, 1993.

27 Al-Kashmiri and Abu Ghuddah, eds., *Al-Tasrih*, 57–61.

28. Al-Kashmiri and Abu Ghuddah, eds., *Al-Tasrih* 56–57.

29. Al-Albani, *Qissat Al-Massih*, 9.

Ibn Hanbal Ash-Shaybani, and Abu Abdullah Ahmad Ibn Muhammad. *Musnad Imam Ahmad Ibn Hanbal.* Translated by Nasiruddin al-Khattab. Edited by Huda Al-Khattab. Riyadh: Maktabah Dar-us-Salam, 2012.

Ibn Kathir, al-Makki. *Tafsir al-Quran al-`Azim.* 10 vols. Beirut: Dar Al-Jil, 1988.

Ibn Majah Al-Qazwini, et al., trans. *The English Translation of "Jami` at-Tirmidhi."* With Arabic text, translated by Nasiruddin al-Khattab. Edited by Abu Tahir Zubair Ali Za`i. Riyadh: Maktabah Dar-us-Salam, 2007.

Jacobs, Joseph, et al. "Jesus of Nazareth." *Jewish Encyclopedia.com* (website). https://jewishencyclopedia.com/articles/8616-jesus-of-nazareth/.

Khuttab, Mustafa, ed. *The Clear Qur'an.* Website. https://theclearquran.org/.

Muslim, ibn al-Hajjaj al-Naysaburi. *Sahih Muslim.* Translated by Nasiruddin Al-Khattab. 7 vols. Houston: Dar-us-Salam, 2007.

3

Writing the Afterlives
From Jesus to the Vilna Gaon

RICHARD A. FREUND[1]

The idea of writing down oral Jewish traditions was problematic from ancient to modern times even for the "People of the Book." Rabbinic tradition viewed with great skepticism the practice of writing down oral rabbinic teachings. The question is, why? Why was it considered inappropriate to write down the teachings of the study house and of its greatest teachers? I think I know why. This chapter is about the afterlives of the teachings of some of the greatest sages of the rabbinic tradition—"From Jesus through the Vilna Gaon"—and asks why it was left to the students of these great masters to edit, write down, and "publish" the words of their teachers.

HUBRIS AND HUTZPAH

There is at least a measure of humility that can be detected in the decision not to publish the oral traditions in general. The rabbis had a deep and

1. Rabbi Professor Richard Freund died on July 14, 2022. This volume is dedicated to his memory.

abiding respect for the written text of the Hebrew Bible. I think they did not want to contribute—even in a small way—to the diluting of the sanctity of the Bible. In the Mishnah, for example, there are a minimal number of direct citations of the Bible. The lack of a direct biblical textual justification to accompany the legal pronouncements of the rabbis seemed to embolden the rabbis of the Mishnah.

In the midrash, these same issues from the Mishnah are presented with a textual justification. This too is problematic since the textual justifications within the midrash were often derived from a rather strained interpretation of a biblical text. The rabbinic respect for the sanctity of the biblical text and the humility of the rabbinic interpretation may have dictated their own unwillingness to write down their teaching in their own generation. That did not stop later generations of rabbis from feeling a sense of ownership of their teachers' oral tradition. I suspect that these later generations of rabbis were guilty of a measure of hubris (or better the Hebrew word, *huzpah*) that they were custodians of the "true" meaning of the text that they had been taught. *Huzpah* dictated that the later generations of students not only would write down and edit the teachings of their teachers but had an obligation to publish the teachings for others to study. The afterlife of rabbinic teachings involved a multigenerational process of oral study, reflection, writing, editing, and publishing. It seems to have served not only the Jews but also other ancient masters among the Greeks.

Orality allows for flexibility—and this dictum's meaning is only approximated by a human pronouncement. Rabbinic citations are cited in rabbinic texts as formulas of comparison such as, "Rabbi Y said of Rabbi X's view-of A-B-C, while Rabbi Z said of Rabbi Y's teaching that it is D-E-F." What started as a way of compensating for the lack of a written "paper trail" of the actual discussion by the original master, became a convention of multiple versions of an oral tradition whose meaning could be understood in different ways and formulations. This format gave the original master's words great flexibility for a changing and often radically different context. It also gave the orality an ongoing place in a world of Jewish written texts.

FROM THE GREEKS TO THE ROMANS TO THE JEWS

Most scholars of religion are aware of the oral nature of the Homeric poetic tradition. They can understand the orality of the African, Buddhist, and Native American traditions, but rarely see the application to our elucidation of the rabbinic ideas inherent in the collected works about Jesus' pronouncements and other oral traditions in Judaism.[2] What I call the "ripple effect" is a long and twisted path for researchers who do not employ a critical methodology and so take every canonical textual statement as if it was pronounced by the master himself.

The ancient Greek court system itself is a study of how fixed, memorized legal formulations were permitted as precedents in trials in Athens.[3] The fact is that oral traditions were seen as reliable as written traditions, and it is only quite late in history, after the development of cheap and easily available writing implements like paper and fixed-leaf papyri in the fifth and sixth centuries CE that the Near East was able to record and fix their textual traditions. One would like to think that the traditions of ancient masters were preserved in simple but fixed canons of oral expressions, but the traditions were most probably products of a later generation with memorized notes of a tradition.

BACK TO THE SOURCES:
READING SOCRATES SYNOPTICALLY

I have been writing about this type of synoptic reading as a genre of ancient but also modern writing. It is seen as a barrier to a full understanding of the historical accounts of literary figures. Instead of an autograph copy from the hand of the master, we are presented with a series of forms, and each form contains kernels of data that often tell us as much about the student as about the master.

Plato is a particularly vexing student because he is such a looming and prolific literary figure to see through to Socrates. Socrates had many students. The three most prominent were Plato, Xenophon, and Aristophanes, and each had totally different approaches to the master's teaching. Each wrote down the "notes" of the ideas of the master, and it is from them that they expanded upon ideas to their re-creation of the meaning of Socrates's

---

2. Parry, "Studies in the Epic Technique" was a groundbreaking article in establishing the nature of how mnemonic devices are embedded in the poetry. This allowed ancients to remember the meter and cadence of what might be the original formulation as it was performed by the master teacher. The theory created an entire discipline as one can see in the annotated bibliography of Foley, *Oral-Formulaic*.

3. Gagarin, *Early Greek Law*.

ideas. In the writings of Xenophon, for example, Socrates is more suicidal than he is in Plato and Aristophanes.[4]

We are dependent upon the versions of these works that survived the Dark Ages when most of these texts were not copied and only revived by a translation mill that was heavily influenced by the Islamic concept of their own legacy. Xenophon's Socrates is far more involved in the daily lives of people and far less aloof and philosophical than he is in Plato's and Aristophanes's works. Plato's *Apology* presents a Socrates unlike the Socrates in Xenophon's *Apology*.

The Clouds by Aristophanes and *The Apology of Socrates* by Plato give Socrates a different tone in his teaching, and these differences give us a sense that either there were three different figures called Socrates, or this is the nature of orality as reflected in the teaching of a master teacher and in the note-taking of the students. Socrates can attract a diverse group of disciples, and separate students hear different messages in the same teaching because they are from different social strata, because they have different skills or interests, or simply because they are themselves not intellectually gifted enough to understand the master's teachings.

Xenophon, who came from a humbler background than Plato, emphasizes Socrates's sometimes-obsessive critiques of individuals while Plato presents Socrates as a critic of society in general, without delving into as many details of who exactly Socrates is critiquing in a given instance. The Socrates of Plato is not deferential of those who will decide his fate at his trial while in Xenophon he is much more deferential to the judges. This may be a reflection of the privileged status that Plato enjoyed versus the status of Xenophon. Xenophon is himself more pious in regard to the divinities of Greece, so his Socrates is less impious. Aristophanes, in his comic caricature of Socrates, captures elements of the master that are absent from Xenophon's and Plato's portraits, but Aristophanes seems closer to Xenophon than to Plato.[5]

For Plato, who wrote about his mentor, at the end of his life, Socrates is the wisest of men in Athens and is an idealist concerned with the morals and improvement of the State. For Aristophanes, who chose to write about the midlife Socrates, Socrates is still a teacher of a dialectic message and he is simply a moral gadfly. Who was Socrates? In the end, he becomes a composite figure, and we end up reading these three and other random

---

4. Anastaplo, "On the Socrates."

5. Petrie, "Aristophanes and Socrates."

accounts synoptically in order to understand both the historical Socrates and the Socrates of Greek philosophy. One may wonder if the presentation of the comedic Socrates by Aristophanes was intended to harm or lessen the sharpness of Socrates's criticism of Athens by presenting him as a harmless teacher of pedantic philosophy. In its historical context, what Aristophanes's play did, however, was elevate the status of Socrates in the eyes of the public so that he suddenly went from a relatively obscure figure for the masses to a well-known person, albeit a caricature of himself.

As we view this some 2,400 years after the fact, we can wonder why Socrates himself did not write his own thoughts—and, more important, what we can learn about public intellectuals who are at the mercy of their students to manage their legacies. This is a well-known problem in antiquity, but it is specifically an issue for Jewish figures, who were faced with the prospect of multiple authors adding elements to their teachings that they never intended to convey.

THE HISTORICAL JESUS AND READING RABBINIC TEXTS SYNOPTICALLY

The case of Jesus is similar, with the dizzying array of views of his teachings from the canonical Gospels to the gnostic gospels. The attempts by the "historical" Jesus scholars and "Q" scholars to reconstruct Jesus' original stances are usually stymied because of the lack of textual evidence to support such reconstructions. The diverse messages from the original oral statements of Jesus as captured by the Gospel writers are often treated as a synoptic "mosaic" or "weave" that can be untangled by researchers employing a series of literary principles.[6] The key, I think, to contextualizing the emphasis on the orality of the tradition is to assume that the oral tradition was a simple mnemonic, a memorizable series of words present in the written versions but expanded in different ways based upon the considerations of the writers. In their "afterlives," therefore, Jesus sayings have not been preserved verbatim but rather serve as signposts by which the individual Gospel writers understand certain meanings behind the orally transmitted "gist" of a teaching.

In the case of Jesus of Nazareth this may be a function of Jewish oral law in general and not just the idiosyncratic tendencies of particular devotees of Jesus in the Greco-Roman world. The Babylonian Talmud expressly

6. Bernier, *Quest for the Historical Jesus*; and Witherington, *Jesus Quest*, for example.

forbids the writing down of the oral tradition of master teachers. Babylonian Talmud, Tractate *Gittin* 60b records this as follows: *Devarim she'be'al peh, eey atah resha'ie le'omram bichsav* ("You are not permitted to transmit the Oral Torah in writing").

This early pronouncement is indicative of an antipathy to written parts of a tradition. The Oral Torah was not permitted to be taught from a written format. *Torah shebeal peh* was meant to be just that—Torah taught completely without any written text. This may be understood in a number of ways. Writing, if done in this period, was a laborious preoccupation of a skilled scribe. The preparing of an animal's skin or parchment was itself a labor-intensive exercise. Arranging the text to be easily copied and recited in antiquity had something in common with sending a Tweet today; material was organized in short chunks rather than in the long narratives that prevailed later. A great teacher's musings were taken down by students and therefore potentially subject to misunderstanding by those students because of the nature of the short expositions that were preserved. When one reads in the early rabbinic collection *Tosefta Zabim* 1.5 that Rabbi Akiva in the second century would "set in order" the teachings for his students and would then caution them by saying, "He who has heard some argument against his fellow student's [rendition] let him come forward and state it" shows just how an oral tradition in this early period would be related to varying versions of the same oral tradition that coexisted at the same time. Also, the Jews in the Greco-Roman world feared that a certain teaching might transmit information that would be used by the authorities (or perhaps other Jewish "heretics") in unintended ways. The fear that a certain rabbinic teaching, laden with culturally rich references, might have unintended consequences once it was "published" made writing an issue. Finally, there is just the nature of the pedagogical enterprise of expositing Jewish oral tradition. Midrash, a form of expansion of a biblical text by a teacher, orally explores the variant ideas inherent in a cryptic ancient tradition without an intent to formally legislate the idea.

There is a story in the Babylonian Talmud, tractate *Menahot* 29b which exemplifies this type of expansion, which seemed to the rabbis to be both appropriate and expansive. In the midrash there, Moses is brought to the academy of Rabbi Akiva thousands of years in the future. In the academy where he is teaching, the rabbi explains an entire tradition that Moses himself cannot understand. When Rabbi Akiva reaches a discussion point, the students ask their teacher: "Rabbi, how did you reach that conclusion?"

Rabbi Akiva answered: "(The source of my information is a tradition that) Moses received at Mount Sinai and passed it on to succeeding generations." The idea that "expansion" and "interpretation" of an oral tradition should be attributed back to a great master—even if he did not actually say it—was a very meaningful part of the tradition.

We know what synoptic reading of the New Testament Gospels must have looked like in the early church thanks to surviving manuscripts of attempts to harmonize them. Synoptic reading of the New Testament meant looking at the four canonical versions of the Gospels with all their similarities and differences and gleaning a story line that fit together neatly, often by accepting and deleting elements that did not fit together easily. We know about this type of synoptic reading because of the second-century CE writer Tatian, whose harmonized *Diatessaron* survived for us to examine in the modern period. While his edited text did not catch on, it provided a window into reading an ancient text synoptically. Tatian sought to combine all the textual material he found in the four canonical Gospels into a single, coherent narrative of Jesus' life and death, and his version tells us much about how readers understood the text even while they had different circulating gospels.

This kind of intellectual quest for the historical figures and circumstances behind the texts in the modern period gives us a sense of what was, I think, a form of early synoptic reading of rabbinic traditions—a kind of reading that was done by the later interpreters. The terminology counts. The rabbis of the first generations (from the first through the third century) are considered the founders of the oral-to-literary transition. *Tannaim* is the term for both "learners" and "oral transmitters." Tannaim are considered the closest to the original oral traditions, and the fourth- and fifth-century *Amoraim,* be they in Israel or Babylonia, are seen as interpreters of the oral traditions. When I read about the opinions of the first-century CE Hillel and Shammai (better: the schools of Bet Hillel and Bet Shammai that organized them) reflecting on ancient oral traditions that are only vaguely expressed in the Bible—about ritual purity, relations between Jews and non-Jews, marriage customs, discipleship, and even some fundamental theological issues—one can see how the tradition of oral-to-written texts that developed in the period following the two destructive rebellions of the Jews against the Romans (in the first and second centuries CE) are 180-degree disputes with only a topic to bind them. The early rabbinic view of how to harmonize or read these aphorisms or traditions was that two parallel but divergent ways of reading were both equally true, but one was chosen as implementable.

So, the saying is, *Elu V'Elu divrei Elohim Hayim* [literally: "both views are the words of the living God"]. As expressed by the Amoraim in the Babylonian Talmud, tractate *Eruvin* 13b, both opinions are considered as divinely inspired. In the generations following Hillel and Shammai (both Tannaim) there are a range of individual opinions and "schools": the opinions held in these schools were collected and edited into a full rabbinic text about Jewish life and law. These edited texts include such collections as *Mechilta D'Rabbi Yishmael* and the *Mechilta of Rabbi Shimon bar Yochai*. Both of these focus on the biblical book of Exodus, but the opinions within the two collections are often diametrically opposed to one another.

As the rabbinic Talmudim and midrashim emerged in the Amoraic period and continued until the last group of *Stammaim* (the final, anonymous editors) put their stamp on the discussions, the trend towards synoptic reading continued even as the writing process for both the Jerusalem and Babylonian Talmud continued through the sixth century and into the seventh century of the Common Era. Writing became the main form of Jewish expression even when there were writers who presented their own form of diverse traditions by writing in different periods and places (such as Maimonides, who found himself totally redoing his early work in his later work in the twelfth century CE). The idea of writing was the key, but the rabbis felt comfortable expanding earlier works or even restating traditions of earlier generations often in a new context.

THE MYSTICAL AND THE LEGAL TRADITIONS: AFTERLIVES OF THREE RABBIS AND THEIR STUDENTS

In the sixteenth century we have the case of two mystics. Rabbi Isaac Luria (1534–72) was born in Jerusalem and died in Safed (Galilee). His student, Rabbi Hayim Vital (1542–1620), was born in Egypt and died on his way back to Safed from Syria. The biggest problem of this period is to distinguish which are the teachings of the master and which are the interpretation of the disciple. This is complicated by the changing nature of rabbinic oral tradition even as the age of the printing press would forever change the immediacy of the teaching.

Notes from Rabbi Luria's lectures on mysticism were not publicly available and became the vehicle for the dissemination of his wisdom only through very dedicated copying at the behest of Rabbi Hayim. While it is possible that the early death of Rabbi Luria provided his enterprising students with the opportunity to move his ideas forward in ways that Luria could never have imagined, the dissemination process—from manuscript copies produced in Safed to later publication of the work titled *Etz Hayim* (Tree of Life, but obviously with a play on words based upon Rabbi Hayim Vital's name)—turned the study of mysticism from an esoteric and private enterprise into a much larger endeavor. Hayim even produced *Peri Etz Hayim* (literally Fruit of the Tree of Life), which dealt with the ritual implications of the system of mysticism.

From the talmudic period there were rabbis who discouraged mystical teaching for the masses and restricted them to certain advanced students. They did not want the general public to hear these doctrines in normative synagogue settings. So, for example, the opening chapters of Ezekiel, which have a rather graphic description of God and a Divine Chariot, were forbidden to be expounded upon in public. The Mishnah (tractate *Hagigah* 2:1) instructs that one may not teach Maaseh Merkavah (the Chariot event). Even then, one may only teach Maaseh Merkavah to someone who is capable of understanding it on his own; the teacher communicates merely chapter headings, the main outlines of the subject matter, from which the disciple may deduce the rest. Writing down such knowledge would allow it to be presented to an unprepared and unknowing public, so it was forbidden. Esoteric or mystical ideas which appeared even in the Bible but were not geared for the learned rabbinic public fundamentally changed rabbinic reading. Rabbinic synoptic reading began to take on altogether new mystical bent.

Whether Isaac Luria was the primary or secondary author of the work ascribed to him has been the subject of intense debate. In his article titled "Which Lurianic Kabbalah?"[7] we can see how Dan Karr attempts to understand why most disciples were willing to list their teacher as the author of their works: because it was known that Luria did not publish his works during his lifetime, and in fact their publication was not complete until the nineteenth century. Karr cites Dr. Shaul Magid at the beginning of his article to demonstrate the problem: "The corpus of Lurianic literature is highly complex and disorganized. Luria himself wrote almost nothing during his brief time in Safed. Most of what exists from the Safed circles is the product of various students, the most prolific and prominent being Rabbi Hayyim Vital and Rabbi Yaakov Hayyim Zemach."[8]

7. Karr, "Which Lurianic Kabbalah?"

8. Magid, "Kabbalah and Postmodern Jewish Philosophy."

The idea that Rabbi Isaac Luria contributed some cryptic statements that were then synthesized by his students, especially Rabbi Hayyim Vital, leads some to ask: "Why would a student pin his teacher's name to a teaching rather than straight away taking credit for an idea?" The idea of a student attaching his/her own insight to the master's teaching seems to be a very ancient tradition that dates back to the Pseudepigrapha in the Greco-Roman period. Many of the writings of the Bible's apocrypha and the pseudepigrapha have this as their foundation. Either to ensure that a work would be taken seriously or to bolster the significance of an idea in a text, authors were willing to ascribe their own ideas to an even earlier period and writer.

Isaac Luria is an example of how this view continued right through the modern period. As a student, I heard and read Professor Gershom Scholem's works on Luria in the 1970s. Professor Scholem always referred to the Lurianic Kabbalah as the product of a real person, Isaac Luria, but with the help of student note-takers. Unfortunately, it does not appear that there were any of the original notes of the master, and the students synthesized the cryptic oral cues of the teacher into a distinctive system.

Scholarship today attributes much more to the students than was originally suspected fifty years ago. Today, it is held that the "inspiration" of Luria provided a small part of the much larger corpus of ideas. Perhaps, it is thought, the nature of mystical thinking required this type of communication. Such communication was imparted from master to student and through the medium of a personal and intimate contact, with words that were themselves a type of revelation.

What we learn from the case of Rabbi Luria is that there is very little that can be in a transmitted in a public and published document. The mystical mentor can present a revelation as a personal "stream of consciousness" that is by nature unruly and nonsystematic but if revealed to gifted students can be made into a meaningful public and published text. Publishing books in the generation before the printing press was still publishing, but it still had a more fluid format. The printing press formalized this fluid nature of handwritten manuscripts and changed the extent to which teaching could be spread. Both the text of the Zohar and the interpretation of Luria were literally being published in the almost the same time period. The most renowned of the initiates of Luria was Rabbi Hayyim Vital, who, according to his master, possessed a unique soul, and who lived a lot longer than his mentor.

One of the other issues not always expressed is the whole problem of literacy. We assume that reading a text is a "given" skill. Today as we peruse most religions, the literacy question or the abilities of a disciple to write down or copy is taken for granted. In earlier periods the idea of literacy of the masses was quite different, and in places like India, the Middle East, and in Africa a student's ability to recite from memory was a highly valued skill. In many indigenous religions, literacy was not always a sign of deep, abiding wisdom but rather a skill set that was a technical ability rather than a prerequisite for discipleship. It may have caused oral recitation to be more free-flowing as opposed to our post-Enlightenment insistence upon the recitation of the canonized and published text.

THE BAAL SHEM TOV AND
THE ORIGINS OF HASIDISM

The idea of a modern oral tradition seems to have developed in tandem with the published word. Hasidism is an excellent example of how this trend developed. The "founder" of Hasidism was Israel Ben Eliezer (1698–1760), born in the Ukraine. He is known as the Baal Shem Tov—literally "the master of the good name" or in a short Hebrew acronym, "Besht"—but is not known for his literary prowess. He did not leave any commentaries or even annotations but rather a more popular form of storytelling and sayings traditions that are different from Isaac Luria's and from those of the Gaon of Vilna.

Shivhei HaBesht (In Praise of the Baal Shem Tov), a set of stories associated with his life and encounters of the Besht, and the *Iggeret HaKodesh* (The Holy Letter) are two examples of the Hasidic traditions. Like the Gaon and Luria, the Besht had disciples, especially Yaakov Yosef of Polonne (1710–1784) and Dov Ber of Mezeritch (1704–1772), and others. However, it is not altogether clear that the study of texts was the primary form of their realization of his teachings. They were more akin to folkloristic oral traditions and inspirational accounts that were spread through the general population, which gave them significance. Where the Besht, the Gaon, and Luria do compare well is that during their lifetimes there were no or few examples of their work available in writing, and even those that came into existence (such as The Holy Letter) include expansions that make them examples of the ongoing history of the Hasidic movement rather than reliable examples of the ideas of the original master, the Besht.

According to Hasidic tradition, The Holy Letter was a real letter that the Baal Shem Tov either wrote or dictated to someone else who wrote it down and sent to his brother-in-law in Israel in 1752. There were multiple versions of the letter that circulated after his death, but the "original" Baal Shem Tov letter—according to researchers—has been amplified and expanded, with all of the versions attributed to the master. There are as many as three or four versions, shorter and longer, that exist of the letter, and it is obvious from internal and external references that some of them have been supplemented. Even the viewpoint of the writer is changed by the editors in some versions of the letter to the third person from the second person.

That Baal Shem Tov was an original thinker who created fully formed rabbinic ideas that guided Hasidic thought in its early period is the way that most followers understand his role. The longer and most meaningful version of the letter echoes the ideas that became fashionable among Hasidic teachers over a hundred years after the Baal Shem's death. Many of these ideas became the guiding principles of the Hasidic movement. This process is one of the most important ways to compare the afterlife issue from the oral tradition to the written form of popular mysticism. Hasidism includes a teaching that the "unification" between each letter and each word of prayer and study reflects a comsic connection between human actions, souls, and divinity. This is a profound idea that echoes throughout Hasidism into the twentieth century.

In his article in the journal *Jewish History*, Moshe Rosman shows us that this idea is not in the shorter versions of the Baal Shem's letter.[9] Thus, we learn an important aspect about the afterlife of a sayings or story tradition—that this is the nature of the preserved elements of the life of the Baal Shem, and that later generations needed to expand even the sayings and the stories to make them both intelligible in and relevant to the life of Hasidism as it existed in later periods.

The *Shivhei HaBesht* (Sayings or Stories) collection has sayings that start with a short, cryptic statement by the master, which was taken down by one disciple, and in the next generation another Hasidic master expanded the saying, understanding it in a more encompassing way. The collection was first compiled by Dov Baer ben Samuel of Linits, the son-in-law of Alexander Shohat, who had acted for several years as Eliezer's scribe. Two editions

9. Rosman, "Hebrew Sources." He even shows that in order to harmonize the letter's contents certain researchers have to posit the existence of a second letter where the Baal Shem appears to ask whether his brother-in-law received his first letter and then has the opportunity to elaborate new ideas of the first letter. He concludes that there was one letter with one conflation or expansion that includes one of the central ideas of Hasidism, and it is placed in the earliest writing of the movement.

also appeared in Yiddish (the spoken language that was also the most read-able), which differ markedly from the Hebrew edition that was set to make it appear to be a standard rabbinic text. The collection was copied many times, and over time the copies became filled with errors. It was printed with the title, *Shivḥei HaBesht* only after Dov Baer ben Samuel's death.

THE GAON OF VILNA (1720–1797) AND THE CENTER OF JEWISH PUBLISHING IN VILNIUS, LITHUANIA

Unlike these earlier examples, the Gaon of Vilna, who died in 1797, was active as a teacher in a period when publishing was quite popular, and the largest publishing house for rabbinic texts was in fact in Vilnius: Romm Publishing House. It became the main purveyor of the Babylonian Talmud as well as most of the main rabbinic texts; the press was originally located in the city of Grodno but moved to Vilnius in 1799.

The Gaon's own specialized institute, for his own special teaching, was on the first floor of his house, where there was a minyan that the Gaon would attend, and which was limited to hand-selected scholars. The group, which later became known as the Gaon's Kloyz, was formed after the death of the Gaon in the most documented way that I have seen. The Vilna Gaon was a copious annotator; there is hardly an ancient Hebrew book of any importance to which he did not provide marginal glosses and notes, or on which he did not write a brief commentary (which were mostly dictated to his pupils). Many maintain that it was his disciples who recorded his comments, if not his editorial notes.

However, nothing of his work was published in his lifetime. The Gaon was very precise in the wording of his commentaries, because he maintained that he was obligated by Torah Law that only the *Torah she'bichtav* (the writ-ten law) is permitted to be written down. The rest of *Torah she'beal peh* (oral law) cannot be written down, unless circumstances require it. This certainly was the case in the early period of rabbinic texts, but later this idea does not seem to be prevalent. This further supports the view that it was his disciples who wrote and published his comments. The Vilna Gaon abided by this view of law by reducing his extensive explanations, which are largely inscrutable to any but advanced Talmudists, to short, often one- and two-word comments.[10]

10. Professor Yosef Rivlin of Bar Ilan University wrote: "There are two diametrically opposed views regarding attribution of the Vilna Gaon's commentaries. One ascribes

The method of the Gaon of Vilna included comparing manuscript versions and retrieving the original version of a rabbinic statement. What is interesting is that the Gaon knew about Rabbi Isaac Luria's reticence to write down his teachings on the Zohar and that his students edited his work. He must have wondered what Luria's original views were, and what were the views of Luria's students embedded in the text.[11]

The Gaon's publishing issue is much more complex. Unlike Luria, who was not a legal specialist but a mystic, the Gaon of Vilnas held unmatched authority in the eighteenth century, and his views continued to be authoritative in the nineteenth and twentieth centuries. Unfortunately, his "writings"—which may have numbered as many as seventy different "books"—had to be authenticated by the Gaon's children and students by the handwriting after his death. The number of the works written by the Gaon is nearly impossible to know since none of his works were published during his lifetime; nor were his works technically books, but rather notations or insights sometimes on a single word or phrase.

It is assumed that printed editions published in the nineteenth century may have been based upon manuscript notes that he wrote and were then added to or expanded by the Gaon's students, who may or may not have had their own notes. Since the Gaon was seen as an authority during his lifetime, there was a serious practical problem almost immediately following his death. The problem was so pronounced that in 1798—only a year after his death!—that the rabbinic Bet-Din in Vilna (the Jewish court) placed a ban upon publishing anything under his name that had not been authenticated by his children or students or both. One of the most expanded areas of his writings has to do with short, cryptic marginal notes on some of the most famous rabbinic study texts—notes that his students expanded into full texts before attributing the whole textual construct to the Gaon.

If there is a lesson for the understanding of the afterlives of figures such as Socrates, Alexander the Great, Jesus, the talmudic rabbis, Rabbi

---

every brilliant refinement to him, and the other denies him any interpretation that has the slightest spark of anything attributable to someone else. The one is based on the fact that there are hardly any extant manuscripts of the Vilna Gaon's commentaries written by his own hand; most of his work was written down by his disciples and published after his death. The other approach seeks to shatter the myth surrounding the Vilna Gaon and sweepingly denies any saying or commentary attributed to him, calling these 'false attributions,' 'an incomprehensible matter,' or 'second hand.' I hope to publish a comprehensive study of this question elsewhere" (Rivlin, "Parashat Ekev 5761/2001," fn. 14).

11. Brill, "Mystical Path."

Isaac Luria, the *Besht*, and the Vilna Gaon, it comes from studying what the disciples may have had to work with when they started. It appears that the most common thread is that the original tradition was indeed an oral tradition that was sometimes accompanied by some written notes from either the master himself or a disciple who was present. These communications were often short, cryptic sayings or stories in need of contextualization, which the disciples often placed together with a version of the original communication. One has to ask if this was also the classical model for the New Testament Gospel accounts.

What we know about the transmission of oral tradition comes from the writings of the Gaon's students, who were very clear about how they understood the words of their charismatic teacher as they expanded on and embellished his words. Rabbi Hayim of Volozhin wrote in his introduction with the sons of the Gaon to the published book titled *Shnot Eliyahu*.[12] In the Mishna order *Zeraim* (Seeds, 1799), published two years after the death of their teacher, it is written: "Now the works on the Mishna and the Jerusalem Talmud Zeraim are not from the writings or words of the great Gaon, may his soul rest in Eden, they were written and collected by the students who heard his words. However, the work on the Jerusalem Talmud was seen by the Gaon for eighteen years, and we heard from the holy mouth of our Rabbi that the editor understood well" (*Shnot Eliyahu* to mishnayot of Seder *Zera'im*, Lemberg, 1799).[13]

The ancient idea of people as "living books" insured that the oral tradition was as important as what later became the published or manuscript copy of a work. The idea of the Jews and the Christians being the "People of the Book" is primarily a Muslim concept but was in the modern period appropriate for the Jews as they became central players in the publishing of Jewish texts. The Jewish publishing world of the 1800s and 1900s is what made published authors out of the Gaon, Isaac Luria, and the Baal Shem Tov, but in their afterlives the number of books formed around their thinking became as numerous as the talmudic and midrashic works from a thousand years earlier.

The Gaon, the Baal Shem Tov, and especially Isaac Luria are read synoptically by their followers, and it is only researchers who seem to notice the

12. The Hebrew title is usually translated as "Years of Elijah" but also means "Teachings of Elijah." This is a rabbinic play on words since the words could mean both "years" and "teachings."

13. Kaminetzky, "Ktav Yad Kodsho shel Rabeinu HaGra" *Yeshurun* 14 (2004) 972, n. 17. Cited in Shuschat, "Place of Manuscripts," 77.

differences that inevitably developed as oral traditions were written down and enshrined in print. It seems that many scholars did not see the benefits of publishing their works even after the printing press would have allowed a wide dissemination. The issue of not publishing ideas during the lifetimes of sages was apparently not an obstacle to the books later becoming classics after their deaths. Their reputations were insured by the study houses and the hagiographies of these saintly figures, which persisted through the time of the publishing of their works and after. If we learn anything from these "afterlives" of the famous thinkers and the works attributed to them, it is the idea that a teacher's message transcended his words.

BIBLIOGRAPHY

Anastaplo, George. "On the Socrates of Xenophon and Plato." *George Anastplo's Blog*, October 1, 2013. https://anastaplo.wordpress.com/2013/10/01/on-the-socrates-of-xenophon-and-of-plato/.

Bernier, Jonathan. *The Quest for the Historical Jesus after the Demise of Authenticity: Toward a Critical Realist Philosophy of History in Jesus Studies*. Library of New Testament Studies 540. London: Bloomsbury T. & T. Clark, 2016.

Brill, Alan. "The Mystical Path of the Vilna Gaon." *Journal of Jewish Thought and Philosophy* 3 (1994) 131–51. https://brill.com/view/journals/jjtp/3/1/article-p131_5.xml/.

Foley, John M. *Oral-Formulaic Theory and Research: An Introduction and Annotated Bibliography*. Garland Folklore Bibliographies 6. Garland Reference Library of the Humanities 400. New York: Garland, 1985.

Gagarin, Michael. *Early Greek Law*. Berkeley: University of California Press, 1986.

Karr, Don. "Which Lurianic Kabbalah?" https://www.academia.edu/30928619/Which_Lurianic_Kabbalah?swp=rr-rw-wc-22423238/.

Magid, Shaul, "Kabbalah and Postmodern Jewish Philosophy-From Theosophy to Midrash: Lurianic Exegesis on Adam and Eve and the Garden of Eden." *Journal of Textual Reasoning*, Old ser., 4 (June 1995). http://jtr.shanti.virginia.edu/textual-reasoning-vol-4-2-june-1995/.

Parry, Milman. "Studies in the Epic Technique of Oral Verse-Making: I. Homer and Homeric Style." *Harvard Studies in Classical Philology* 41 (1930) 73–147.

Petrie, R. "Aristophanes and Socrates." *Mind* 20 (1911) 507–20. https://www.jstor.org/stable/2249174?seq=14#metadata_info_tab_contents/.

Rivlin, Yosef. "Parashat Ekev 5761/2001" (August 10, 2001). Bar Ilan University Parashat Study Center. https://www2.biu.ac.il/JH/Parasha/eng/ekev/riv.html/.

Rosman, Moshe. "Hebrew Sources on the Baal Shem Tov: Usability vs. Reliability." In "Toward a New History of Hasidism," edited by A. Rapoport-Albert et al. Special issue, *Jewish History* 27.2/4 (2013) 156–58.

Shuschat, Raphael. "The Place of Manuscripts in the Research of the Vilna Gaon's Writings." *Studia Judaica* 21 (2014) 76–94.

Witherington, Ben, III. *The Jesus Quest: The Third Search for the Jew of Nazareth*. 2nd ed. Downers Grove, IL: InterVarsity, 1997.

4

The "Disappeared" Jesus and the Emancipation of European Jewry

Lorraine J. Parkinson

The raison d'être of Karl Hübner, the main character in Aharon Appelfeld's novel *The Conversion*,[1] which he shared with many western European Jews of the early twentieth century, likely had its genesis in the rationalist thinking and ideals of the European Enlightenment (starting in the seventeenth century and reaching into the nineteenth). German Jewish philosophers and reformers such as Moses Mendelssohn and David Friedländer had profoundly influenced western European Jewry through their enthusiastic adoption of Enlightenment rationalism. For them, although Judaism was rational law, it was now bereft of any ancient Jewish soul or tribal bonds. Their response was to incorporate that law into an ideal of unified human brotherhood based on the moral universe of German philosopher Immanuel Kant (1724–1804). Through the encouragement of Mendelssohn, Friedländer, and others, who hoped to achieve a final and definitive emancipation of European Jews, this movement arose for equality between Jews and Christians.

1. Appelfeld, *Conversion*.

In March 1770, Moses Mendelssohn wrote these words to Johann Caspar Lavater, a Swiss Christian theologian:

> Are the designations Christianity and Judaism tied up with . . . particular doctrines? What difference does it make? In our ears these names will be no more inimical than Cartesians and Leibnizians. What a happy world we would live in if all men accepted and practiced the truths that the best Christians and the best Jews have in common.[2]

It is perfectly rational to argue here that in such a movement the "disappeared" Jesus of Nazareth, overlaid and obscured by the weight of christological doctrine, might reemerge. The unified humanity imagined by the Enlightenment thinkers had at its base the principles of justice, equality, compassion, and peacemaking inherent in the Hebrew Scriptures and taught by Jesus. The feeling was that the way might be opening for a unity of Christians and Jews unheard of in the whole history of the two faiths. Yet in the real world of the eighteenth and nineteenth centuries, the reality of Jewish emancipation met the obstacle of a conscious if untroubled Christian destruction of Judaism, an indication of anti-Semitic norms in the church. That harsh reality played out in "conversions" of Jews to Christianity: It became apparent to aspirational Jewish men that by way of the baptismal font they might become free and equal in European society. Our question must be, where was Jesus the Jew in the willingness of the church to conduct such baptisms? He was, as in most of Christian history, the "Disappeared" Jesus.

The degree of optimism then for relations between Christians and Jews was to be short-lived. The old teachings of contempt for Judaism, influencing relationships between Jews and the religion of Jesus Christ, had by no means disappeared in the eighteenth century. Jesus himself had been so comprehensively separated from his own faith ("he was a Christian, wasn't he?") that the connection with his own people was barely understood. Jesus was mostly believed to have rejected his own faith as he founded the new religion of Christianity. An intriguing example of the rejection of rational Enlightenment thought within the Church of England led to the writing of the well-known hymn "The Church's One Foundation." In 1861 the Church of England bishop of Natal, South Africa, John Colenso, was charged with: "impugning the doctrines, amongst others, of Atonement, Justification, Regeneration, Inspiration of Holy Scripture, the grace of the Sacraments and

---

2. Mendelssohn, *Gesammelte Schriften*, 7:317–18.

the Hypostatic Union. Also of depraving the Book of Common Prayer."[3] Colenso was the quintessential Enlightenment scholar, excelling in mathematics and espousing a nonliteral view of scripture. He converted many Zulus to Christianity, and during his translation of the Hebrew Scriptures into the Zulu language, he contended that the numerical discrepancies found in Genesis warranted doubts concerning the historical accuracy of the Bible. He was also opposed to the doctrine of the eternal punishment of sinners. At his heresy trial the bishop of Cape Town, Robert Gray, defended the "catholic faith" against Colenso's heresies. Colenso was deposed but not excommunicated. He said to a friend, "I intend to fight the battle of liberty of thought and speech for the clergy." His trial was the catalyst for the first Lambeth Conference in 1867.

It was Gray's defense of the faith against Colenso that inspired Samuel John Stone, rector of All-Hallows-by-the-Wall, in London, to write, in 1866, "The Church's One Foundation." Its first verse summarizes its content:

> The church's one foundation
> is Jesus Christ her Lord:
> she is his new creation
> by water and the word;
> from heaven he came and sought her
> to be his holy bride;
> with his own blood he bought her,
> and for her life he died.

That Jesus would have been horrified by the rejection of Judaism and establishment of a new (and Gentile) religion, with himself lauded as its founder, was unthinkable to most Christians.

By the end of 1770, Mendelssohn had come to realize that the vast majority of Christians, including even the best educated such as Lavater, could not admire and respect a virtuous Jew without endeavoring to convert him.[4] Conversion was, after all, a primary motif of Christendom. This revelation prompted an immediate reversal of Mendelssohn's tendency to prevarication when he was challenged to defend Judaism against Christianity. Yet despite his own change of heart, Mendelssohn's reformist legacy lived on. Throughout the following century, assimilating German Jews, particularly those from highly educated middle classes, came to regard the faith into which they were born as an "unnecessary separation between

---

3. Day, *Robert Gray*, 32.

4. Meyer, *Origins of the Modern Jew*, 33–34.

[themselves] and [their] gentile environment."[5] In 1811, in a letter to Chancellor Hardenberg, David Friedländer claimed that during the preceding five to eight years, fifty cases of baptism had occurred in the 405 established Jewish families in Berlin. He also estimated that the proportion would be similar in provincial cities such as Breslau and Königsberg.[6]

Clearly, the desire to convert (and be baptized) depended on the willingness of the church to offer the sacrament of baptism. Potential converts often sought baptism out of political and social expediency, and significantly, the church did not demand evidence of pietistic conviction. For the acculturated Jews who did not convert, the metaphysical basis of the old natural religion had crumbled away. It was to be replaced by an equally rational faith, but grounded in the moral imperative, which may be expressed as a rationally moral will that must always be followed despite natural desires to the contrary.[7] The key to understanding the stance of Enlightenment thinkers appears in Kant's view that the presence of a self-governing reason in each person demonstrates definitive grounds for regarding each person as of equal worth and as of deserving equal respect. Surely the "disappeared" Jesus who taught universal principles of inclusion and justice is here seen emerging from the doctrinal shadows.

Although Aaron Appelfeld's book is set among provincial Austrian Jews in the early twentieth century, much of the Enlightenment era's rationalist attitude toward Jewish conversion to Christianity remains evident in the thinking of his cast of characters. The story traces the personal effect of conversion on the civil servant Karl Hübner, plus several of his childhood friends who convert for the sake of their careers in business and professional life. Significantly, only a few convert with their parents' blessing; most do it on their own. Several people tell Hübner they know about his baptism because of the chiming church bells that announce each new baptism. The chimes are different from those announcing ordinary services or church festivals. Their note is joyful and triumphant, as the whole city is informed that one more Jew has entered the fold of the church.

Nonetheless, for those Jews already converted, the bells are sobering, as they signify another nail in the coffin of the old Jewish community. For Hübner, as for other Jews, there is a lingering Jewish "voice" in the background of their lives, which from time to time unsettles their planned

5. Meyer, *Origins of the Modern Jew*, 87.

6. Katz, *Out of the Ghetto*, 121.

7. Katz, *Out of the Ghetto*, 86.

existence, creating a subtle longing for something indefinable. This leads him at one point to physically defend the old rabbi against intruders into his run-down synagogue, even though Hübner himself gives no allegiance to the practice of the Jewish faith.

The book begins with Hübner's own baptismal service and then moves back to his school days and the beginnings of his acquaintance with Father Merser, the priest who would eventually baptize him. Through the medium of Hübner's story, Appelfeld develops the motif of the Jew as outsider seeking entry into a society which rejects his ancestral religion and culture. The pervasive impression of Jews in the novel is that of a people who have become separated from the heart and soul of their faith, and whose cultural accoutrements merely serve to hold them back from social acceptance and civic advancement. For Hübner and his Jewish friends, the subtle persuasion toward conversion begins in their school days. Although it is said kindly enough, Father Merser's instruction to the Jewish children to leave the classroom during religious lessons carries the impression that:

> the world was divided into two, the higher beings who were permitted to hear the secrets of faith, and those to whom it was forbidden.[8]

This, along with schoolyard taunts from Christian children and well-aimed rocks on the way home, reinforces the sense of isolation he and the other Jewish children experience. Accordingly, almost every Jewish child who graduates from the gymnasium converts. Yet Hübner is one of the last among his group of Jewish friends to be baptized, out of respect for his parents. His reason for converting is clear—he is applying for the position of municipal secretary, and he feels that conversion will tip the scales in his favor. The ambivalence he feels is echoed by a woman who comes to his baptism. "I did it while my parents were still living," she says, "and I regret it to this day. Things like this should be done secretly, under the cover of night, don't you think?[9]"

Appelfeld reveals something of the church's attitude toward these conversions from expediency, as he weaves into the story the activities of Father Merser. From Hübner's childhood, Father Merser is the watcher in the background, taking an interest in the lives of the Jews in the city, ready to offer baptism to any who seek his counsel. Nowhere is the reader invited

8. Appelfeld, *Conversion*, 21.

9. Appelfeld, *Conversion*, 3.

into the thoughts of Father Merser, so his persona remains enigmatic, and his motivation unexpressed. There are, however, several incidents which, when taken together, reveal the thinking behind his actions. They are also an indicator of the European church's general attitude to the conversion of Jews, two generations before the Holocaust.

The overriding impression is that Father Merser has no scruples against conversions that are clearly not from religious conviction. The most blatant example is probably the ninety-year-old man who converts in order to gain entry to the Catholic old folks' home, where there is better heating. Yet for most, the reason is more subtle and important, and the preparation more lengthy and discreet. The words Appelfeld uses to describe the baptismal services seem to reflect an acknowledgment by both the church and the candidates for baptism that something is happening which is not of the same order as genuine conversion.

In the first sentence of the book, Hübner's baptism is described as "short, subdued, and without ostentation."[10] The candidate's feelings indicate his ambivalence: "He hadn't expected the transition to be like this. The pain was so subtle he could barely feel it. If anything of the ceremony stuck in his mind, it was Father Merser's sturdy fingers gripping the brass vessels on the altar."[11] In the discreet celebration after the ceremony one of the guests, who had previously converted to advance his career in law, describes Father Merser as "very pleasant" but also "very tactful." Nonetheless, although Hübner remembers a childhood friend once saying, "A ceremony like this is no more than a tonsillectomy," he does feel different, "as if his legs were weighed down." The ambiguity of the atmosphere is complete when Father Merser embraces him in a warm and fatherly manner. "It was clear that the tall, distinguished man was not only fond of him, but also respected him." Father Merser looked like someone who has "brought a ship safely to harbor."[12]

Hübner's preparation for the baptism is unremarkable, and probably representative of many such conversions. He seeks out the company of the priest in a social setting, and Father Merser does not broach the subject of conversion. Yet gradually the subject of their conversations turns toward the church, and eventually Hübner decides for himself to read the New Testament. He finds himself repelled by the miracles, but during his struggle

10. Appelfeld, *Conversion*, 3.

11. Appelfeld, *Conversion*, 6.

12. Appelfeld, *Conversion*, 10.

his mother appears to him in dreams, night after night, telling him that if his career requires him to convert, he must do it. Eventually he tells the priest of his decision, and Father Merser's simple response is, "I'm pleased."

This naturally begs the question of why the church was so willing to baptize those who were less than convicted by the Christian faith. Historically, Christian doctrine stated that the conversion of the Jews was necessary before the coming of the kingdom of God and the return of Jesus the Messiah/Christ. That led to countless historical instances of forced baptisms, where it was felt that the power of the font would overcome any spiritual reluctance on the part of the baptized. Forced baptisms had ceased by the time of the Reformation in Europe, and the alternative had become almost complete segregation of Jews into ghettoes, so they could not "contaminate" Christians with their unbelief. The assimilation of Jews into European society from the eighteenth century signaled a new religious tolerance in which Jews were free to follow their own faith within gentile society. By the late nineteenth and early twentieth centuries, the conversion of Jews was a voluntary phenomenon, although nonetheless influenced by a pervasive if understated anti-Semitism.

Appelfeld's descriptions of clear anti-Semitic utterances and actions among the citizens of the city are few, but probably best summed up by the comment of a Christian woman working in Hübner's office. After his baptism, she says to a fellow worker:

> Soon there won't be any Jews left. Father Merser is baptizing them one by one. But I don't trust them. A Jew, even after he's been baptized, is still a Jew. He'll always cheat you or betray you.[13]

Father Merser, therefore, seemed to represent a church no longer prepared to baptize Jews forcibly, consign them to ghettoes, or slaughter them as "Christ-killers." For many clergy their subtle encouragement to baptism was doubtless undertaken from personal goodwill toward individual Jews. Nonetheless, the underlying aim was the eventual disappearance of the Jewish faith (inadvertently or otherwise, along with Jesus the Jew).

The irony in Hübner's case is that while his baptism does indeed influence his current appointment as municipal clerk, it is this change in his life that brings back many poignant reminders of his discarded Jewish heritage and sharpens memories of his parents. From economic necessity they had traded the strong community of a rural Jewish village for life as shopkeepers

13. Appelfeld, *Conversion*, 35.

in the run-down Jewish shops in the city center. The first reminder for Hübner is a conversation with Professor Zauber, a Christian teacher with a love for Hasidism and the rural synagogues in the Carpathian Mountains.

Zauber urges him to go to the Carpathians himself: "One must go there to see the true servants of God."

"Strange," said Hübner, "It's hard for me to imagine Jews devoted to faith." Another reminder of his heritage comes as he travels to his aunt's funeral in an outlying Jewish village and converses with the villagers. Every word of Yiddish, every assumption that he has not converted, "jolts his body as if they reveal his deepest flaws." Most importantly, the third reminder comes from the return to Hübner's life of a woman who was maid in his parents' home, and who has adopted the practice and spirit of his parents' faith. Gloria's presence reminds him of his bar mitzvah, and walking to synagogue with his father. Through her, the inner conflict reaches its peak, and he finds himself falling in love with her.

In the end, a political confrontation with an old (converted) adversary over the eviction of Jewish shopkeepers from the city center takes its toll, and Hübner decides to resign from his cherished appointment and seek his lost integrity in the mountains of his ancestors. For a time there is happiness with Gloria, and a reclaiming of his Jewish identity. But eventually he knows he must rage against the anti-Semitism of the local peasants, and their revenge begins to destroy the life he and Gloria have built. Their choice is between either fleeing to the city or taking a stand for his Jewishness. He decides to stay, and he and Gloria perish in the flames of hatred.

Appelfeld's book is stunning in the power of its understatement, and chillingly clear in its portrayal of the "other Holocaust"—the destruction of Jewishness by conversion. For the Christian reader, there is no escaping the increasingly uncomfortable truth the story carries. Whereas it is disturbing enough for a Christian to admit to the manner in which the church participated in the development of anti-Semitic hatred through the ages, this book also demands an explanation for the shameful way the sacrament of baptism was used in an attempt to destroy the faith of Jesus' own people.

This exploration of the attempted emancipation of European Jews points to the phenomenon of the "disappeared" and "reappearing" Jesus, as the religious and cultural norms of European Christendom underwent reform. In the twenty-first century this spiritual and theological phenomenon has by no means "disappeared" from the life and conversation of Christianity. The twentieth and twenty-first centuries have seen similar divisions in belief between liberal and traditional Christians, as has been the case since the Enlightenment. For many in traditional churches, Jesus of Nazareth remains in the shadows, taking second place (at the most) to the Christ of faith. What Immanuel Kant called "self-imposed nonage" (the inability to use one's own understanding without another's guidance) is the norm for a majority of churchgoers. To have the courage to use one's own understanding is therefore the motto of the Enlightenment. Doctrines and dogma are the manacles of "nonage." Release from those restraints permits followers of Jesus to walk free into the responsibilities and privileges of the twenty-first century. Conversion of people of other faiths to Christianity is increasingly seen to be as irrelevant as it is mindlessly disrespectful.

Far from upholding the traditional Christian motif of conversion for Jews, progressive Christians often note that they hold more in common with Jews who call themselves progressive than they do with many traditional Christians. A prominent example of the work of progressive Judaism to promote *Tikkun Olam* ("repair of the world") is Rabbi Michael Lerner, whose online magazine is called *Tikkun*. It is a spiritual as well as a social voice, whose raison d'être is stated this way: "We are a prophetic voice for peace, love, environmental sanity, social transformation, and unabashedly utopian aspirations for the world that can be. We speak to, and hear from, people from all communities, all races, all religions, all ethnicities, and all ages."[14] Their commitment is to "speak truth to power." In that regard, Rabbi Lerner often promotes a "Caring Society":

> In a capitalist society, we judge our institutions to be productive and efficient and rational to the extent that they maximize money and power. In "the Caring Society" a new bottom line would judge our economy, our corporations, our government policies, our legal system, our education system, our cultural systems, and even some of our personal behavior to be rational, productive and efficient to the extent that they maximize our capacities to be loving and caring, kind and generous, attuned to social, economic and environmental justice for everyone on the planet, committed to overcome every form of racism, sexism, homophobia, anti-Semitism, and Islamophobia, responding to each other as intrinsically valuable (or in religious terms, sacred beings) rather than simply valuing them to the extent that they can deliver something to satisfy our personal needs, and responding to the universe and our mother Earth with awe, wonder, and radical amazement, rather

14. *Tikkun.org/*, "About Tikkun."

than valuing them only to the extent that we can turn them into commodities to sell in the capitalist marketplace.[15]

It cannot be surprising to Christians that this voice comes from Jesus' own people, with their heritage of the prophetic faith that inspired him. This interfaith approach to the spiritual and social health of the world carries with it universal principles of justice and compassion that are the foundation stones of the world's major religions. At the time of the Enlightenment, in accord with the principles of capitalism, the church largely relegated justice and compassion (particularly with regard to the slave trade) to the shadows, along with the "disappeared Jesus."

Encouragingly, the afterlife of the "reappeared" Jesus in the twenty-first century does not depend exclusively on the conviction of progressive theologians that Christianity can now look past the dogma of Christendom to the call to follow Jesus of Nazareth. That conviction is coming increasingly from Christians across the theological spectrum, including voices from mainstream denominations and Evangelical churches. The American Evangelical writer and preacher Jim Wallis has recently written *Christ in Crisis: Why We Need to Reclaim Jesus.* Wallis diagnoses the moral crisis of his own society as due to a fundamental flaw:

> We have become disconnected from Jesus. We are not standing and acting in his name, with his values, action, and inspiration. We have lost Jesus—lost our connection to him. This explains why our actions and words lack the power evident in the early church.[16]

The year 2020 is the scene of humanity's greatest fear for the future of life on earth since the world wars, the Cold War (with its threat of nuclear annihilation), and the effects of climate change. The latest fear is for the very future of humanity, as a worldwide fight continues to preserve human life against the "virus from hell," COVID-19. This era of fear and uncertainty has sparked pessimism and optimism in probably equal proportions. Each is an opposite side of the one human coin. Fear can be a compulsion to surrender or to flee from reality. Pessimism adopts that response. Optimism sees the reason for fear but lifts its gaze to hope and action. Hope more and more sees the future of human life through unified human cooperation and creativity. The deep hope embedded in humanity is the inspiration of much of the work of American ecologist and founder of EarthSave, John Robbins. He writes:

15. Lerner, "Don't Waste an Economic Meltdown."

16. Wallis, *Christ in Crisis,* 11.

I look out into the world and I see a deep night of unthinkable cruelty and blindness. Undaunted, however, I look within the human heart and find something of love there, something that cares and shines out into the dark universe like a bright beacon. And in the shining of that light within, I feel the dreams and prayers of all beings. In the shining of that beacon I feel all of our hopes for a better future. In the shining of the human heartlight there is the strength to do what must be done.[17]

In a time of greater uncertainty than usual for many, whether churched or unchurched, Jesus of Nazareth is again reappearing from the shadows. Ironically, the teachings he espoused, taken to the world outside his native Palestine through the gentile church he would have disowned, are key to broader recognition of the oneness of humanity. In that oneness all are included; no one is an outsider in need of conversion. Human connectedness is the basis of universal principles of justice, peace, equality in difference and compassion. Such connectedness thrives on a rational and scientific as well as a spiritual approach to the human condition. It remains to be seen whether for the church and for the world, the "afterlife" of the teachings of Jesus of Nazareth will now be irreversibly established, connecting people of all faiths and no faith in peace and healing for humanity and for mother Earth. The hope is that the "reappearing" Jesus of the twenty-first century will remain in the light; as a beacon of hope for sorely distressed humanity.

BIBLIOGRAPHY

Appelfeld, Aharon. *The Conversion*. Translated from the Hebrew by Jeffrey M. Green. New York: Schocken, 1998.

Day, E. Hermitage. *Robert Gray: First Bishop of Cape Town*. Little Books in Religion. London: SPCK, 1930.

Katz, Jacob. *Out of the Ghetto: The Social Background of the Jewish Emancipation, 1770–1870*. 1973. Reprint, New York: Schocken, 1978.

Lerner, Michael. "Don't Waste an Economic Meltdown: A Strategy to Replace Capitalism." *Tikkun*, April 29, 2020. https://www.tikkun.org/dont-waste-an-economic-meltdown/.

Mendelssohn, Moses. *Gesammelte Schriften, Jubiläumsausgabe*. Edited by I. Elbogen et al. 7 vols. (incomplete). Berlin: Akademie, 1929–1938.

Meyer, Michael A. *The Origins of the Modern Jew: Jewish Identity and European Culture in Germany, 1749–1824*. Detroit: Wayne State University Press, 1967.

Robbins, John. *Diet for a New America*. Walpole, NH: Stillpoint, 1987.

Tikkun.org/. "About Tikkun." https://www.tikkun.org/about-tikkun/.

Wallis, Jim. *Christ in Crisis: Why We Need to Reclaim Jesus*. San Francisco: HarperOne, 2019.

17. Robbins, *Diet for a New America*.

5

Jesus and Contemporary Jewish Identity

Richard E. Sherwin

The ins and outs of the troublesome legacy of Jesus for contemporary Jews have been recognized, discussed and debated by Jewish scholars in Europe since the nineteenth century, and—except for such of it as may appear with Jesus in my poems—are out of my province as a Jewish poet in the twentieth and early twenty-first centuries. I am not a scholar, but undoubtedly have been influenced over my life's decades by readings, allusions, implications, and references to the work and opinions of such scholars. This it seems to me is inevitable for most Jews born and raised in the Western diaspora. I would go further and suggest there is little if any contemporary Judaism in the West that has not been seriously affected by having been embedded in diverse Christian cultures. And similarly, for Judaisms once embedded in Muslim cultures. Consciously and unconsciously, aggressively and defensively, diaspora Judaisms respond to the dominant non-Jewish cultures in order to keep defining and defending their distinctiveness; their borders of agreement with collective mores; and disagreements ethnically, religiously, and nationally.

I find myself troubled nonetheless by the figure of Jesus as a Jew because it cannot be separated totally from its functions within the dominant Christian cultures. I pluralize Christianities and cultures because I personally have lived in, been exposed to, and traveled among different aspects of the Christian West. And while I shall avoid biobloggery as much as possible in this presentation of such of my Jewish Jesus poems, neither they nor I manage to escape the troublesome origins, alliances, and assaults on my emotions, pieties, and experiences of divinity. Something of those experiences is reflected in these poems. Or at least, the poems do not manage to escape them.

Now for some escape clauses: I have never had a discussion with Jews whether Reform, Conservative, or Orthodox—let alone the other Jewish associations—about Jesus as a Jew. Any kind of Jew. Whatever the viability of the topic among Jewish scholars past and present, I have found none among the Jews I have lived and prayed with.

When I asked my Israeli offspring what they thought of Jesus, the few replies I got were useless. Jesus was something at most the outside world of gentiles concerned itself with. Jews just were not involved in it, except as one tolerates the beliefs of others as one expects one's own to be. A matter of polite indifference. My poetic inclusions of a Jewish Jesus seem eccentric at best, a diasporic hangover at worst, to my few Israeli readers. Perhaps a useful meme for such readers overseas who have religious concerns which my poems do not directly violate. I have no idea what English-reading Christians make of them, except that those concerned with the matter of the historical Jesus might find them tangentially relevant. In brief, for the Jews I know, Jesus has no afterlife; he has no life at all.

For me, personally, having gone through my hard drive's holdings from the 1960s and 1970s onwards, it is clear I neither escape the figure of the Jewish Jesus as troublesome, nor am I able to separate it from its entanglements with Christianities' behaviors to Jews. Those indeed are undoubtedly historical—real—and the various aspects of my life (body, mind, and soul) have all been—and probably still are—affected by them.

All this brief selection of some sixteen out of at least a hundred of my poems including Jesus as Jew can hope to do, is to reflect for good and bad, whole and part, of such diasporic Christianities as my Judaisms are tainted, hued, colored by. Do these poems claim to say truths about Christian behaviors to Jews? Yes. Do they or I assume the truths are at any time the whole truth and nothing but the truth? No. I leave to courts, divine (as in Job) and human (as in the International Criminal Court), such assumptions.

As far as I can tell, few if any of my Jewish Jesus poems escape the impact of the *Sho'ah* (aka the European sacrifice of Jews and Jewry to whatever combination of Christian trinity and pagan gods it could offer up my people for a "holocaust"). And almost as a corollary, all my Jewish Jesus poems assume Jesus—Jew to the Nazis, savior to the antinomians—was pulled down from churches and shipped with his crosses stripped of loincloth and mystery to the gas, furnaces, pits, ashes, and ions now fertilizing cannibalistic European pagan reality. This transportation, my poems presume, created the spiritual vacuum which contemporary Muslim immigrants seem to be filling, as part of the intellectual armory of the left-wing elite and the jihadi *reconquista* of Europe.

True or not, fantasy or not, this is the world my Jewish Jesus poems exist in. And in part explains how Jesus as a Jew got burnt out of theology and got ingathered into Zionist Israel, which has embodied my poems since I immigrated from the USA to Israel in 1964. It was not one of my spiritual goals in coming to Israel to deal with Christian remnants, but rather to parochialize and intensify my own Jewish identity. Yet, I confuse or complicate Jesus as a Jew in my at least partially sympathetic poetry he exists in, willy nilly.

My first (and only other) essay at explaining my orthodox Zionist nationalist entanglement with a Jewish Jesus tried to trace what I understood in 2008 of its skeins in my poetic development in a talk given at an SBL seminar in Auckland, New Zealand.[1] This essay (hopefully the last one) will not repeat that excursus but focus on my experiences poetically not with Jesus as Jew *then*, but Jesus as Jew *now* in my poems. My Jewish Jesuses are primarily from poems written between 2008 and 2020. As it were, my future (and I suspect, final) sympathetic take on the figure of Jesus as my poems represent and hopefully not mangle it.

Jesus as Jew inescapably means for me Jews as some aspect of Jesus. One entails the other, having been annealed in the Nazi Christian furnaces, themselves perhaps encouraged and desired centuries ago in the works of Martin Luther. I assume this identification will dwindle and vanish as holocaust, *Sho'ah*, and who knows, Jews go the way of all flesh whose spirits the Lord may not deign to preserve.

---

1. Sherwin, "Influence of Jesus."

The latest entanglement of Jesus and Jew in a poem first: politically incorrect, satirical, sad, and eternal:

NOW ALL JEWS ARE WHITE AND PRIVILEGED

now all jews are white and privileged
the good old days when jews were black are gone
koons and kikes and katholiks no hedging
white jews like i was bleached and spat upon

unbelieved among believers saved
never knowing why or for how long
skating razors edges by the graves
nimble bleeding flaming crosses dodged

ah well its over finally at last
all jews are white oppressors of the world
blacks the only victims colored black
hating jews and casting swine white pearls

whitewash blackwash pagans killing jews
leftwing rightwing wash out jesus too

The particular populist betrayal by Western clerics underlying this poem began with the Nazis achieving the concordat of the soon to become Pope Pius XII. It since appears to have spread successfully to the Western universities, media, and political powers. It merged successfully with such black Jew-hating as can accommodate anti-Zionist Islam and Marxist intent to overthrow republics politically and economically. Down Jews, and you down Jesus from whatever prophetic or divine reality ascribed to him.

At the same time, I see imminent catastrophe, I know I cannot help but believe Gd's ingathering of diasporas to Israel signals at least a delay of total destruction, a gap in time and space that allows rebirth of at least some Jews' individual national religiousness to occur. So, a contrary poem of a different "now" for Jewish Jesuses, since I do not and cannot extricate myself from the collectives of my people.

ITS ME I SEE IN JESUS AS A JEW

its me i see in jesus as a jew
no prophet god messiah just a man
up and down the country prosecuting
himself his sins to virtue as he can

diasporations past and future warding
all catastrophes escaped paroled
inflicted as the Lord might will our soul
to flesh and jew unable to avoid

he didnt choose his bioblogs or saul
chanting plain or chopping up one Gd
he did his time and nows escaped them all
for galilees renewed in jewish law

here i am antique like him untethered
times and climates changed and freedoms weathered

The poem assumes Jesus in churches was imprisoned in the role of Gd, and tortured to encourage *mea culpa* responses to his worshipers' sins. The Jewish survival and reconfirmation in the State of Israel to some degree qualifies the "original sin" of Saul of Tarsus and to some degree its churched sequels:

I CAN HANDLE JESUS AS A JEW

i can handle jesus as a jew
haredim are far more violent
on their opponents than anything he said
it's when i come to gentiles i'm confused

paul says he studied with gamliel
the pharisee most tolerant of christians
how come paul says he persecuted them
and then took gentiles as his jesus mission

i think damascus road revealed to him
how gentiles were the way he dodged himself
avoiding jews and jewish converts left
him all the pagan world to school of sin

his vision christed gentiles devilled jews
converted empires and made himself anew

In some ways, Saul interests me more than Jesus—even though Jesus is the subject of four divergent gospel blogs. I have another poem merging Saul of Tarsus with King Saul, both as unlikely prophets, with which I will conclude this essay. But meanwhile back to Christendom and its current Jesuses . . . Once you start splitting up divinity, who is to say where it stops or ends? Hinduism and Buddhism are sophisticated cases that polytheism need not involve the Christian traditions of Jew hatred.

I have given up asking myself why I do not simply turn or have not simply turned my back at least poetically on the European civilizations which so horrifically holocausted us and then abandoned our saved and saving remnant and still subvert politically Israeli Jews in favor of some vision of Palestinianism they cooked up for proof of Jews having deserved European destruction and not deserving survival. Maybe I remember such remnant glories of Christian music and arts and even architecture, let alone their focus on Jesus as figure of renewal, rebirth, to the degree I cannot ignore their sacrificing their secular remnants of Christianity and Enlightenment to the lowest level of Muslim jihadism. And all in the name of the ashes of belated Christian charity they furnaced with Jesus. I have nothing to poeticize about possible Christian renewal and Jesus-less rechurching the West.

So this caricature summary of the current situation: a *Kaddish* for European Christendom.

VIVE LA FRANCE MOSQUÉE

moslems resurrect the western dhimmis
sponging off the jizya contributions
freely given lest imams solutions
raise the rapist mob to faithful killings

all west elite and left wing mobs
of moslem diplomats and pagan liars
corpses headless just as in their lives
rot before the public they had robbed

whos left to care that no ones left to hear
the horn of roland blown too late the troops
of charlemagne sold out to media scoops
and eurocrats betraying europes heirs

the jews are fled and jesus with them gone
empty churches empty souls stuffed mosques

I have seen a steady principled Western, European abandonment of standards of communal and personal responsibility and behavior that can only encourage the violence that occurs when different communities are forced to live side by side. And so, my fury at the Brussel bigots running whatever they run, and organize against Israel, Jews, and naturally "Jesus as Jew." And yes, I *do* blame rulers more than people, for it is the rulers who direct the mobs that pogrom the horrors: therefore, Stoking Eurocrats:

YOU HAD AT LEAST
FIVE HUNDRED YEARS TO LEARN

you had at least five hundred years to learn
youre each responsible for all the others
instead you fired your furnaces to burn
the jews and jesuses who were your brothers

and now your worshipped selfie citizens
are conquered group by group by terrorists
and you remain self blinded to the dens
of moslems bombing you to dhimmi bliss

communitarian sharia law
has just begun to smother all of you
islam dismembers citizens as flaws
its body politic expels like Jews

and then the pyres and then your ashes inking
korans your children learn and call it thinking

I very much hope the current breath of peace between Middle Eastern Sunni countries and Israel will spread to lessen the jihadi results achieved among European Muslim immigrant communities of radical imams and other teachers in right-wing madrassas and mosques. If so, it will take time. Meanwhile, the best of Europe is under attack: the people who want to behave decently and are abandoned by their politicians. As Jews and Jesus were, and are.

Islam, and even European Christendom, let alone the corrupt intellectuality and mobocracy of worldwide media, are not my business. I know of their past greatness, and their possible future glories, as well as their current declines. My "business" parochially as an eccentric English-speaking-and-writing Jewish Israeli is where my poetry and heart should create. And usually does. But along with the intensity of nationalist Zionism comes not only my commitment to orthopractic Judaism—and the web of commandment spirituality, ritual, and study—but also a biographical and moral concern to pay my dues to the Christian and secular communities and individuals that kept me alive, educated me beyond my capacities, and nourished my professional and personal careers. Which means I experience what I see as their vulnerabilities and sufferings instinctively as part of an inescapable watching brief acquired during the benevolent periods of Western culture.

The period from about 1945 to 1955 when the "news" of the *Sho'ah* was publicized to about 1973 when the Muslims almost succeeded in destroying Israel, was comparatively golden for Jews in the United States and much of Europe. Regret, embarrassment, atonement: whatever the motives, anti-Semitism and Jew-hatred were forbidden public expression from about 1955 when I came out of four years in the USAF to do four years in UCLA and then another three at Yale, and two at Carleton College, and I left for Israel. I had during this period the very good fortune to meet intelligent, kind, devoted Christians—professors, ministers, priests, and laypersons—who confirmed the value of both the classical education I received and the Jewish heritage I was in the process of recuperating via rabbis and ex-GIs at Hillel. They showed me how one lives a full mental, physical, and spiritual life, worth whatever it took to achieve and maintain it. This was an incredible platform on which my later immersion in Israeli life was firmly established, and still constitutes both model and obligation to defend.

There was no way I could dismiss these gifts. I refused ignoring them, just as conversely in Israel I refused switching totally to Hebrew, unwilling to let the country or the community or Gd deprecate or ignore that diaspora Jews were immersed by divine plan. The songs we sang in a once strange land were no longer totally an Israelite foreignness, nor all that unholy to offer up in English on returning to the Promised Land from Babylon.

Oddly, I came to understand and accept this perpetual living in but not of, at the rim not the center, of Israeli Zionism, Judaisms, and languages, and thus was able to accept the figure of a Jewish Jesus as at least as Jewish as I managed to be, not only from any direct Christian influence, but also by indirection. My Californian experiences before during and after UCLA had fixed my poetic and mental attention on the Zen Buddhism popular in the fifties and persisting throughout my adult life. I have been taken by the figures of the eccentric Zen (Japanese) Ch'an (Chinese) recluses in flight from the chaos of war and the intrigues of mandarin rule of empire. These eccentrics also became models for and justification in part for my conflicted duties as citizen soldier (two armies), householder and professor on the one hand, and on the other, my need to escape at least mentally, by a form of internal reclusion, the pressures of daily conformity to such duties without which my life in Israel would be for me both impossible and a sin.

This split personality was difficult to manage gracefully. What helped me manage it was both Jewish (the divide between Kabbalistic individual mysticisms and talmudic commandment-based community duty) and East Asian (the accepted duality of Confucian commitment to public duty and Taoist/Ch'an flight towards spiritual enlightenment at odds at times with social legal custom and behavior). With such awarenesses, right or wrong, the figure of Jesus as Jewish eccentric both dutiful and in opposition to many public customs, helping the helpless, curing the ill, feeding the poor, made sense to me living in the geography and customs out of which he had been extracted, cross-purposed, and deified by the gospel biobloggers and Paul's antinomianisms. He and something of me were wandering the same terrain, physically, spiritually, and geographically. Without the foreigners and diasporaters, he became a Jew I could live with.

We both participated at least poetically in "the eternal Jew" in the promised land of Gd. And unlike Johnny Cash's Jesus, we could differ but walk together . . . a union of time and space and language and religion in that sometime lonesome valley:

IVE WALKED WHERE JESUS
MAY HAVE WALKED

ive walked where Jesus may have walked
it sometimes jacked my spirit up a bit

the same old Jew i always was in part
mind and whims and idols gobble heart

nazareth and capernaum and sea
sephoris synagogues remember me

ive been around too long since i was born
Gds my shepherd still and me still shorn

Jewish fishermen expecting fish
pulled up worlds of wider nets for casting
bodysoul salvations hungry dish
hunger feeding hunger everlasting

mine the kosher diet Gd commands
of remnant hosts his promises have landed

The figure of a Jewish Jesus actually helped me accept my eccentricities *vis á vis* my colleagues and parishioners and friends and . . . family. Granted I had been as it were prepared for existing so by the long immersion in the works and lives of the Chinese eccentrics and Japanese monkpoets, wanderers all, while enjoying a kind of Carthusian stability at least internally, by these historical and geographical connections with ambient and personal divinity.

The omnipresence of spiritual experiences overriding distances of all kinds worked as a mental image of divine omnipresence, I think. Something like my merging of Jew and Jesus and Ch'an (and in other works not discussed of the Japanese poets Saigyo and Basho—and the wild monk, Ikkyu Sojun):

OBVIOUSLY OBSESSED WITH CHINESE MYSTICS

obviously obsessed with chinese mystics
safely dead enlightened centuries
han shan shih te feng kan and all their breed
their tragedies outlived in verse and pics

saint this magician that and oddball always
prayed to preyed on meditated models
cultures crumbling into civil slaughter
up and down the social ranks still fought for

they survived and i who imitated
their reclusions zenning cliffs and waves
dutied familied and soldiered saving
israel assaulted by our neighbors

distance here and now and there and then
Jesus jewed by asian poets zen

That these eccentrics outlasted their countries' historical chaos, horrors, and wars, and that their countries and cultures survived all this as well, further encouraged me to commit to my Gd, country, and family while developing internal reclusions as spiritual topographies of survival. Any blame from Jesus for the catastrophes to nation and people he was identified with by gentiles after his death was removed.

As Jesus became more sympathetically Jewish and like me eccentric, Christianity seemed concurrently to be emptied out of spiritual reality, the presence of Gd . . . Or, perhaps, the reverse: as I saw Christianity losing hold of the population of Europe first, then the USA mainstream Protestant and Catholic churches, I felt more sympathetic to the figure of Jesus, who more easily seemed another case of the rejected Jewish identification with liberal, Western Christian secular values—the Jews intellectually, socially, and religiously abandoned again, as "unacceptables." Jesus had become one of the Western "deplorables"—the Nazis institutionalized such rejection, encouraged by the pope's abandonment of liberal German Christianities, thereby setting groundwork for European *Sho'ah*. I had begun fearing the Western Protestant establishments as theologizing and politicizing their abandonment of the post–World War II concordat against Jew-hating. The difference between their traditional supersessionism (theological erasure of Judaism and Jews) and the rise of public, institutional Jew-hating again, I saw occurring with the Presbyterian and Quaker identification with Palestinian anti-Zionism. They all posit Israel—the old people, the new nation—as some form of corrupt neo-Nazism, and revel with the remnants of Eurocracy in every Muslim suffering for which they could blame Jews. Whitewash, pink wash, black wash—the whole LGBT etc—"woke" rainbow slandering every version of Jew or Jesus that did not idolize Islam as victim of Western orientalisms, colonial occupations, male chauvinism, and whatever else could be used to confirm the lies of Hitler, Stalin, and their worshipers.

This of course led me to allege poetically—ever since Egypt's Nasser employed Nazi fugitives and KGB advisors—that the Arab propaganda machines had successfully made the *Protocols of the Elders of Zion* into the Koran's New Testament. Muslim traditional belief in Jews as devils got modernized into Jewish worldwide conspiracies, for which the KGB's secular Russian orthodoxy forged the documentation. Since little if any textual analysis reigned concerning the Koran, this pagan Christian blasphemy was taken as truth throughout much of the Muslim world . . . , which had become the paymaster for most violent Muslim imams and jihadi religious education throughout the formerly Christian Europe and West. All its subsequent riots, prostitution, schooling gangs, and spontaneous beheadings followed.

By 2017 I was exhausted. Juggling the icons of Jew and Jewish Jesus which my Western "woke"ness created—and living with the tensions of a thriving and I believe righteous Israel perpetually slandered, subverted, and even by its allies condescended to—I desired at least the temporary "rest" the Lord provides creation with: the Sabbath. This poem's prosaic form is a withdrawal from sonnet declaration into prosaic, three-stanza tanka, my preferred imitation of un/free verse.

SABBATHS HERE LETS REST

sabbaths here lets rest.
jesus and jews you murdered
all the worlds you made
unenlightenments your best
mecca and moscow prayed to

protocols of zion
koran and other nameless
forgeries your shameless
shepherds and lambs and lions
shearers shorn and beasts blameless

oh hell theres nothing
idolaters in brussels
cant swallow as true
except for israels Gd
because the god of the jews

Obviously the "rest" is a temporary cease-fire. Not believed in, but ironically hoped for and perhaps even half believed: that if I had said bluntly what I saw Europeans (and now the English-speaking Westerners "awoke" to religious fervor and asleep to reason) doing, they would give it up. They did not. Once you get the taste for murdering Jews and "killing" Jesus with behavior, you no longer feel obliged to repent with a *mea culpa*. Slander and subversion come easy. Fortunately, the rejected Jewish Jesus had at least my Israeli poetry to home in; divinity passport and credibility all erased. Like most Jewish refugees, even the UN does not want him, or us.

Neither Jewish Jesus nor I abandoned our awarenesses of Western paganisms, Islamic *reconquistas*, and the decline of reason into political religiosities intersectionalized: my poems developed parochially either parallel to or in at least partial response to such awareness. They focused on the harmonies and conflicts of internal worlds in Israeli Judaisms—*Halachah* (the commandments of ritual and spiritual duties) and *Kabbalah* (the heightening of individual and collective awarenesses of Gd's presence in our worlds). Without these parallel presences in my life, there is no way I could have endured watching the decline of my Western past cultures, and their turn against Jews everywhere.

Some Western Christian Evangelicals apparently were immune or partially impervious to such abandonments. This did not make it easier for me to accept them or their beliefs, since like most Western Jewry I had grown up with liberalized anti-Christian antisupersessionist attempts to convert or consume our Gd-given religion, nation, ethnicity, and peoplehood. The best I could poeticize was my limited newer tolerance of and admiration for Christians for whom Jesus was still a center of their lives.

OUTSIDE ISRAEL

outside israel
its the faith of the pagans
as keeps me a Jew
I find more in common with
a hard-shelled baptist's life style

than an agnostic
Jew's and since theres no way I
believe their beliefs
or deny the truth of their
living im forced back to the

only Gd I can
stomach for long: israel's
rock and sometime (some
times no time) redeemer whose
uncomfortable worlds mine

And even this qualified admiration of daily life and my rejection of Jesus as personal savior became even more admirable when it stands firm against all the "fake news" about Jewish Jesus. Even though that began with early Christianity—and segued into the *Protocols*—separating Jesus from his Jewishness so his people could be demonized:

THE FIRST FAKE NEWS THAT JESUS WAS A JEW

the first fake news that Jesus was a Jew
the second was the romans crucified him
the truth of course is Jesus wasnt Jewish
and romans loved him while the Jews denied him

no one reads the gospels now and then
illiterates the pagans read the churches
there in stone the latin truth is said
Jews killed god betraying him to murders

the Jewish bibles lies the new ones thinner
lawless loving praising roman winners
moslems slimmed it down to feed the crowds
moses up and Jews and Jesus down

truths a power game for mobs and rulers
fakery the fairy tales pre schoolered

Although it clearly is some version of the historical Jesus which I find my poetry unable to ignore, I also realize this version of Jewish Jesus exists ahistorically within the words and worlds of my poems, be they satirical, political, at least half historically referential to the former statuses of Jesus in European cultures, and . . . yet . . . embarrassingly personal and at least partially spiritual. While I have selected from the four gospel bioblographies what I can accept and understand as Jewish, it is clear that the unhistorical, unsubstantiated, mythical, and magical details ascribed to him also enter my poems and life.

ALMOST EIGHTY THREE AND WINDING UP

almost eighty three and winding up
comfortably my more and less decades
always wondering if i'll wake up
when i wake up from soul and mind ive made

at night i give whats left of me to Gd
hoping something usefuls here for there
morning thanking whats returned of all
i knew i gave and know still unaware

plank by thinning plank i place before me
jesusing the swamps that seem firm land
these commandments now the Lord still chores me
island planked by island hand by hand

where ive been and why and where i am
Gd only knows and judges whats the man

The poem converts the magic tale of Jesus walking on the Sea of Galilee's stormy waves to console his frightened disciples into a very personal spiritual struggle through the swamplands of my murky unconsciousnesses daily and nightly to become and preserve whatever Jewishness I entail. Whoever thinks the worlds of belief in Gd's commandments, persistence in the worlds of spiritual survival, and ritual prayer make life simpler or easier, thinks of a world I have never met, heard of, or was able to breathe in. Let alone pray in. Here Jesus is so absorbed into my Jewish world, that even the unbelieved stories of his actions, become "planks" for my soul's desperate struggles to survive obediently night by nightmare. Any metaphor is gratefully grabbed and used.

To balance out what seems as absolute confirmation of a life internally and externally committed to Gd and Judaisms, which aspects of Jesus as Jew have infiltrated, I feel obliged to offer as support of my eccentricities, my near atheism, which remains a permanent if not dialogic at least argumentative part of my soul.

I'D SOONER DIE

I'd sooner die
for lemon meringue pie
than Gd

I'd soon trust
in a good crisp crust
than pie in anyone's sky

let moslems and jews
have yahweh and allah
i'll stick to Jesus
and a be-el-tea
on toast if you please

meringues less frothy than Gd
the lemon more substantial

crusted right together
and pie on earth outglories
Gd and satan together

and as for pigs lets face it
they taste better than they smell
on the hoof tho any oven
sweet savors even germans
in hell

besides whats Gd got to do
with anything important
better up whatever
than finger electric sockets

no pie
no sky
just Gd
no wonder
Im flawed

The worst part of the lemon meringue poem is that it has always been part of my spiritual experience. Often in the form of BLT or apple pie with ice cream and a hamburger. I did not grow up as an observant Jew, let alone a pretender to piety. Like many Jews one generation out of the European Pale of Settlement (Belarus, Ukraine, Poland, Lithuania, Latvia and others), I had a "religious grandfather." But then as a mentor generalized satirically, everyone had a religious grandfather. Yes. Perhaps. But, still . . . perhaps my one-year Boston Latin School's semiclassical exposure glued onto the secularity of my other grandfather, who always seemed more in tune with Bostonian puritanisms than pieties. Whatever the origins and associations, I have enjoyed and written a few thoroughly reductive atheist poems. And this one, after all, at least tips its tongue to Christian diets. Let alone the churches and Euronations' condemnation of everything *kosher* to Jews. While it confirms my plights: no matter what I feel or think or believe or wish, Gd permeates the entire mélange inhabiting me.

Atheism withal, doubts and skepticisms included, it seems clear that my poems accepted Jesus as another type of Israeli Jew almost to degree that he and Israeli Jews were slandered, rejected, and finally ejected from international organizations (Christian, pagan, and agnostic) and those of various powerful nations, allegedly allies, frenemies, and adversaries. On the one hand, I have found no single Israeli Judaism controlling admission into Israeli culture, so there was and is always room for the eccentric to wander in, passportless or forged, and settle down. On the other hand, I have also found no wide interest across the divers Israeli Judaisms in either Jesus—Jewish or not—or my eccentric English-language poems at all, let alone those with any Jesus inside. This has its upside as freeing me and my poems to do as they may. And the downside, my external representations of politics, nationality, and religion, as well as their internal pieties and mysticisms, are comfortably irrelevant and therefore harmless to Israeli literatures and cultures.

I shall close this attempt, this essay at assaying my Jewish-Jesus poems, with a few internal pieties. They are even less accessible as such because they are embedded inextricably in the ritual Israeli calendar, at once religious even for seculars, and collective for the impious, and open to kabbalistic implications for all.

KRISTALLNACHT TODAY

kristallnacht today
            pace Jeremy Taylor

there may be holy living
there may be holy dying
and if I miss the latter
it wont be for lack of trying

todays the shattered crystals
of my assimilations
I cant say ive not missed them
for all my shredded faiths in

shudder just how stupid
trusting antisemites
left and right and center
piously self righteous

the sphere of heaven splinters
christians hunting Jews
revenge for Jesus sinning
against their pagan truths

nowhere safe this planet
commanded here to live
good Lord my heart is cracking
and loves no glue to give

there may be holy living
weve tried five thousand years
there may be holy dying
that weve proven here

neither one much matters
except expressing You
shatter me all shattered
every fragment true

I composed this in 2007 in Little Rock, Arkansas. It goes back to 1938 when I was five years old, living in Boston, thank heavens, and trying to read *Hans Brinker and the Silver Skates,* the first book with more words than pictures I had received as a birthday present. This was also unsurprisingly the book that established my interest and admiration in Holland as a country which I had heard had protected Jews. I was dismayed when I heard how they had abandoned Dutch Jews so thoroughly—from royalty down through church and people. *Kristallnacht* goes back at least as far as 1933, my birth year, when Hitler came into power. And forward to the *Sho'ah,* which the Israel government, calendar, and religious memory engrave into Israeli Jewish awareness, even if citizens' lives and families might fail to do so. Its origins go pastward to pagan pogroms and forward to . . . The title, of course, parodies the mid-seventeenth-century books by Taylor—parodies because for all the books' popularities, the offspring of Christians worried less about their own souls than about wiping out Jews. And I have to live with and make sense of Gd allowing this. Then and . . .

Finally, Jesus becomes the world's justification for hating and hounding Jews. Pagans in all their forms simply will not and apparently cannot accept a Jew as representative of Gd, even when he is dressed in pagan ritual and theology, split three ways to diminishment of the divine, and stripped to a loincloth immodestly but acceptably for its exposures of agony on the Roman cross. Many of my poems deal with this rejection, this transference of fury onto the Jewish people, who did not accept either such a composite icon. As ancient Greek Alexandrians pogromed Jews because they could lose their land to Roman occupation forces but still maintain culture, language, religion, and integrity; so too modern paganries.

All of which leaves me with two conclusions. One, the world—not only Muslim—rejects Jesus as divine, messiah or not, whatever wrath it expends on Jews for persisting as unbelievers, as murderers of the divine it would not accept to begin with. Two, what for me at least remains my focus on immortal reality, the Jewish people is forever covenanted with Gd, and Israel is simply our most recent incarnation of such.

WHAT IF JESUS WAS A JEW

what if Jesus was a Jew
and not the gentile gentiles think
the romans had to execute
or crown him king of Jewish kings

what if saul was on his own
and not the rabbis agent at all
hunting nazarenes to sow
his private creed encoding paul

what if Gd has never died
not even from his own repenting
forcing jonah into silence
job paid twice for theft and testings

what if Jews are all there is
and chosen still to live Gds trust
and all the others chose to kiss
off either flesh or soul as dust

And leaping back to 1986 before my poetic migrations with Jesus, with no Jewish Jesus appearing separately, part of eternal Jewish peoples:

WE ARE THE POET

we are the poet
people, the makers of words
that answer the Lords
commandments to live not die
we are the lovers of Gd

animals who try
to walk like men not to sink
beneath the simple
ones the beasts who cannot sin
we do not praise thoughtlessness

what nations could do
to erase our poems theyve
done, do, and will do
the Lord has pulled us from the
smoke and ashes soap and lye

the nations raped us
trashed us drooling for pure blood
our genes are mongrel
our people chooses God the
only God who chooses us

In conclusion, there seems to be no conclusion. I do not know if the Jewish people and covenant ever will consider a Jewish Jesus as worth incorporating into its ritual lives, secular or religious, national or individual. Some complex of my diasporic lives seems to have made such incorporation, such inclusion, necessary. But then, I know I am eccentric, barely tangential to Israeli Jewish culture, existence, significance, survival. I knew this likely enough before I immigrated to Israel in 1964. And have had sufficient decades of participating in the miracles of restored Jewish self-rule to find this acceptable. Between Romans and Hellenisms, Egyptians and Syrians, Christendoms and Islams, this Jew and that Jesus, at least so far I have not had to choose as perhaps had Israel's two Sauls between their lethal careers and royalties, among the chaoses it seems divinity creates realities from, while humans Jews and gentiles alike try to stay alive . . . which unfortunately all too often seems to be what we have to accept as thriving.

IS SAUL AMONG THE PROPHETS GOSSIP GOES

is saul among the prophets gossip goes
his politics and feet dont dance so good
he woke to david and damascus road
psalms poor Jesus doublecrossed in wood

holy historys a clusterfuck
who was really who and what they did
or didnt marketed like mortgaged junk
gamblers buy and sell their souls to fiddle

here judeas where it comes together
been there done that temples tabernacles
Gd makes meaning out of changeless weather
freedom out of chaos rabbis shackle

lawless pagan moslems slaughtering
christians neither paul nor Jesus spring

All my Jewish Jesuses seem to suffer from the fates of hope and failure the rest of us do. He was never a viable messiah candidate for the Jewry conditioned by the Babylon it returned from and the talmudic religions it brought inside itself. But even in the gospel bioblogs he was Jewish enough to be concerned with the possibility every Jewish male is perforce entangled with, however briefly or permanently. The immanence of messiah engendered in every Jewish male. Then willy nilly as an icon he did become horrifically ominous of the fate of many European Jews. From all of this my biography and therefore poetry springs—feebly and eccentrically and so very Jewishly for this past nine decades.

Shortly after this chapter was completed, the following poem from 1970 was found among some old personal papers.[2] The poem suggests my poetic fascination with the Jewish Jesus started earlier than I recalled, while also suggesting there has been no positive change in the intervening fifty years.

BETHLEHEM 1970

It's hard to remember Christmas
so near to Bethlehem.
Santa Claus and Muzak carols
and jingling cash-register bells
never got this far southeast.

And here the Army's Salvation
is deadly serious; the band is silent
when all the faithful come
to listen to loudspeakers chant
Latin, Greek, Arabic
from the bowels of the cradling church;
our soldiers have to guard them from
Herod's terrorists.

2. This poem was published in the *Jerusalem Post* (Thursday, December 24, 1970, page 30) alongside a feature about Holy Land Pilgrimages.

It's hard for innocence to get born
so close to Bethlehem, especially
a man-child, and a Jew
for all the birth-joy and the covenant
knows a hard life's waiting
up on Skull Hill for him.

It's bitter cold, Judean December,
with only brandy faith
to warm you over birthing pain
and through the nights
when snowfires indicate the high
but do not warm the morning
blood.

And when I do remember the many mansions
of glittering toys and myrrh
and centrally heated wise men starring
from Wall Street to Harlem
through the concrete hills and desert parks,
the great broad ways of night,
I thank God [sic!] for silence and darkness.

One radiance, one super-nova, one explosion
more
and who can tell what innocence will end
and where?

BIBLIOGRAPHY

Sherwin, Richard E. "The Influence of Jesus on My Jewish-Zionist Poems, 1964–2008." In *Problems in Translating Texts about Jesus: Proceedings from the Society of Biblical Literature International Meeting, 2008*, edited by Mishael M. Caspi and John T. Greene, 269–320. Hors serie. Lewiston, NY: Mellen, 2011.

6

Jesus as a Yogi in Hinduism

Vishal Sharma

This chapter explores one of the less familiar afterlives of Jesus. The religious significance of Christ is explored here from within the Yogi practices of Hinduism and in such a way that the daily relevance of his holy life and instructions are clearly delineated. It has long been recognized that the Johannine Christ is a figure congenial to Eastern modes of thought and experience. There are countless similarities between the Hindu scripture of Bhagavad Gita and the Gospel of John. The Bhagavad Gita says that God incarnates Himself at different times to fulfill a particular mission, or to reestablish the spirit of religion whenever virtue declines and evil prevails. Jesus, the Christ, came to the world to reestablish the spirit of religion in the Jews and other people who then existed in that part of the world. As such, he is recognized by many Hindu saints as an incarnation of God alongside Rama, Krishna, Buddha, and Chaitanya.

Swami Vivekananda, the founder of Ramakrishna Mission, and a key figure in the introduction of Indian philosophy of Yoga to the Western world tells us:

Each soul is potentially divine. The goal is to manifest this divine within, by controlling nature, external and internal. Do this either by work or worship, or psychic control, or philosophy, by one, or more, or all of these—and be free. This is the whole of religion. Doctrines, or dogmas, or rituals, or books, or temples, or forms, are but secondary details.[1]

The central message of Jesus is to seek the kingdom of God first, and he teaches a method by which we can reach the state of perfection, in which there will be no pain. Therefore, the teachings of Jesus can be integrated into Hindu belief and practice.

There is considerable misunderstanding of the word *Yoga* in the West. It is often associated with physical fitness, rope tricks, fortune telling, burial alive, thought reading, thought transference, and so forth. However, Yoga forms one of the six orthodox systems or schools of Hinduism. Yoga introduces the methods of the discipline of body and mind, and was founded by the ancient sage Maharishi Patanjali of India. Yoga has eight steps, but the uninitiated masses equate it to physical postures, exercises, and stretches, which is just the third step. The Yoga system actually includes following ethical values and attitudes in order to cleanse the mind and tendencies, performing physical postures in order to keep the body healthy and supple for doing deep and long meditation, practicing psychophysiological breathing techniques in order to control the life force, engaging in interiorization and concentration of the mind, and finally committing to meditation practices. The goal of Yoga is complete absorption of the mind in God by stilling the alternating waves of consciousness. Thus, an adept Yoga practitioner (Yogi) achieves the state of Self-realization, which means the realization that our true Self is not the ego, but God, the vast ocean of Spirit which manifests for a time the little wave of awareness that we now see as our self. That is why Jesus said, "the kingdom of God is within you" (Luke 17:21 KJV).

In this chapter, I am offering extensive citations from the teachings and practices of the great Yogi-saint, Paramahansa Yogananda. This will provide an insight into one significant contemporary afterlife of Jesus in a community of spiritual practice—an afterlife which is very different from traditional Catholic and Orthodox forms of Christianity.

1. Swami Vivekananda, *Complete Works*, 1:119.

PARAMAHANSA YOGANANDA

The pioneering father of Yoga in the West, Paramahansa Yogananda, has uplifted the lives of millions through his Self-Realization Fellowship teachings.[2] This beloved world teacher has come to be recognized as one of the greatest emissaries to the West of India's ancient wisdom. His life and teachings continue to be a source of light and inspiration to people of all races, cultures, and creeds.

Yogananda was born in 1893 in India, and from his earliest years it was evident to those around him that the depth of his awareness and experience of the spiritual was far beyond the ordinary. In 1910 he met and became a disciple of the revered Swami Sri Yukteswar Giri. In the hermitage of this great master of Yoga he spent the better part of the next ten years, receiving Sri Yukteswar's strict but loving spiritual discipline. At their very first meeting, and on many occasions thereafter, Sri Yukteswar told the young disciple that he had been chosen as the one to disseminate the ancient science of Yoga in America and worldwide. After graduating from Calcutta University in 1915, he took formal vows as a monk of India's venerable monastic Swami Order.

Yogananda began his life's work with the founding, in 1917, of a "how-to-live" school for boys, where modern educational methods were combined with Yoga training and instruction in spiritual ideals. One day in 1920 while meditating, Yogananda had a divine vision showing him that now was the time to begin his work in the West. The next day he was invited to serve as India's delegate to an international congress of religious leaders convening later that year in Boston. Shortly before his departure, Mahavatar Babaji, the deathless master who revived in this age the ancient science of Kriya Yoga, which is a part of Raja Yoga (the royal or highest Yoga), visited Yogananda. Babaji said to Yogananda:

> You are the one I have chosen to spread the message of Kriya Yoga in the West . . . Long ago I met your guru Yukteswar . . . I told him then I would send you to him for training. Kriya Yoga, the scientific technique of God-realization, will ultimately spread in all lands, and aid in harmonizing the nations through man's personal, transcendental perception of the Infinite Father.[3]

2. Key texts for understanding the wisdom and the influence of Yogananda include Yogananda, *Autobiography*; Yogananda, *God Talks with Arjuna*; and Yogananda, *Second Coming*.

3. Yogananda, *Autobiography*, "I Go to America."

Yogananda emphasized the underlying unity of the world's great religions, and taught universally applicable methods for attaining direct personal experience of God. To serious students of his teachings he taught the soul-awakening techniques of Kriya Yoga, initiating thousands of men and women during his thirty years in the West. Yogananda's final years were spent largely in seclusion, as he labored intensely to complete his writings—including his voluminous commentaries on the Bhagavad Gita and the teachings of Jesus Christ in the four Gospels.

On March 7, 1952, the great guru, exhibiting the powers of a supreme yogi, made a conscious exit from the body at the time of physical death. His passing was marked by a phenomenon, which is extraordinary but not unique and has been displayed by great yogis in the past—for three weeks afterwards, his body did not decay. A notarized statement signed by the director of Forest Lawn Memorial Park testified:

> No physical disintegration was visible in his body even twenty days after death . . . This state of perfect preservation of a body is, so far as we know from mortuary annals, an unparalleled one . . . Yogananda's body was apparently in a phenomenal state of immutability . . . no odor of decay emanated from his body at any time . . . for these reasons we state again that the case of Paramhansa Yogananda is unique in our experience.[4]

Yogananda's mission bequeathed to him by his gurus was to present to the West actual techniques to commune with God and show the underlying harmony between the original teachings of Yoga and Christianity. His organization, the Los Angeles–based Self-Realization Fellowship, compiled his teachings and published them as a book.[5] This is the first detailed interpretation of the four Gospels by a Hindu. The guru did not focus on a literal return of Jesus. Rather, he said, the significant second coming involved a return of the "Christ consciousness," of divine intelligence, wisdom, and perception that was incarnate in Jesus and other masters, such as Krishna of India. According to Yogananda, as this spreads among seekers, it will bring peace and harmony.

---

4. Excerpt from the notarized letter by the Los Angeles Mortuary Director, Harry T. Rowe to Self-Realization Fellowship dated May 16, 1952.

5. Yogananda, *Second Coming*.

JESUS IN THE MYSTICAL EXPERIENCE OF PARAMAHANSA YOGANANDA

The path to God or enlightenment through meditation is not distinctive to the Yoga system of Hinduism. It is also found in Sufism of Islam, Kabbalah of Judaism, monastic Buddhism, and contemplative Christianity. Christian mystics such as Teresa of Avila, Meister Eckhart, and John of the Cross have described experiences of divine union that uncannily resemble the Yoga experience. In many accounts, deep meditators report hearing a "cosmic hum," then perceiving a light in their brain's frontal lobe and experiencing a blissful, expanded sense of self. Yogananda said:

> We think of the baby Jesus as helpless in his crib, dependent on his mother's milk and care; yet within that tiny form was the Infinite Christ, the Light of the universe in which we are all dancing as motion-picture shadows. During one of our daylong Christmas meditations, when I prayed to see the baby Christ, the light of the spiritual eye in my forehead opened its rays, and I saw Jesus as an infant. He appeared in such beauty and power of God. All the forces of nature were playing in that baby-face. In the light of those eyes the universe trembled—waiting for the command of those eyes. Such was the infant the Wise Men beheld—a little child over whom the angels stood watch, and in whom the whole universal consciousness was manifest.[6]

Yogananda drew parallels between the Christian Trinity of Father, Son, and Holy Spirit and the Yoga concept of Sat, Tat, and Aum. Both traditions use a trinity to distinguish among the transcendent, divine reality; its immanence in creation; and a sacred, cosmic vibration that sustains the universe. Bible passages used to exclude non-Christians from salvation have been misconstrued. Some Christians believe, for instance, that Jesus' saying that "no one comes to the Father except through me" (John 14:6), requires a belief in Jesus as God and personal savior. Yogananda, however, asserts that Jesus was referring to the need to achieve the same "Christ consciousness" that he personified as a way to achieve oneness with God. "Christ has been much misinterpreted by the world," Yogananda wrote. "Even the most elementary principles of his teachings have been desecrated, and their esoteric depths have been forgotten."[7]

---

6. Yogananda, *Second Coming*, 61.

7. Yogananda, *Second Coming*, 89.

Many of Yogananda's assertions would enhance Christian faith, because they affirm the resurrection and other accounts of Jesus' experiences. Here is an extended citation of Yogananda's account of his visionary encounters with Christ:

> From personal experience I know the reality of his life and miracles, for I have seen him many, many times, and communed with him, and received his direct confirmation about these matters. He has come to me often as the baby Jesus and as the young Christ. I have seen him as he was before his crucifixion, his face very sad; and I have seen him in the glorious form in which he appeared after his resurrection. Jesus did not have a light complexion with blue eyes and blond hair as many Western painters have depicted him. His eyes were dark brown, and he had the olive-colored skin of his Asiatic heritage. His nose was a little flattened at the tip. His moustache, sparse beard, and long hair were black. His face and body were beautifully formed.
>
> It is an erroneous assumption of limited minds that great ones such as Jesus, Krishna, and other divine incarnations are gone from the earth when they are no longer visible to human sight. This is not so. When a liberated master has dissolved his body in Spirit, and yet manifests in form to receptive devotees (as Jesus has appeared throughout the centuries since his passing, such as to Saint Francis, Saint Teresa, and many others of East and West), it means he has an ongoing role to play in the destiny of the world. Even when masters have completed the specific role for which they took on a physical incarnation, it is the divinely ordained task of some to look after the welfare of humanity and assist in guiding its progress.
>
> Jesus Christ is very much alive and active today. In Spirit and occasionally taking on a flesh-and-blood form, he is working unseen by the masses for the regeneration of the world. With his all-embracing love, Jesus is not content merely to enjoy his blissful consciousness in Heaven. He is deeply concerned for mankind and wishes to give his followers the means to attain the divine freedom of entry into God's Infinite Kingdom. He is disappointed because many are the churches and temples founded in his name, often prosperous and powerful, but where is the communion that he stressed—actual contact with God? Jesus wants temples to be established in human souls, first and foremost; then established outwardly in physical places of worship. Instead, there are countless huge edifices with vast congregations being indoctrinated in

churchianity, but few souls who are really in touch with Christ through deep prayer and meditation.[8]

In *The Second Coming of Christ*, he expands further on his encounters with Christ:

My singular desire to discern rightly the true meaning of Christ's words was given wondrous confirmation one night during a period when I was working on these interpretations. It was in the Hermitage at Encinitas, California. I was sitting in my darkened room in meditation, praying deeply from my soul, when suddenly the blackness gave way to a celestial opal-blue effulgence. The entire room was like an opal flame. In that light the radiant form of the blessed Lord Jesus appeared.

His face was divine. His appearance was of a young man in his twenties, with sparse beard and moustache; his long black hair, parted in the middle, had a golden light about it. His feet were not touching the floor. His eyes were the most beautiful, the most loving eyes I have ever seen. The whole universe I saw glistening in those eyes. They were infinitely changing, and with each transition of expression I intuitively understood the wisdom conveyed. In his glorious eyes I felt the power that upholds and commands the myriad worlds.

As he gazed down at me, a Holy Grail appeared at his mouth. It descended to my lips and touched them; then went up again to Jesus. After a few moments of rapt silent communion, he said to me: "Thou dost drink of the same cup of which I drink." At that I bowed down. I was joyous beyond dreams to receive the testimony of his blessings, of his presence. Exactly the words that he said to me in this vision he also said to Thomas, which I never read before. His words meant that I was drinking of his wisdom through the Holy Grail of his perceptions which he has dropped in my consciousness, and he was pleased. He approved very dearly and blessed me for writing these interpretations. This I can say without pride, because the interpretation of Christ's words herein is not mine. It has been given to me.[9]

---

8. Yogananda, *Second Coming*, xxvii.

9. Yogananda, *Second Coming*, xxxi.

JESUS AND KRISHNA
AS GUIDES FOR RAJA YOGA

Bhagavan Krishna is worshiped by millions of Hindus as an incarnation of God and as the supreme God in his own right. He is the central character in the ancient Hindu epic *Mahabharat*, of which the Bhagavad Gita is a part. He probably lived in the third millennium before Christ, but the historical facts of his life are interwoven with a maze of legend and mythology.

The main purpose of Lord Krishna's birth was to free earth from wickedness and ignorance. He played a variety of roles during his stay in the world. In his childhood he was a cowherd. There are many stories and legends that portray him as an ideal son, an ideal brother, an ideal husband, an ideal friend, and an ideal king. He is the embodiment of all the highest ideals of man. But most of all, Sri Krishna taught the supreme truths of Yoga to his disciple Arjuna for the benefit of humankind. That is why he is also known as the Lord of Yoga.

Referring to Yoga's sure and methodical efficacy, Bhagavan Krishna says to Arjuna in the Bhagavad Gita: "The yogi is deemed greater than body-disciplining ascetics, greater even than the followers of the path of wisdom or of the path of action; be thou, O Arjuna, a yogi!"(6:46).[10]

A yogi is someone who can declare: "I am the Self," just as Jesus said, "I and the Father are one" (John 10:29). The real power of Yoga lies in its power to transform individuals. Jesus demonstrated that in his life. He was also a Raja Yogi, as we know from the display of his extraordinary powers. A Raja Yogi established in meditation can easily display those powers. To seekers of truth they are a by-product, not a primary result of Yoga practices.

An example of Jesus' mastery over the materialistic laws of earthly life are seen in the act of resurrection, something that has been understood by accomplished yogis of India for thousands of years. These yogis consider Jesus to be a realized yogi: one who knew and had mastered the spiritual science of life and death, God-communion and God-union.

In the Bhagavad Gita, Krishna says: "Thus always keeping the mind steadfast, the Yogi of subdued mind attains the peace residing in Me, the peace that culminates in freedom. Verily, the supreme bliss comes to that Yogi, of perfect tranquil mind, with passions quieted, and freed from taint." (6:15, 27).

---

10. All quotations from the Bhagavad Gita are from the English translation in Yogananda, *God Talks with Arjuna*.

Swami Abhedananda was a renowned Hindu monk and a disciple of Ramakrishna Paramahansa (the spiritual guru of Swami Vivekananda). He wrote of Jesus:

> The powers and works of this meek, gentle, self-sacrificing Divine man, who is worshipped throughout Christendom as the ideal Incarnation of God and the Savior of mankind, have proved that he was a perfect type of one who is called in India a true Yogi.[11]

JESUS WITHIN HINDU TRADITION OF YOGA

Yogananda writes in his *Autobiography* that Jesus appeared to the Yoga master Babaji and asked him to send someone to the West to spread the teachings of original Christianity. Jesus told Babaji that his followers need-ed to learn how to receive him through deep meditation, as beautifully de-scribed in the verse, "As many as received Him, to them He gave the power to become children of God" (John 1:12). He said that although his followers still do good works, they have lost the ability to commune inwardly with God. Because of Jesus' request, Paramahansa Yogananda came to the West. Thus, Jesus Christ is placed on the altar of all students of the teachings of Self-Realization Fellowship, known in India as the Yogoda Satsanga Society of India. Jesus is one of their supreme gurus, and the students pray daily to Him for help and guidance. Once in a year just before Christmas thousands of devotees around the world join in an all-day special Christmas medi-tation dedicated to honoring the birth of Christ, physically and in their consciousness.

Legends abound concerning the worship of the infant Jesus by the "wise men from the east" (Matt 2:1–12). A common tradition is that they were magi, a priestly class of mystics among ancient Persians credited with esoteric powers. In such traditions, the Wise Men were three in number, commensurate with the New Testament account of the offering of three kinds of gifts: gold, frankincense, and myrrh.

There is a very strong tradition among the yogi community in India— preserved in oral tales and ancient manuscripts,—that the wise men of the East who made their way to the infant Jesus in Bethlehem were, in fact, great sages of India. They named him Isa, which means "Lord" in Sanskrit. The star they followed to find the infant Jesus was not a physical celestial

---

11. Swami Abhedananda, *How to Be a Yogi*, 168.

body. It can be understood as the omniscient "wisdom star of infinite perception" in the spiritual eye, located between the eyebrows, which the wise men accessed through deep meditation.

In popular Hindu tradition, Jesus later traveled to India, where he practiced Yoga meditation with the great sages there. Such traditions provide a midrashic elaboration of gaps in the biblical narratives to deepen the sense that Jesus was truly at home in the East as much as in the Christian West.

This is not to say that Hindus believe Jesus learned everything from his spiritual mentors and associates in India. Rather, avatars (incarnations) are believed to come with their own endowment of wisdom. Jesus' store of divine realization was merely awakened and molded to fit his unique mission by his sojourn among the Hindu pundits, Buddhist monks, and particularly the great masters of Yoga from whom he purportedly received initiation in the esoteric science of God-union through meditation. From the knowledge he had gleaned, and from the wisdom brought forth from his soul in deep meditation, he distilled for the masses simple parables of the ideal principles by which to govern one's life in the sight of God. But to those close disciples who were ready to receive it, he taught the deeper mysteries.

> And when he was alone, they that were about him with the twelve asked of him the parable. And he said unto them, Unto you it is given to know the mystery of the kingdom of God: but unto them that are without, all *these* things are done in parables: That seeing they may see, and not perceive; and hearing they may hear, and not understand; lest at any time they should be converted, and *their* sins should be forgiven them. (Mark 4:10–12 KJV)

Yogananda observes that the complex symbolism in the New Testament book of Revelation of Saint John accords exactly with the Yoga science of God-realization."[12] He further says: "My purpose in noting the broader narratives of Jesus' life available in ancient records is not to insinuate their authenticity or opine as to their factualness, but rather to suggest their plausibility against the background of India's vast spiritual tradition."[13]

For a yogi, the best way to know a liberated master is to have direct knowledge through intuitive, divine communion with that soul. Through the centuries many mystics have known Jesus Christ in this way: Saint

12. Yogananda, *Second Coming*, 87.
13. Yogananda, *Second Coming*, 69.

Francis of Assisi and Saint Teresa of Avila as well as many others. The Hindu yogi Paramahansa Yogananda many times experienced the manifested presence of Jesus.

On the teaching of Jesus, "If therefore thine eye be single, thy whole body shall be full of light (Matt 6:22 KJV)," Yogananda commented:

> Any devotee who, by the practice of yoga meditation, knows how to focus his inward gaze at the point between the eyebrows, finds that the light traveling through the optic nerves into the two physical eyes becomes concentrated instead into the single visible spiritual eye. The two physical eyes perceive only limited portions at a time of the world of relativity; the vision of the spiritual eye is spherical and can see into omnipresence. By deep meditation the devotee penetrates his consciousness and life force through the tricolored lights of the spiritual eye into the macrocosmic manifestation of the Trinity. When the Wise Men saw a star intimating to them the birth of Christ, they were beholding through the wisdom-star of infinite perception in their spiritual eye where the Christ Consciousness was newly manifested in the body of infant Jesus.[14]

THE KINGDOM WITHIN

Chapter 2 of Yogananda's commentary on the Bhagavad Gita, *God Talks with Arjuna*, beautifully describes how a yogi realizes the true nature of his soul:

> The advanced student should meditate deeply until his thoughts become dissolved into intuition. In the lake of intuition, free from the waves of thought, the yogi can see the unruffled reflection of the moon of the soul. Forgetting his dreams of the body, he knows that the soul exists behind the screen of thoughts and is therefore unknown to them. When the yogi perceives the soul as made in the image of Spirit, he knows himself to be unchangeable, unmanifested, ever calm, like the Spirit. All devotees should meditate and interiorize their consciousness until they realize the true nature of the soul.[15]

---

14. Yogananda, *Second Coming*, 61.

15. Yogananda, *God Talks with Arjuna*, ch. 2.

Yogananda taught that Jesus, who began his journey as a human being like all of us, eventually became one with God. He then agreed to return to Earth to help others attain the same. "To him that overcometh will I grant to sit with me in my throne, even as I also overcame, and am set down with my Father in his throne" (Rev 3:21 KJV). In the Hindu tradition, such a one is called an *avatar*, meaning "the descent of divinity into flesh." Jesus was his given name. Christ was his title. For a yogi, "Christ" refers to the "Christ Consciousness," the highest state of consciousness that one can attain spiritually, wherein one is completely immersed in God's presence within and all around, or as the Bible says, wherein one lives into the mystery of that "kingdom of God [which] is within you" (Luke 17:21 KJV).

We noted earlier that Jesus is described in the Gospels (Mark 4:10–12 and parallels) as reserving esoteric instruction for his closest disciples. Yogananda interprets this as follows:

> When Jesus was asked by his disciples why he taught the people in the subtle illustrations of parables, he answered, "Because it is so ordained that you who are my real disciples, living a spiritualized life and disciplining your actions according to my teachings, deserve by virtue of your inner awakening in your meditations to understand the truth of the arcane mysteries of heaven and how to attain the kingdom of God, Cosmic Consciousness hidden behind the vibratory creation of cosmic delusion. But ordinary people, unprepared in their receptivity, are not able either to comprehend or to practice the deeper wisdom-truths. From parables, they glean according to their understanding simpler truths from the wisdom I send out to them. By practical application of what they are able to receive, they make some progress toward redemption."[16]

JESUS INSPIRING ORIENTAL SPIRITUALISM

When an incarnation comes, the world is blessed even though as John 1:11 tells us, "He came unto His own and His own received Him not." Those who are in the world during the lifetime of an incarnation are truly blessed. God is fully manifest in Him, just as the wave. Swami Vivekananda understood this when he said of Christ: "If I as an Oriental, have to worship Jesus of Nazareth, there is only one way left to me, that is, to worship Him as God

---

16. Yogananda, *Second Coming*, 693.

and nothing else."[17] This shows how an Oriental spiritual personality considers Jesus.

In a broad sense, many Hindus do not actually see Jesus as a Christian at all. Of course Jesus did not describe himself as a Christian either. The term was not used during His lifetime. Jesus would simply have understood himself as a faithful Jew seeking to live into the mystery of the kingdom within. In Hindu thought, church or temple membership or belief is not as important as spiritual practice or path. As there is no central religious authority (*magisterium* in Western terms) in Hinduism; everyone is entitled to hold his own spiritual and philosophical opinion. It is difficult then to understand someone's spirituality simply by looking at their religious trappings. Therefore in India it is more common to hear someone ask, "What is your practice?" than, "What do you believe?"

Hindu yogis demonstrate spirituality by behavior and practice. They look for evidence of humility, tolerance, and nonviolence. Can we control our senses and our mind? Are we aware of others' suffering, and are we willing to give up our comfort to help them? On these criteria Jesus measures up as a yogi, as a holy man. He preached a universal message, love of God and love of others, which was beyond any sectarianism or selfishness. Jesus was one of those people who appealed from heart to heart, and that is what makes him such a great Oriental saint. In certain Hindu traditions Jesus is unequivocally considered a divine incarnation sent to us for a specific mission to fulfil God's will on earth.

Paramahansa Yogananda writes in the Introduction to *The Second Coming of Christ*:

> To reestablish God in the temples of souls through revival of the original teachings of God-communion as propounded by Christ and Krishna is why I was sent to the West by Mahavatar Babaji, the deathless Yogi-Christ of modern India, whose existence was revealed to the world at large for the first time in 1946 in *Autobiography of a Yogi*.
>
> Babaji is ever in communion with Christ; together they send out vibrations of redemption and have planned the spiritual technique of salvation for this age. The work of these two fully illumined masters—one with a body, and one without a body—is to inspire the nations to forsake wars, race hatreds, religious sectarianism, and the boomerang evils of materialism. Babaji is well aware of the trend of modern times, especially of the influence and

17. Swami Vivekananda, *Complete Works*, 4:143.

complexities of Western civilization, and realizes the necessity of spreading the self-liberations of Yoga equally in the West and in the East.

It was Mahavatar Babaji who, in consonance with the wish of Christ, devolved upon me the tremendous task of properly interpreting for the world the profound meaning of Jesus' words. In 1894 Babaji instructed my guru, Swami Sri Yukteswar, to write a comparative study of the harmony between the Christian and Hindu scriptures from the point of view of India's Sanatana Dharma, eternal truth (Holy Science). Babaji further told my Guru that I would be sent to him to train for my mission in the West: to teach, side by side, original Christianity as taught by Jesus Christ and original Yoga as taught by Bhagavan Krishna.[18]

CONCLUSION

In his life and teachings, Jesus imparted deep truths, which he himself received through direct experience and communion with the divine. One may refer to this state of consciousness by many names, such as Christ Consciousness, or God Realization. Christ Consciousness is beyond the dogma of religion, and can only be known through experience, not by virtue of ritual, location, costume, or temple. Yogananda defines self-realization as

> The knowing—in body, mind, and soul—that we are one with the omnipresence of God; that we do not have to pray that it come to us, that we are not merely near it at all times, but that God's omnipresence is our omnipresence; that we are just as much a part of Him now as we ever will be. All we have to do is improve our knowing.[19]

For his Hindu devotees, Jesus Christ demonstrated and taught that through direct personal practice in the various techniques of Yoga and meditation, transcendental consciousness may be achieved. The Yoga treatises contain step-by-step and in-depth methods following which faithfully anyone may awake the energy centers in the spine, and thus open the gateways into what Jesus called the kingdom of God. This distinctive and unique afterlife of Jesus as a practitioner and teacher of the science of Yoga represents a significant spiritual asset for people in both India and the West.

18. Yogananda, *Second Coming*, xxviii.
19. Yogananda, *Second Coming*, xxi.

BIBLIOGRAPHY

Abhedananda, Swami. *Vedânta Philosophy: How to Be a Yogi*. New York: Vedanta Society, 1902.

Vivekananda, Swami. *Complete Works of Swami Vivekananda*. 8 vol. Mayavati, India: Advaita Ashrama, 1947.

Yogananda, Paramahansa. *Autobiography of a Yogi*. Los Angeles: Self-Realization Fellowship, 1954.

———. *God Talks with Arjuna: The Bhagavad Gita*. Los Angeles: Self-Realization Fellowship, 1995.

———. *The Second Coming of Christ: The Resurrection of the Christ within You*. Los Angeles: Self-Realization Fellowship, 2004.

———. *The Yoga of Jesus: Understanding the Hidden Teachings of the Gospels*. Los Angeles, Self-Realization Fellowship, 2007.

———. *Where There Is Light: Insight and Inspiration for Meeting Life's Challenges*. Expanded ed. Los Angeles: Self-Realization Fellowship, 2016.

7

Ruist (Confucian) Receptions of Jesus in Late Imperial China

RYAN PINO & BIN SONG

The history of encounters between Ru (Confucian)[1] and Christian traditions in China is a long and storied one, commencing with fits and starts in the seventh century CE when a delegation of Christians arrived from Central Asia at the court of the Tang dynasty. The exchange between the two traditions attained a more explicit and enduring form, however, with Jesuit missions to China in the latter half of the sixteenth century. Building on these missionaries' scholastic engagement with Ruism for the sake of evangelizing literati steeped in the Ru Classics, the Western enterprise of historicizing Ruism (along with other Chinese traditions) and

1. *Confucianism* is a misnomer devised by early Christian missionaries in the nineteenth century to refer to the Ru ("civilized human") tradition with a primary purpose of religious comparison, just as Islam was once called *Muhammadanism* in a similar historical context. A detailed explanation of the history of the nomenclature of *Confucianism* can be found in Swain, *Confucianism in China*, 3–22; and Sun, *Confucianism as a World Religion*, 45–76. Following the reflective scholarly trend regarding nomenclature, in this chapter "Confucianism" is written as "Ruism" or "the Ru tradition," and "Confucian" or "Confucianist" is written as "Ru" or "Ruist."

recording its intersections with Christianity also arose. This has evolved to the present to include scholarship of both varying secular academic and Christian missiological types. Perhaps because of the Christian roots of this enterprise, while a substantial amount of scholarship has attended to the historical interaction between Ruism and Christianity, the vast majority has approached the encounter with Christianity foregrounded.

As a result, scholarship on Ru-Christian encounters, whether historical or theologically constructive, has largely prioritized the efforts of missionaries and Chinese Christians to contextualize the Christian faith in China, with Ruism being a major influence in such a context. In contrast, far fewer attempts have been made to survey *Ruist* receptions of Christianity. Unsurprisingly, then, in the more specific case of Ruist receptions of the person and teachings of Jesus himself, studies are even fewer and farther between. This gap in scholarship is understandable, not only due to the backgrounds of many scholars writing about Ruist-Christian encounters, but also to the distinct natures of the two traditions. After all, only Christianity is overtly evangelistic and an import to China. The downside of not framing the encounters in an equally Ru-focused way, however, is that scholars may occlude adequate observation of Ruist perspectives rooted in historical events, intellectual trends, and economic and sociopolitical realities within the broader Chinese context. At the same time, an equal hazard can be anticipated if historians of Ruism neglect encounters with Christianity in Chinese history due to an assumption that such encounters were altogether peripheral and polemical.

Thus, because Ruist receptions of Jesus have been so understated, a single chapter cannot cover all the ground needed to fill the significant gaps in scholarship, nor can a comprehensive reception history be attempted here. After all, these receptions have been as sundry as the receivers have been many. Instead, we aim to outline some of the major identifiable *types* of Ruist receptions of Jesus in the history of Ru-Christian encounter, hopefully to provide a framework and impetus for further, more focused research along similar lines. Accordingly, we identify Ruist receptions of Jesus under the following six types:

1. anti-Christian rejection

2. skepticism

3. ambivalent hospitality

4. reformist/comparative appropriation

5. "Confucian Christian" acceptance

6. Christian-exclusivist replacement

The last two types are conversional in nature, often entailing a religious allegiance to Jesus in some sense, such as through creedal self-identification as a Christian, or church affiliation. The other types are more ambivalent or adverse in kind. However, even these less accepting types are not mutually exclusive, as each type is broadly generalizing and can overlap with others on a spectrum. A given individual's overall reception of Jesus may even manifest more than one type simultaneously.

Some of these types have also been period-specific (especially the fourth and sixth) due to larger trends in Ruism vis-à-vis the state at a given historical moment, while others have found expressions throughout various epochs of Chinese and Ru history, including during both the Ming and Qing dynasties (ending in 1911), during the Republican period (1911–1949), and so on. Accordingly, we organize our discussion of these types more or less chronologically and focus primarily on the late imperial period (from circa the seventeenth to the early twentieth century). Thus, a caveat needs to be added from the outset: since types 4 and 5 appear either at the very end of or after the imperial period (i.e., post-1911) and hence exceed the due scope of this chapter, our treatment of these two types is much shorter than others. Most importantly, what all types demonstrate collectively is that there is in fact no clear dichotomy between wholesale acceptance and rejection, but rather that each Ruist reception of Jesus has been unique to itself, shaped both by broader trends in Ruism at a given point of history and by individual contexts and concerns. Through the following taxonomic and historical treatments, therefore, we intend simply to furnish a basic framework for scholars to advance within a largely uncharted area.

ANTI-CHRISTIAN AND SKEPTICAL RECEPTIONS OF JESUS IN LATE IMPERIAL CHINA

Within the paltry picture we have painted of scholarship on Ruist receptions of Jesus, it should be noted that a number of important historical studies of Chinese-Western relations can provide at least a partial foundation. Most significantly, several have highlighted a major mode of Ruist response to

Christianity in late imperial China: anti-Christian polemics.[2] Yet because of the topical and temporal limits of such studies, they have been largely episodic in nature. They have also tended to focus on Ruist reactions to Christianity in general as a foreign tradition of learning and a metaphysical supposition of a transcendent Creator in contrast with dominant Ruist (especially Neo-Confucian) positions on these matters. Nevertheless, they do highlight a number of receptions of Jesus specifically, at least in the extent to which such receptions speak to these more general points of contention.

For example, Paul Cohen has identified a centuries-long "anti-Christian tradition" in imperial Chinese history rooted in an antithesis between "orthodoxy" (*zhengdao*) and "heterodoxy" (*xie* / *zuodao*). This antithesis, moreover, was informed by the ideal of the ancient sages (*shengren* / *shengxian*) and revered in Ru tradition,[3] and indeed, the notion of sagehood plays a role in nearly all Ruist receptions of Jesus. Accordingly, starting with the earliest of polemical texts, such as Ru astronomer Yang Guangxian's *I Cannot Do Otherwise* (*Budeyi*) in 1664, Jesus was assessed in comparison with such exemplary figures as the sage-kings Yao and Shun, virtuous rulers like King Wen and the Duke of Zhou, as well as Kongzi (Confucius) and Mengzi (Mencius). And by these particular standards, Jesus was often found wanting. Some Ru were simply perplexed by claims about Jesus as God incarnate and of God as triune, seeing no need to accept such apparent paradoxes when China's past sages were fully human but nonetheless comparable with, or even seemingly superior to, Christ in virtuous attainment. On this score, Jesus was especially derided as a criminal executed for sedition, as this was thought to be incongruous with a truly sagely character, much less a divine one.

One later representative of such anti-Christian polemics, Liang Tingnan (1796–1861), in his "Discussion of the Obstacles Confronting the Entry of Christianity into China" (*Yesujiao Nan Ru Zhongguo Shuo*), levels the critiques that Jesus' teachings are shallow and suspect, and also that his miracles are no different from Daoist priests' magical performances. Moreover, Jesus' apparent proscription of concubinage is chided as contradictory to filial piety, which is an important virtue in Ru tradition and in Chinese culture broadly, due to the potential of having no descendants

---

2. Noteworthy examples include Cohen, *China and Christianity*; Gernet, *China and the Christian Impact*; and Mungello, *Great Encounter*.

3. Cohen, *China and Christianity*, 4–5.

to continue one's lineage.[4] Another withering rejection is that of Wei Yuan (1794–1856), who charges in his scathing "Examination of Catholicism" (*Tianzhujiao Kao*) that Jesus was actually an inheritor of the teachings of demon-like Rakshasas of Hindu tradition and was killed not by crucifixion, as traditionally claimed, but rather by a traitorous wife.[5] In a particularly heated (though perchance stoked) exchange with Protestant missionary Griffith John (1831–1912), one Ru scholar allegedly exclaimed, "If you say anything derogatory of our holy sage (Kongzi), I assure you I would rather go to hell with him than with your Jesus Christ to heaven!"[6]

More recently, D. E. Mungello has identified other key factors underlying anti-Christian sentiment in late imperial China. Among these, at least three were directly related to Ruist influences of some sort: "Confucian religious skepticism and agnosticism" about spirits and deities, Neo-Confucian cosmology (i.e., a nontheistic, qi-based monism), and the conflict between Christian monogamy and Chinese concubinage practices at the time.[7] A fourth major factor, ethnocentrism, was also partially influenced by a conception of Ru orthodoxy as handed down from the ancient sages via Kongzi and his disciples in a chain called the "Lineage of the Way" (*Dao-tong*); consequently, such a view of Ru tradition colored the way some received foreign teachings, for by virtue of being foreign such teachings' proponents were de facto nonparticipants in the *Dao-tong*.[8] Thus, among the many possible points of contention, it was Jesus' *foreignness*—and not necessarily the manner of his life or teachings—that was objectionable to many Ru in late imperial China. Despite the undeniable influence of certain Ru perspectives on *Dao-tong*, however, this raises a critical question: is such ethnocentric thinking really fundamental to Ruism in general? Clearly not, for other Ru of the period did not find Jesus' foreignness a barrier to openness or even acceptance. To the contrary, they saw this point as having no real bearing on the coherence of Jesus' life and teachings with the Ru tradition. To these figures we now turn.

4. Cohen, *China and Christianity*, 42–43.

5. Cohen, *China and Christianity*, 36–39.

6. Cohen, *China and Christianity*, 80.

7. Mungello, *Great Encounter*, 53–61. Other factors included the fear that Christianity was a subversive sect like the notorious White Lotus Society, the concern that church construction would upset the harmonious balance of nature in accordance with *fengshui* principles, suspicion that European priests would seduce Chinese women, and the belief that Christian missionaries practiced alchemy.

8. Mungello, *Great Encounter*, 53–54.

AMBIVALENT HOSPITALITY

Lest one assumes from the above that Ruist receptions of Jesus in late imperial China were altogether negative, it is important to note that both hospitable and conversional responses were also to be found. Indeed, were it not for both types, Jesuit efforts in China would have likely floundered, if not failed, from the outset. Because of Ruism's dominance both intellectually and politically at the time of the Jesuits' (and later, Protestants') arrival, the acceptance, authorization, and friendship of various Ru officials were necessary for missionaries to take up residence, travel within the empire, and commence evangelistic work.

Furthermore, because of the stratified nature of imperial Chinese society, Jesuits and later missionaries made it a top priority to gain the favor, and hopefully conversion, of literati elites. This was a major reason for Matteo Ricci's fateful decision to adopt a strategy of supplementing Ruism and displacing Buddhism, to study the Ru Classics, and to dress in literati garb. (Prior to this he had worn robes resembling a Buddhist monk's.) These efforts—combined with the introduction of European mnemonic techniques, cartography, and astronomical knowledge—impressed a number of Chinese literati, gaining both curiosity and support. Nevertheless, largely because of dominant notions of sagehood and an impersonal understanding of "Heaven" (*Tian*) or the "Lord on High" (*Shangdi*), missionary presentations of Christianity to Ru literati often foregrounded moral teachings rather than more provocative or particular details. Thus, Ricci and his fellow Jesuits often avoided displaying the crucifix in official circles and delayed discussions of Jesus' crucifixion and resurrection until later in the catechesis of potential literati converts.

As a result, among the numerous Ru scholars and officials who befriended Ricci and company but did not embrace Christian doctrines, it is not clear in each case how much was disclosed about Jesus specifically.[9] Tellingly, it was not only at the behest of a literatus acquaintance that Ricci swapped his Buddhist garb for a Ruist persona, but it was also after numerous conversations with the Ru scholar Zhang Huang that Ricci was inspired to seek parallels between the Ru Classics and Christian principles in a way that sidelined controversial doctrines like Christ's death.[10] Even

9. On some of Ricci's friends in high places, see Hsia, *Jesuit in the Forbidden City,* 90, 120–25.

10. Hsia, *Jesuit in the Forbidden City,* 136, 224.

Ricci's famous dialogue between a Chinese and a Western scholar, *The True Meaning of the Lord of Heaven* (*Tianzhu Shiyi*), only briefly discusses Jesus as the incarnate "Lord of Heaven" (*Tianzhu*) and makes no mention of the crucifixion.[11]

Notwithstanding Jesuit claims about Jesus as *Tianzhu* incarnate, then, those who were sympathetic to the missionaries but not accepting of their entire message were, at most, willing to accept Jesus as a figure comparable to certain sages of antiquity (and thus in no small light), but not as higher than a sage. Because of this, such receptions of Jesus were hospitable but ambivalent, evidencing a certain level of acceptance of Jesus and his teachings as expressive of truths compatible with Ruist understandings, but not as offering anything so novel as to necessitate conversion to Christianity. If anything, Jesus may have been seen to reiterate what was already transmitted by the Chinese sages.

This raises a crucial point of context. Chinese society at the time of the Jesuits' arrival was characterized by intellectual ferment and experimentation, as well as a loosening of Ru orthodoxy in certain circles of influence. While some Ru were staunch defenders of a competitively exclusivist form of orthodoxy, others demonstrated a radical willingness to harmonize diverse teachings like Buddhism and Daoism (and, likewise, newer imports like Christianity) in a way that minimized differences. Accordingly, the hospitality extended by some to Christian missionaries' message about Christ was often an outgrowth of their larger orientation within this intellectually fecund milieu. Conversely, sharp critics of Christ, like those seen above, often expressed this criticism in line with more broadly conservative positions on the nature of Ru orthodoxy itself. Similarly, in later periods marked by predominantly conservative attitudes politically and intellectually—such as after the notorious Chinese Rites Controversy in the early eighteenth century—correspondingly sharper criticisms of Jesus Christ were raised.[12]

"CONFUCIAN CHRISTIAN" RECEPTIONS

In light of the above discussion, some of the most remarkable receptions of Jesus in late imperial China were by those who converted to Christianity

---

11. For more nuanced discussions, see Criveller, *Preaching Christ*; Standaert, *Illustrated "Life of Christ"*; and Song, *Giulio Aleni*.

12. On the causes and casualties of the Rites Controversy, see Mungello, ed., *Chinese Rites Controversy*.

but still unequivocally identified as Ru. (Some have even gone so far as to label such figures "Confucian Christians."[13]) Among these, a number of prominent examples are relatively renowned, such as the "Three Pillars of Chinese Christianity," Xu Guangqi, Li Zhizao, and Yang Tingyun (Xu, for instance, was a grand secretary, one of the highest positions in the Ming dynasty bureaucracy).[14] While each of these individuals' conversions was unique, they generally accepted Ricci's notion of "supplementing Ruism" with Christianity. Consequently, their understandings of Jesus were both informed by and informative of their orientation within Ru tradition as well, including their interpretations of the Ru Classics and the ancient sages.

One way this Ru-Christian fusion manifested was with respect to history and the Classics. Since Ru converts to Christianity generally followed the line of argument in Ricci's *Tianzhu Shiyi* that Neo-Confucian interpretations arising in the Song dynasty (960–1276 CE) had obscured teachings about the worship of a monotheistic deity in the ancient Classics, their acceptance of the figure of Jesus also entailed a concomitant rereading of the Classics not widely held at the time. Thus, to the extent that these converts accepted and defended such a reading on overtly Ruist terms, they also represented a distinctive lineage of thought within Ruism in their own right.

The same can be said for how some Ru Christians framed their discussions of Jesus in light of the ancient sages. For example, in an apologetic work called *Shengshui Jiyan*, presented as a dialogue between two scholars, Yang Tingyun (1562–1627) defends his Jesuit friends, whom he calls "Western Ru." At one point, the Christian scholar in the conversation is confronted: "You were born and grew up in China, and you have studied the Way of Yao, Shun, the Duke of Zhou and Kongzi. But one day, guests came from afar . . . and you rejected what you have learned and followed them."[15] In response to this charge, which juxtaposes these foreigners' learning with the way of China's ancient sages, Yang cites the Neo-Confucian scholar Lu Xiangshan (1139–1192 CE):

> Xiangshan said: 'Within the four seas, this mind and this principle are the same.' If one confines them to a specific place, they are

13. See Rule, "Jesus of the 'Confucian Christians'"; and Rule, "Life and Thoughts."

14. Other notable figures fitting the ascription of "Ru Christian" include Qu Rukui (1549–1612), Li Yingshi (fl. ca. 1600), Han Lin (1601–1644), Zhang Xingyao (1633–after 1715), Zhu Zongyuan (1626–1666), Qiu Sheng (before 1663–after 1706), and the later diplomat Xu Jingcheng (1845–1900).

15. Adapted from Standaert, *Yang Tingyun*, 200.

false. Their words are all in accord with the orthodox principle and there is real evidence for it. In every matter, they surely talk about Heaven, and when talking about Heaven they surely speak about a Lord. They want people to take the unselfishness of Heaven as an example, and to love themselves according to this mind, which is to love people according to this mind; this is what is meant by 'Reverencing Heaven.' This is the correct vein of humanity that successively has been transmitted from Yao, Shun, the Duke of Zhou and Kongzi on . . . The Westerners know Heaven and serve Heaven, in a true and real way, with diligence, not simply with ears and mouth. They share in one way . . . It completely agrees with the Way of Yao, Shun, the Duke of Zhou and Kongzi. Therefore, I rejoice to have contacts with them, and to honor their teachers and instructions. How can those who correctly and perfectly study the Way of [the sages] be said to act contrary to them?[16]

Yang thus draws a clear connection between Christianity and the orthodox transmission of the ancient sages, yet he does so in a more explicitly Neo-Confucian way through appeal to the universality of principle (*li*) and the human heart-mind (*xin*), which are to be properly accorded with in following the example of Heaven, i.e., through reverencing the Lord of Heaven worshiped by Christians. His evocation of Lu Xiangshan is likely an allusion to a famous passage in which Lu argues for the essential unity of the universe and the human heart-mind:

Sages appeared tens of thousands of generations ago. They shared this mind; they shared this principle. Sages will appear tens of thousands of years to come. They will share this mind; they will share this principle. In the Southern or Northern Seas, in the Western or Eastern seas sages appear. They share this mind; they share this principle.[17]

Yang adapts these notions in a novel way, though, arguing that because all share the same heart-mind and principle, it is proper for all to reverence the Lord of Heaven. To do so on account of this shared heart-mind and principle is not to betray the sages of past generations; rather, it is to follow their examples more closely, for they also spoke of "reverencing Heaven." Such a presentation rebuts any notion that the orthodox Lineage of the Way is somehow an exclusively Chinese inheritance. Instead, foreign figures like Jesus may also be links in this lineage. No doubt aware of the qualms of

16. Standaert, *Yang Tingyun*, 200–201.

17. Following de Bary et al., comps., *Sources of Chinese Tradition*, 510.

the literati, however, in his apologetic dialogue Yang parallels Ricci in not mentioning more scandalous aspects of the Jesus-narrative such as the crucifixion. Rather than presenting Jesus as a savior who redeems humanity from sin through his death and resurrection, Yang presents Jesus as the perfect exemplar who comes from heaven and becomes human in order to show the fullest way for all to "revere Heaven and love men" in turn.[18]

Later Ru Christians, who wrote in the same vein as apologist-converts like Yang would present Jesus in similar ways in responses to critics. Because of this, some have deemed these figures' religious commitments as distinct from those of their Jesuit counterparts, labeling the converts' faith variously as "*Tianzhu*-ism" or "Confucian monotheism," implying a belief in the Christian God but with a diluted Christology.[19] This reading is not entirely fair, though, because these apologetic presentations of Jesus within a sagely paradigm say just as much about the intended audience as they do about the authors. Furthermore, other types of writings by early generations of Ru Christians, such as poems, essays, letters, and diaries, evince rich reflections on Jesus' divinity, passion, and resurrection, as well as on the need to explain these thornier points of doctrine in a Ru-accommodating way.[20]

CONTINUATION OF RU-CHRISTIAN FUSION IN THE NINETEENTH CENTURY

Moving closer to the twilight of imperial China, factors like Christianity's proscription after the Rites Controversy precluded a distinctively Ru-Christian tradition from continuing in any robust sense. Furthermore, when Protestant missionaries began to seek Chinese converts in the nineteenth century, most of them were highly critical of the tradition and saw it more as a barrier to evangelism than a potential point of connection. Nevertheless, some missionaries (such as James Legge, Timothy Richard, and Karl Gützlaff) opted to build on the legacy of Catholic missions by seeking a path of dialogue with Ruism. Faced with many of the same criticisms from literati as their predecessors, though, they found few conversions in higher circles. Indeed, during the final decades of the Qing dynasty's decline and the consequent waning of Ruism's political weddedness to the

18. Lai, "Jesus in the *Shengshui Jiyan*," 532.

19. See Zürcher, "Jesuit Accommodation," 50.

20. See Rule, "Jesus of the 'Confucian Christians,'" 508–509; and Mungello, *Great Encounter*, 20–31.

imperial state, the vast majority of converts to Christianity did not come from literati backgrounds. This, however, has led to false impressions both that serious dialogues between Ruism and Christianity ceased until the twentieth century, and that there were few to no self-identifying Ru converts to Christianity in the late Qing period.[21]

Nevertheless, a closer look at Chinese-language sources from the time, including missionary periodicals like *Jiaohui Xinbao* (*Church News*), printed from 1868 to 1874, and *Wanguo Gongbao* (*Review of the Times*), printed between 1874 and 1907, reveals a surprising amount of Chinese Christian writing—pieces that are clearly conversant with Ru tradition. In fact, the total number of Chinese contributors to the two magazines above exceeded a thousand over their publication runs, and at least thirty-six different Chinese Christian authors wrote specifically on Ruism. Some individuals even wrote dozens of articles on the subject.[22] A number of these Chinese Christians, moreover, described themselves as Ru and presented themselves as knowledgeable enough to carry on nuanced discussions on the Classics with other scholars.

Though a number of examples could be raised here, one such figure who stands out is Zhang Ding, a Ru scholar-turned-pastor who penned a book of more than thirty chapters titled *A Discussion on the Errors of Ruism* (*Rujiao Bian Miu*), which was serialized in *Wanguo Gongbao* in 1878. Possibly the most extensive text of its kind by a nineteenth-century Chinese convert, Zhang's *Discussion* interestingly parallels a number of arguments and strategies used by earlier Ru Christian converts from the Catholic mission (despite being written by a Protestant). In fact, its title notwithstanding, the book shows a striking amount of sympathy toward Ruism on the balance, adopting a position of supplementing what is thought to be lacking in Ruism with Christian teachings. Likewise, a striking omission in Zhang's book is Jesus' crucifixion. A noteworthy pattern is thus repeated. Still, extensive work remains to be done in uncovering the manner and motivations of nineteenth-century Ru receptions of Jesus such as that of

---

21. For instance, Paulos Huang writes in an extensive study on Ru-Christian dialogue that "after Ricci's dialogue with Confucians in the 17th century, the dialogue was stopped and was not begun again until the beginning of the 20th century." Huang, *Confronting Confucian Understandings*, 9.

22. This was tallied with the use of several indices: Bennett, comp., *Research Guide to the Chiao-hui Hsin-pao*; Bennett, comp., *Research Guide to the Wan-Kuo Kung-Pao*; and *Wanguo Gongbao: Zongmu, Suoyin*.

Zhang Ding, as well as in examining the broader instances of Ru-Christian dialogue that such receptions engendered.

RECEPTIONS OF JESUS AT AND AFTER THE END OF IMPERIAL CHINA

The twilight years of imperial China brought with them unprecedented political, economic, and religious shifts that directly affected the role of Ruism within Chinese society. In the face of existential threats both foreign and domestic (not the least of which being repeated Chinese humiliation at the hands of European powers), a spate of reform-minded intellectuals began to seek new paths for strengthening and stabilizing the Chinese state. In line with this broader trend, one of the primary ways in which Jesus began to play an instigative role in Ru thought was in being seen as a reform figure: a prophet who stands against oppression and coercion, lifts up the needs and the suffering of the masses, and offers a new vision for a more peaceful and just society. At the same time, the perceived strength of European powers relative to the declining Chinese state led some to posit (partially at the suggestion of Christian missionaries who championed a Christian civilizational discourse) that one key to such strength was the guiding force of the Christian religion in Western civilization.

Among the most prominent of the era's Ru reformists who sought insights from Western culture and religion was Kang Youwei (1858–1927), a pivotal player in the abortive Hundred Days' Reform of 1898 who continued for decades to seek the Chinese nation's rejuvenation by retooling and revitalizing Ruism's place within it. Informed by his studies of Christianity's role in Western civilization, Kang envisioned reform partially through the establishment of a state religion styled "Kongjiao" (or "Confucianity"[23]) on par with the place of Christianity (especially Protestantism, due to its inherently reformational origins[24]) in certain European nations. Kang was particularly impressed by the potential for social transformation provided by church institutions, but he was also inspired by the central and singular role of Jesus within Christianity. More specifically, Kang found the monotheistic worship of Christians to be vital to the strength of Western nations, writing,

---

23. Sun, *Confucianism as a World Religion*, 42–43.

24. Liang even referred to Kang as the "Martin Luther of the Confucian religion"— an especially apt appellation considering Kang's admiration for the Protestant reformer. Liang, "Nanhai Kang," 486.

"Americans and Europeans only pray to the Heavenly God, and their temples only worship the religious founder [i.e. Jesus Christ] . . . This serves to guard their innate goodness and makes them orderly and deferential."[25]

Rather than calling for an adoption of Christianity, however, Kang instead strove to reorient Ruism in a similar way around its founding sage, Kongzi. As a result, he promoted Kongzi as a messianic "uncrowned king," the rightful receiver of Heaven's Mandate, and the progenitor of true Chinese civilization, whose sole veneration could serve as a religious replacement for the dominant imperial Ruism rooted in the Neo-Confucian philosophy of Zhu Xi. With Kongzi essentially apotheosized to parallel a monotheistic deity, Kang even called for the establishment of Kongzi temples throughout the land and the removal of all other sages from existing temples.[26] In light of this, Kang Youwei's unique reception of Jesus can be rightly labeled a reformist/comparative appropriation, as his comparative learning for the sake of Ruist reform led him to reconsider and then reconfigure the status of Kongzi within Ruism in light of Jesus' status within Christianity. One of Kang's most prominent students, Liang Qichao, even admitted that Kang's overt intention was to frame Kongzi as a figure on par with Jesus.[27] While various Ruist religious movements have continued to the present which partially owe their legacy to Kang's Kongjiao movement, his own attempts were met with criticism and floundered by the 1920s for various political and well-argued philosophical reasons. However, like Kang before them, other Ru scholars have continued in diverse ways to engage in comparative learning and dialogical development vis-à-vis other traditions and figures like Jesus in the decades since—a more recent history of engagements well beyond the scope of this chapter.

Finally, a sixth type of Ruist reception of Jesus, wholesale replacement by acceptance of an exclusivist Christian framework, need only be mentioned in passing. This type is largely (though not entirely) specific to the early twentieth century due to unique political realities of the time, which saw the rapid demise of Ruism's association with the imperial political system. One example of this type would be Fan Zimei (1866–1936), a Ru scholar and one-time supporter of Kang Youwei's reform movement. Disillusioned after the failure of the Hundred Days' Reform and influenced by the Christian civilizing discourse of certain missionaries, Fan eventually

25. Huang, *Kang Youwei*, 456.

26. Huang, *Kang Youwei*, 464–69.

27. Kuo, "Christian Civilization," 250.

converted to Christianity in 1901. In doing so, he initially renounced "false Confucian civilization" in favor of "true Christian civilization."[28] Such a stark dichotomy would likely not have been deemed necessary in earlier times of dominant Ru political influence, or in later times of relative decoupling of Ruism from political spheres, however; and even later in Fan's own life he regained an appreciation for Ruism as an ally to Christianity for the revitalization of Chinese society in the face of cultural confusion, moral decline, and the encroachment of materialism. His later writings would thus echo the work of other twentieth-century Chinese theologians to seek rapprochement between the Christian and Ru traditions for the sake of theological contextualization and national rejuvenation.[29]

CONCLUSION

As indicated by the above discussions, Ruist receptions of Jesus at various points in Chinese history have been reflective of broader concerns with respect to Ru orthodoxy at those times. Meanwhile, these receptions have also been specific to the nature and teachings of Jesus himself, particularly in relation to exemplary figures within the Ru tradition such as Kongzi and the sages of antiquity. What is compelling, then, is how such diverse receptions highlight particularities of Ru thought and practice that might not stand out otherwise. While receptions of Jesus may appear peripheral in the broader sweep of Ru tradition, they are nonetheless significant in shedding unique light on the boundaries and contours of the tradition as a whole, including on the ways in which certain self-identifying Ru have negotiated the boundaries of Ru orthodoxy and their position within it. In this regard, much important work remains to be done.

Such receptions can also highlight the phenomenon of multitraditional belonging in imperial Chinese history. In the case of late Ming "Confucian Christians," for instance, we find a wholehearted acceptance of Christianity and of Jesus himself without rejection of core Ruist commitments; and yet a definite reevaluation of Ruism, particularly in terms of how to interpret the Ru Classics, did emerge as a result. Thus, observing how these figures identified themselves as simultaneously Ru and Christian can raise insights for thinking more creatively about various forms of religious (or, for that

---

28. Ying, "Fan Zimei," 67–68.

29. Notable in this regard are Zhao Zichen (1888–1979) and Wu Leichuan (1870–1944). For case studies on these and others, see Starr, *Chinese Theology*.

matter, multireligious) commitment, the boundaries of tradition, and the myriad ways in which religious identity is formed and transformed through interreligious encounter, whether positive or polemical.

Finally, the cases above clearly speak to how Ruism's relation to Chinese politics at different points in history has influenced Ruist receptions of Christianity in general and of Jesus in particular. For example, while total abandonment of Ruism by late Ming converts would have been practically unthinkable, the later decline of Ruism's influence within Chinese politics engendered new possibilities for creative, comparative, and critical Ruist receptions of Jesus. As the dynamic relationship between Ruism and the Chinese state continues to evolve still today, then, this is an important historical lesson for considering how Ruism may continue to play a part in interreligious dialogue as well. In any case, what we see exemplified here is that throughout Chinese history, numerous serious engagements with the figure and teachings of Jesus have played (and likely will continue to play) an instigative role in both reforming and reinforcing the contours of the Ru tradition in ways both large and small.

BIBLIOGRAPHY

Bennett, Adrian A., comp. *Research Guide to the "Chiao-hui Hsin-pao," 1868–1874*. San Francisco: Chinese Materials Center, 1975.

———, comp. *Research Guide to the "Wan-Kuo Kung-Pao," 1874–1883*. San Francisco: Chinese Materials Center, 1976.

Cohen, Paul A. *China and Christianity: The Missionary Movement and the Growth of Chinese Antiforeignism, 1860–1870*. Harvard East Asian Series 11. Annali (Fondazione civiltà bresciana) 10. Cambridge: Harvard University Press, 1963.

Criveller, Gianni. *Preaching Christ in Late Ming China: The Jesuits' Presentation of Christ from Matteo Ricci to Giulio Aleni*. Variétés sinologiques 86. Taipei: Taipei Ricci Institute, 1997.

De Bary, William Theodore, et al., comps. *Sources of Chinese Tradition*. 2 vols. Introduction to Oriental Civilizations. New York: Columbia University Press, 1964.

Gernet, Jacques. *China and the Christian Impact: A Conflict of Cultures*. Translated by Janet Lloyd. Cambridge: Cambridge University Press, 1985.

Hsia, R. Po-Chia. *A Jesuit in the Forbidden City: Matteo Ricci, 1552–1610*. Oxford: Oxford University Press, 2010.

Huang, Paulos. *Confronting Confucian Understandings of the Christian Doctrine of Salvation*. Studies in Systematic Theology 3. Leiden: Brill, 2009.

Huang, Zhangjian. *Kang Youwei wuxu zhen zouyi*. Taipei: Institute of History and Philology, 1974.

Kuo, Ya-pei. "'Christian Civilization' and the Confucian Church: The Origin of Secularist Politics in Modern China." *Past and Present* 218 (February 2013) 235–64.

Lai, Whalen. "Jesus in the *Shengshui Jiyan* of Yang Tingyun." In *The Chinese Face of Jesus Christ*, edited by Roman Malek, 2:517–37. 4 vols. in 6 bks. Monumenta Serica Monograph Series 50. Sankt Augustin, Germany: Institut Monumenta Serica, 2003.

Liang, Qichao. "Nanhai Kang Xiansheng Zhuan." In *Liang Qichao Quanji*, edited by Zhang Pingxing, 2:481–99. 21 vols. Beijing: Beijing Chubanshe, 1999.

Mungello, D. E., ed. *The Chinese Rites Controversy: Its History and Meaning*. Monumenta Serica Monograph Series 33. Nettetal, Germany: Steyler, 1994.

———. *The Great Encounter of China and the West, 1500–1800*. 4th ed. Critical Issues in World and International History. Lanham, MD: Rowman & Littlefield, 2013.

Rule, Paul. "The Jesus of the 'Confucian Christians' of the Seventeenth Century." In *The Chinese Face of Jesus Christ*, edited by Roman Malek, 2:499–516. 4 vols. in 6 bks. Monumenta Serica Monograph Series 50. Sankt Augustin, Germany: Institut Monumenta Serica, 2002.

———. "The Life and Thoughts of 17th Century Chinese Christians." In *Silent Force: Native Converts in the Catholic China Mission*, edited by Rachel Lu Yan and Philip Vanhaelemeersch, 11–36. Leuven Chinese Studies 20. Leuven: Ferdinand Verbiest Institute, 2009.

Song, Gang. *Giulio Aleni, "Kouduo richao," and Christian-Confucian Dialogism in Late Ming Fujian*. Monumenta Serica Monograph Series 69. Sankt Augustin, Germany: Institut Monumenta Serica, 2018.

Standaert, Nicolas, SJ. *An Illustrated "Life of Christ" Presented to the Chinese Emperor: The History of Jincheng shuxiang (1640)*. Monumenta Serica Monograph Series 59. Sankt Augustin, Germany: Institut Monumenta Serica, 2007.

———. *Yang Tingyun, Confucian and Christian in Late Ming China: His Life and Thought*. Sinica Leidensia 19. Leiden: Brill, 1988.

Starr, Chloë. *Chinese Theology: Text and Context*. New Haven: Yale University Press, 2016.

Sun, Anna. *Confucianism as a World Religion: Contested Histories and Contemporary Realities*. Princeton: Princeton University Press, 2013.

Swain, Tony. *Confucianism in China: An Introduction*. London: Bloomsbury Academic, 2017.

Wanguo Gongbao: Zongmu, Suoyin. Shanghai: Shanghai Shudian Chubanshe, 2015.

Ying, Fuk-Tsang. "Fan Zimei: Between Tradition and Modernity." In *Salt and Light: Lives of Faith that Shaped Modern China*, edited by Carol Hamrin with Stacey Bieler, 1:64–78. 2 vols. Studies in Chinese Christianity. Eugene, OR: Pickwick Publications, 2009.

Zürcher, Erik. "Jesuit Accommodation and the Chinese Cultural Imperative." In *The Chinese Rites Controversy*, edited by D. E. Mungello, 31–64. Monumenta Serica Monograph Series 33. Nettetal, Germany: Steyler, 1994.

8

The Christology of Joseph Smith

A. Keith Thompson

In his 2012 examination of the theology of the Mormon Prophet, Joseph Smith,[1] Stephen Webb wrote that Joseph Smith

> knew more about theology and philosophy than it was reasonable for anyone in his position to know as if he were dipping into the deep, collective unconsciousness of Christianity with a very long pen . . . Smith identifies Jesus Christ not only with God but also with the eternal power that fuels the cosmos and the laws by which that power is regulated. Everything radiates with the energy of Jesus. This is truly the beginning of a Christological metaphysics of matter.[2]

In this chapter I explore the metaphysical consequences that Webb considered flow from Smith's Christology and some other ideas that I have considered as I have reflected on Webb's work.[3] Webb's list includes the com-

1. Webb, *Jesus Christ, Eternal God*.

2. Webb, *Jesus Christ, Eternal God*, 253–54.

3. This chapter is an amended version of a paper originally presented at the 2019 St Andrew's 3rd Theology Symposium, 'The Importance of Christology for the 21st Century' held 20–21 September 2019 at St Andrew's Greek Orthodox Theological College, Redfern, Sydney.

plete mortality and passibility of Christ, his resurrected anthropomorphism, the rejection of Platonic immaterialism (including the idea of ex nihilo creation), the idea that despite his materiality Christ nonetheless permeates all things, and a very developed notion of what *imitatio dei* means.

My additions to Webb's list are not really additions so much as they are consequences. That is, if Christ really does have a resurrected anthropomorphic body composed of heavenly flesh, why is it that Christianity has been obsessed with the idea of his immateriality since Saint Augustine but more particularly since Archbishop Thomas Cranmer opined in 1553 that the Trinitarian Christian God is without body, parts, and passions? Is the Christian God really impassible? Is that conclusion inescapable if we believe Jesus must be a spirit to be capable of dwelling within us? What difference would it have made to Christian reflection and theological insight if we had spent more time pondering the nature of flesh that could pass through walls and roofs and yet consume broiled fish and honeycomb?

The chapter is divided into three parts. In the first I set out, Lewis-like, how Webb was surprised by the consequences of Smith's theology,[4] and what happens when we think outside established theological boxes and reconsider the nature of God and matter itself in new ways. In the second part, I discuss Joseph Smith's theology and how it manifests consistent development unbound by the traditions that have channeled Christian theological reflection for centuries. In part 3, I suggest that breaking Webb's shackles enables new insight into the nature of matter and light, but also into time and how a possible Father, Son, and Holy Ghost can be personally engaged in every human life. I conclude that reflection upon Joseph Smith's theology has enabled Stephen Webb to identify a new universe for Christian reflection.

THINKING OUTSIDE THE BOX

When C. S. Lewis became a Christian, he challenged many theological paradigms. Examples include his insistence that human beings are gods in embryo.[5] Though the idea of deification or *theosis* is nothing new in Eastern Christianity,[6] Western Christianity is full of insistence that the idea that man might become like God is close to the blasphemy with which rabbinical

4. Lewis, *Surprised by Joy.*

5. Lewis, *Weight of Glory*, 46.

6. See for example, Russell, *Deification.*

Jews charged Jesus during his mortal ministry.[7] Stephen Webb has similarly suggested that Christian theological paradigms set in the decades following the Nicene Council in the fourth century CE have stifled the vision of Christian theologians ever since. In *Jesus Christ, Eternal God: Heavenly Flesh and the Metaphysics of Matter*, Stephen Webb has done that in part by drawing attention to the theology and particularly the Christology of the original Mormon Prophet, Joseph Smith. He has written, for example, that "no theology has ever managed to capture the essential sameness of Jesus with us,"[8] and he asks

> What if Tertullian had been more successful in his explication of the materiality of the soul? What if the monks of Egypt had won their battle in defense of anthropomorphism? What if Augustine had not read the books of the Platonists?[9]

But Stephen Webb concedes that it "requires something like an intellectual if not [a] spiritual conversion" to take Joseph Smith's theology seriously because "suspicion of Mormonism runs so high."[10] Webb summarizes Smith's theology of theosis:

> Divine power consists of the mastery of life and death—the power to create, to suffer and sacrifice for others, and to become greater in the process. Since we participate in that power, eternal life is a matter of learning 'how to be gods yourselves . . . by going from a small capacity to a great one; from grace to grace, from exaltation to exaltation, until you attain to the resurrection of the dead, and are able to dwell in everlasting burnings, and to sit in glory, as do those who sit enthroned in everlasting power.' Divinization never looked so real.[11]

Webb observes that Joseph Smith's view of matter and light follows

> the Gospel of John, [in calling] Christ the light of the world, but he takes this metaphor in a decidedly metaphysical direction. This is the light, he says, 'which is in all things; which giveth life to all things; which is the law by which all things are governed; even the power of God.' Smith identifies Jesus Christ not only with God

7. See Slick, "What is Theosis?"; Blackwell, "Man Is a God in Ruins," says that "the idea is virtually unknown in the Protestant tradition."

8. Webb, *Jesus Christ, Eternal God*, 243.

9. Webb, *Jesus Christ, Eternal God*, 244.

10. Webb, *Jesus Christ, Eternal God*, 244.

11. Webb, *Jesus Christ, Eternal God*, 256.

but also with both the eternal power that fuels the cosmos and the laws by which that power is regulated. Everything radiates with the energy of Jesus. This is truly the beginning of a Christological metaphysics of matter.[12]

Webb also considered Mormon christological scholarship most useful because it does not begin with doubt about the credibility of the witnesses of Christ's resurrection. He applauds Mormonism's recognition that Christ was not anti-institutional, and Webb wants to further explore its von Balthasar–like theology of Christ's descent into hell to preach to the spirits in prison and the similarity of Catholic and Mormon traditions when it comes to Christ's bloody sweat in the garden of Gethsemane.[13] But what seems to have surprised Webb the most was that Joseph Smith seemed to have contemplated and understood all these possibilities, and that they were connected together in his discourses in an entirely seamless and logical way.

What Webb wants to ponder more carefully is

- that despite the materiality of Christ, his goodness, energy, and power might still be able to permeate the entire universe;

- that a plan for the literal divinization of every human being was made in heaven before the foundations of the world were laid, and that the plan called for Christ to sweat blood in a sacrificial atonement; and

- that Christ had literally descended to hell in order to free and redeem the spirits imprisoned there.[14]

I now add my own summary reflections on the consequences of Joseph Smith's insights even though I have been marinated in the theology of the Church of Jesus Christ of Latter-day Saints since my childhood.

SMITH'S VISIONARY THEOLOGY

Joseph Smith's first vision, in upstate New York, probably happened on March 26, 1820.[15] He affirmed afterwards that

[t]he Father has a body of flesh and bones as tangible as man's; the Son also; but the Holy Ghost has not a body of flesh and bones, but

12. Webb, *Jesus Christ, Eternal God,* 254.
13. Personal correspondence in the possession of the author.
14. Personal correspondence in the possession of the author.
15. Lefgren and Pratt, "Oh, How Lovely."

is a personage of Spirit. Were it not so, the Holy Ghost could not dwell in us. (*Doctrine and Covenants* 130:22)

Stephen Webb writes that this vision and the consequential theology, "unleashed a squall of fresh air on the question of who Jesus Christ really is."[16] Webb continues, "Jesus and human beings partake of the same eternal properties . . . [but] Jesus has priority." Though the LDS social view of the Trinity can be mischaracterized as both subordinationism and Arianism,[17] the independence of the members of the Godhead is infinitely less than their oneness. And there is an Eastern flavor to their view of the Godhead as a sort of monarchy in which it does not matter whether Jesus was always God. The fact is that he is God now. And that is why Webb asks the question, what would have happened to Christian theology if "the best theological minds had dedicated themselves to explicating all the implications of the heavenly flesh position"?[18]

Joseph Smith's confident view that God and Christ are separate beings but that God presides, connects with the idea of monarchy in the Godhead, which has prevailed in Eastern Christianity since the creedal *filioque* clause separated East and West. For Joseph Smith that idea of monarchy was reaffirmed by the fact that the Father spoke only to introduce the Son with words that recall Matthew's when Jesus is baptized (Matt 3:17): This is my Beloved Son—Hear Him! (*Pearl of Great Price*, Joseph Smith History 1:17).

But Joseph Smith did not rely on inference. As he put it:

> I had actually seen a light, and in the midst of that light I saw two Personages, and they did in reality speak to me; and though I was hated and persecuted for saying that I had seen a vision, yet it was true . . . I knew it, and I knew that God knew it, and I could not deny it, neither dared I do it; at least I knew that by so doing I would offend God, and come under condemnation. (*Pearl of Great Price*, 1:25)

Joseph Smith's expression of testimony resonates with what Stephen Webb writes of the LDS view of the New Testament gospel witnesses:

> it is in exegeting scripture that Mormonism will prove its usefulness to the rest of Christianity . . . so much modern [Christology] scholarship begins with doubt about the credibility of witnesses,

16. Webb, *Jesus Christ, Eternal God*, 246.

17. Webb, *Jesus Christ, Eternal God*, 246.

18. Webb, *Jesus Christ, Eternal God*, 247–48.

dismissal of God's direct involvement in history, and what is probably worst of all, an unearned sense of moral superiority over our forefathers . . . The Saints have . . . confidence in the tangible and ongoing reality of God's verbal communication as the primary form of divine revelation . . . and . . . the living office of a prophet. (*Book of Mormon*, Moroni 7:27)

Joseph Smith has taught the Latter-day Saints that visions and miracles and angelic ministry have not "ceased because Christ hath ascended into heaven, and sat down on the right hand of God" (*Book of Mormon*, Moroni 7:27). These fruits of the Spirit can be confidently expected by those "of strong faith and a firm mind in every form of godliness" (*Book of Mormon*, Moroni 7:30).

Deification

The lost Christian teaching that humans ought to aspire to become as God while living as mortals has always been presented by Latter-day Saints as a primary reason why Joseph Smith was called to restore the fulness of Christ's gospel truth to the earth. Among those who have accepted Joseph Smith's teaching, there has been far too much philosophizing about godliness and not enough emphasis on its transformative power. (*Pearl of Great Price*, Jospeph Smith History 1:19)[19] While the young Joseph may not have fully appreciated the significance of the instruction he received in his First Vision when he was fourteen years old, in his later revelations he claimed that the Holy Ghost impressed its significance upon him at regular intervals.[20] Examples include the 1829 instruction that godliness is an essential attribute of those who seek to participate in God's work (*Doctrine and Covenants* 4:6), the 1832 instruction that the power of godliness is not manifest to men in the flesh without gospel ordinances administered by the authority of the greater priesthood (*Doctrine and Covenants* 84:19–22), and the 1844 funeral discourse, which Webb refers to in detail:

> Here, then, is eternal life—to know the only wise and true God; and you have got to learn how to be gods yourselves, and to be

19. In addition to *The Pearl of Great Price* referenced above, see Webb, *Jesus Christ, Eternal God*, 249.

20. Compare John 14:26 where Jesus promises his disciples that the other Comforter would bring all things that he had taught them to their remembrance as they continued their ministries.

kings and priests to God, the same as all gods have done before you, namely, by going from one small degree to another, and from a small capacity to a great one; from grace to grace, from exaltation to exaltation, until you attain to the resurrection of the dead, and are able to dwell in everlasting burnings, and to sit in glory, as do those who sit enthroned in everlasting power.[21]

This is not "deification . . . as a metaphor" or even as in Norman Russell's mature spiritual doctrine.[22] For Latter-day Saints, Christ was teaching his disciples through a modern-day prophet that he expects his followers to completely overcome the evils of their lives and to become as perfect as they can while still in the flesh (compare Matt 5:48 and 1 John 3:1–3). While in this teaching deification is made possible by the grace of Christ (*Book of Mormon*, 2 Nephi 25:23–27), it is the intended result of human striving aided by the ministry of the Godhead:

> We consider that God has created man with a mind capable of instruction, and a faculty which may be enlarged in proportion to the heed and diligence given to the light communicated from heaven to the intellect; and that the nearer man approaches perfection, the clearer are his views, and the greater his enjoyments, till he has overcome the evils of his life and lost every desire for sin; and like the ancients, arrives at that point of faith where he is wrapped in the power and glory of his Maker, and is caught up to dwell with Him. But we consider that this is a station to which no man ever arrived in a moment.[23]

Preexistence

Though Webb acknowledges that Joseph Smith's teaching of preexistence was not original, he observed that Joseph Smith developed it much more than Origen. For Origen, there was a plan laid before the foundation of this world where Jesus Christ as the oldest spirit son of God was called and fore-ordained as the atoning redeemer of the world.[24] As that chosen lamb of

21. Smith, comp., *Teachings*, 346–47 (part of the King Follet funeral discourse, delivered April 7, 1844, less than three months before Joseph Smith was murdered).

22. Russell, *Deification*, 1.

23. Smith, comp., *Teachings*, 51 (originally written by Joseph Smith in a letter to brethren in Missouri on January 22, 1834).

24. Webb, *Jesus Christ, Eternal God*, 201. See also Givens, *When Souls Had Wings,*

God, Jesus Christ was the original type for all the sacrifices of the righteous patriarchs. Only when that symbolism was ignored or corrupted were ancient sacrifices rejected (*Pearl of Great Price*, Moses 5:5–12; compare also Gen 4:3–7). In Joseph Smith's theology, all the prophets of antiquity knew that Jesus Christ was coming as the redeeming Lamb of God and many of them knew him by name (*Book of Mormon*, Jacob 7:11; see also 2 Nephi 10:3 and Mosiah 3:8):

> [Jesus] came to earth fully himself, not just fully divine in an abstract way. He comes to earth with a personality, we could say, that is already fully developed, and power that is obviously otherworldly.[25]

It was not just the Redeemer who existed with God before this earth was formed: "Man was also in the beginning with God. Intelligence, or the light of truth, was not created or made, neither indeed can be" (*Doctrine and Covenants* 93:29). And indeed God

> had shown unto . . . Abraham, the intelligences that were organized before the world was . . . and he stood in the midst of them, and he said: These I will make my rulers . . . and he said unto . . . Abraham, thou art one of them; thou was chosen before thou wast born. (*Pearl of Great Price*, Abraham 3:22)

Joseph Smith's doctrine of preexistence held that every person who would be born on earth was likewise a fully formed spirit child of God and came to earth with a preexisting personality and foreordained divine potential. Those who proved themselves by doing everything God would command would "have glory added upon their heads for ever and ever" (*Pearl of Great Price*, Abraham 25–26).

The Sinlessness of Jesus

Though traditional Christianity has been uncertain whether Jesus' experience with temptation was the same as that of other mortals in part because of passages in the New Testament book of Hebrews (for example 2:18 and 4:15), Joseph Smith was unequivocal. He said that in 1829 Jesus had affirmed his complete humanity when he described his experience in Gethsemane and at Calvary in these terms:

95–98 citing Elizabeth A. Clark and referring to Origen's *De Principiis*.

25. Personal correspondence in the possession of the author.

For behold, I, God, have suffered these things for all, that they might not suffer if they would repent;

But if they would not repent they must suffer even as I;

Which suffering caused myself, even God, the greatest of all, to tremble because of pain, and to bleed at every pore, and to suffer both body and spirit—and would that I might not drink the bitter cup, and shrink—

Nevertheless, glory be to the Father, and I partook and finished my preparation unto the children of men. (*Doctrine and Covenants* 19:16–19)

And Joseph Smith said he was given further instruction about the nature of Christ's mortality during the winters of 1832 and 1839. He said that Christ had taught him that he had "suffered temptations but gave no heed unto them" (*Doctrine and Covenants* 20:22) and that "he comprehended all things" because he had "descended below all things . . . that he might be in all and through all things, the light of truth" (*Doctrine and Covenants* 88:6; compare with 122:8).

As Stephen Webb has said, when Joseph Smith taught that Jesus is "the light of the world," he really did mean that Jesus Christ was at the center of everything. He could not comprehend and ascend to govern everything unless he had descended below it all.[26] Jesus has experienced everything we have experienced or can experience and more, and he has overcome it all and showed us that we can do the same.

Stephen Webb has said he had experienced joy after working "on Von Balthasar's theology of Christ's descent into hell, [when he discovered] the Mormon understanding of spirit prisons and the idea" that Jesus preached there and organized missionary work to continue in his absence.[27]

Preaching to the Spirits in Prison

Joseph Smith's teaching elaborated Peter's brief reference to Christ's ministry to the spirits in prison while his body lay in the tomb (e.g., see 1 Pet 3:18–20; 4:6),[28] but so did his nephew and fifth successor in the presidency of the Church of Jesus Christ of Latter-day Saints (*Doctrine and Covenants* 138).

26. Webb, *Jesus Christ, Eternal God*, 254.

27. Personal correspondence in the possession of the author.

28. For example, when revising the translation of John 5:29 in the New Testament by the gift and power of God, Joseph Smith and Sidney Rigdon are said to have jointly received an extended and detailed vision of the nature of the resurrection of man in the

Balthasar's theological concentration on Peter's teaching has prompted discussion of the *Catechism of the Catholic Church* by both Pope John Paul II and Pope Benedict XVI.[29] Essentially that teaching is that the gospel reached the dead through Christ's descent while his body lay in the tomb. The consequence is that the dead will also receive the glory of salvation. Balthasar saw Christ's descent as part of his passion and assumption of the sins of the entire human race.[30] Both of the popes believed Christ's passion was complete before the descent.[31] The LDS teaching about the period in Christ's life between his death and resurrection holds that his preaching to the spirits in prison "was the culmination of [his] ministry" and was seen in the light of the resurrection rather than as a prolongation of his experience of the cross.[32] In LDS understanding Christ's death was swallowed up in his victory, as Paul might have said, quoting Isaiah (see 1 Cor 15:54, alluding to Isa 25:8).

Joseph Smith's teaching on this period between Christ's death and resurrection added to the teaching of the prophet Alma the Younger in the Book of Mormon:

> Now, concerning the state of the soul between death and the resurrection—Behold, it has been made known unto me by an angel, that the spirits of all men, as soon as they are departed from this mortal body, yea, the spirits of all men, whether they be good or evil, are taken home to that God who gave them life.
>
> And then shall it come to pass, that the spirits of those who are righteous are received into a state of happiness which is called paradise, a state of rest, a state of peace, where they rest from all their troubles and from all care, and sorrow.
>
> And then shall it come to pass, that the spirits of the wicked, yea, who are evil—for behold, they have no part nor portion of the Spirit of the Lord; for behold they chose evil works rather than good; therefore the spirit of the devil did enter into them, and take

---

world to come. That revelation is set out in *Doctrine and Covenants 76*.

29. See Pitstick, *Christ's Descent*.

30. Webb says that in his *Mysterium Paschale*, Balthasar placed "the emphasis of Holy Saturday on the suffering of Christ . . . Christ suffer[ed] a physical death on the cross and a spiritual death in hell." Holy Saturday was for Balthasar, "the furthest reach of Christ's suffering on behalf of sinners [, which] makes it the climax of the cross. The cross thus casts its shadow over Jesus' death, so that even while his body is in repose his soul suffers inconceivable torment." (Personal correspondence in the possession of the author).

31. Pitstick, *Christ's Descent*.

32. Personal correspondence in the possession of the author.

possession of their house—and these shall be cast into outer darkness; there shall be weeping, and wailing, and gnashing of teeth,
and this because of their own iniquity, being led captive by the will
of the devil. (*Book of Mormon*, Alma 40:11–13)

Joseph Smith's nephew Joseph F. Smith was the fifth president of the
LDS Church. His 1918 revelation elaborated the LDS doctrine of the re-
demption of the dead. He taught that Christ's primary work among the
spirits of the dead during the period between his death and resurrection
was to organize the righteous as missionaries to cross the bridge his atonement had built and then to preach the gospel to those who had been dis-
obedient to truth during mortality (*Doctrine and Covenants* 138:11–30).

I conclude this section of this chapter with one further aspect of LDS
teaching about Christ's eternal nature that draws Stephen Webb's attention.
And that was the insight that God and matter are made of the same stuff.

The Eternal Nature of Matter

Webb puts it this way:

> Smith's idea of divine embodiment would have been part of the
> theological mainstream prior to Origen and Augustine . . . he
> would have agreed with the Neo-Platonists and the Christians
> that the Gnostics erred in identifying matter with evil . . . but he
> would not have shared the . . . [Christian] solution in attribut-
> ing infinity to God . . . Christian theologians have long connected
> the rational, knowable character of the world with the doctrine of
> creation out of nothing. God's infinity is the reason for matter's
> finitude. The consensus of the Church Fathers held that any blur-
> ring of the line between God and matter threatened both God's
> freedom and matter's status as finite and mundane . . . Mormon-
> ism is willing to make God much more knowable (much more like
> us) than traditional theism . . . Augustine is the classic example
> . . . He thought that if God did not create the world willfully, then
> physical substance would be a force as eternal, powerful and mys-
> terious as God himself . . . [But i]f God makes the world out of
> himself, does it necessarily have all the attributes of the divine?
> . . . [And] if God does not create matter out of nothing, then God
> merely shapes (or adds form to) the matter that is already there,
> and that means that God is neither infinite nor omnipotent . . .
> The Mormon Church stakes its whole theology on the coherence
> of the idea that God formed the world from a material substance

that is not totally unlike his own divine nature . . . At the very least, Mormonism presents a prod to theological thought at the precise time when . . . [we do not know how to respond to environmental] urgency . . . We need to know what matter is for, where it comes from, and to what extent it is identical to what we are.[33]

Joseph Smith outlined what Webb called his "metaphysics of matter" in an 1832 revelation and in an offhand 1843 comment to a Methodist preacher. The 1832 revelation follows the Gospel of John when Joseph Smith calls Christ "the light of the world" (compare John 8:12)[34] but Joseph Smith took "the metaphor in a decidedly metaphysical direction."[35]

He . . . ascended up on high, as also he descended below all things . . . that he might be in all and through all things, the light of truth;

Which truth shineth. This is the light of Christ. As also he is in the sun, and the light of the sun, and the power thereof by which it was made . . .

And the light which shineth which giveth you light, is through him who enlighteneth your eyes, which is the same light that quickeneth your understandings;

Which light proceedeth forth from the presence of God to fill the immensity of space—

The light which is in all things, which giveth life to all things, which is the law by which all things are governed, even the power of God . . . who is in the midst of all things. (*Doctrine and Covenants* 88:6–13)

Smith's confidence in the trustworthiness of matter controlled by Jesus was complete. "The universe is not big enough to hold the majesty of God's ingenuity" (*Doctrine and Covenants* 88:6–13). Smith said simply:

There is no such thing as immaterial matter. All spirit is matter, but it is more fine or pure, and can only be discerned by purer eyes; We cannot see it; but when our bodies are purified we shall see that it is all matter. (*Doctrine and Covenants* 131:7–8)

Webb is surprised by the consistency of Joseph Smith's thought. God had not created the world *ex nihilo*; he had formed it from matter and intelligence that can neither be created or destroyed.[36] God's omnipotence is

---

33. Webb, *Jesus Christ, Eternal God*, 249–53.

34. In addition to John 8:12, see Webb, *Jesus Christ, Eternal God*, 254.

35. Webb, *Jesus Christ, Eternal God*, 254.

36. Webb, *Jesus Christ, Eternal God*, 257.

premised in his "mastery of life and death, the power to 'create', to suffer and sacrifice for others."[37]

This chapter is not the place to discuss the nature of the revelations Joseph Smith claimed, but it is appropriate to consider some of the consequences this theology has for Christian understanding.

THE THEOLOGICAL CONSEQUENCES OF JOSEPH SMITH'S CHRISTOLOGY

In this part, I discuss three of the consequences for Christian theology that flow from the insights of Joseph Smith. The first concerns Joseph Smith's insistence that Christ has a resurrected anthropomorphic body. The second is that Jesus Christ is implicated in the very metaphysics of matter, and the third is that the activities of the Godhead are not circumscribed by time.

Jesus Christ Has a Resurrected Body

Though Christ's two appearances through sealed doors in the upper room where the disciples were gathered might have occasioned considerable reflection, the great Christian theologians seem to have left that subject alone. That seems to be because they thought that a resurrected and finite body limited God and foreclosed the power that he must possess to control matter. Thus Webb asks the question, What would have happened to Christian theology if "the best theological minds had dedicated themselves to explicating all the implications of the heavenly flesh position"?[38] Why hasn't Christian theology spent more time working out the consequences of Christ's resurrected insistence that he had a body in which Thomas could feel both the nail and spear marks, and which could prepare and eat human food—fish and honeycomb (Luke 24:36–43; John 20:19–28; 21:4–13)?

What might we learn if we continue to reflect upon how a physical body could enter a room with closed doors, or how the influence of the corporeal Godhead could be spread through time and space? Reflection on only those two ideas might have seen Christian theology ponder both the different densities of matter, which are not all observable by human eyes, and the nature of time itself if it is only measured to man (*Book of Mormon*,

---

37. Webb, *Jesus Christ, Eternal God*, 256.
38. Webb, *Jesus Christ, Eternal God*, 247–48.

Alma 40:8; but compare also with 2 Pet 3:8 and with *Pearl of Great Price*, Abraham 3:4).

Matter Has Different Densities

Traditional Christianity holds that there are heavenly beings known as angels, and that they can reveal themselves to humans as they please. For example, the recipients of the New Testament book of Hebrews were taught that Christians ought to be hospitable as some had entertained angels unaware when they took care of strangers (13:2). Though some interpreters have allegorized the reference, it is not clear that allegory was intended.

The account of the heavenly host that appeared to the shepherds in the fields near Bethlehem sometime between 6 and 4 BCE (Luke 2:8–15) suggests that those angels were unseen for some time before they allowed the shepherds to see them (note the word "suddenly" in 2:13). It was the same in the Hebrew Old Testament for Elisha's servant Gehazi, who could not see that "they that be with us are more than they that be with them" (2 Kgs 6:14–23, esp. vv. 16–17 KJV).

The very idea of transcendence—that there are spiritual things that we cannot perceive or comprehend with our five physical senses—celebrates the unseen dimensions of existence, including of human existence. William Wordsworth's poem "Ode on Intimations of Immortality"[39] suggests that all humans come to earth as spirit beings trailing clouds of glory, and that heaven lies about us in our infancy. Wordsworth's almost secular déjà vu idea also suggests that there is a shadow-on-the-wall quality to mortal human existence, though Mormon Christians think that Plato took that immateriality idea too far.

If, as Joseph Smith recorded in section 131 of the *Doctrine and Covenants* (131:7, 8), in the Mormon canon,

> There is no such thing as immaterial matter. All spirit is matter, but it is more fine or pure, and can only be discerned by purer eyes[,]

is there more that we cannot see because we do not exercise sufficient faith? And if that is so, how can human beings find and exercise the faith they need in order to see more transcendent visions?

---

39. Completed in 1804, this poem was published in *Poems in Two Volumes* in 1807.

Other thoughts that flow naturally from such reflection once mortal eyes have been opened by a member of the Godhead[40] include that our eyes can be opened to all kinds of revealed knowledge in all kinds of ways. What if Saint Augustine had pondered the five different accounts of Christ's coming and going from his disciples during his forty-day postresurrection ministry? (These include the two visits through the closed doors of the upper room, celebrated in Luke 24; the two departures from atop the Mount of Olives, narrated in Luke 24:50–51 and Acts 1:9–11; and the Galilean breakfast detailed in John 21:1–22.) What might Saint Augustine have learned if reflective inquiry had opened his mind to revelation about Christ's corporeal resurrected nature?

Joseph Smith told of five visits from the Angel Moroni during one twenty-four-hour sand he described at least four of the departures with the following summary:

> I saw the light in the room begin to gather immediately around the person of him who had been speaking to me, and it continued to do so until the room was left dark, except just around him; when instantly I saw, as it were, a conduit open right up into heaven, and he ascended till he entirely disappeared, and the room was left as it had been before this heavenly light had made its appearance. (*Pearl of Great Price*, Joseph Smith History 1:43)

He also provided a detailed description of this angel's arrivals and what he looked like (*Pearl of Great Price*, Joseph Smith History 1:30–32). A re-creation of that farm cottage and room in upper New York State, like the re-created upper room in Jerusalem, includes both walls and a ceiling.

Time Is Only Measured to Man
(*Book of Mormon*, Alma 41:8)

Science fiction literature is replete with expressions of the idea that time is a dimension that humans do not fully understand. In cosmos centers in the

---

40. For example, consider again the story of Elisha and his servant Gehazi recounted in 2 Kgs 6:14–23. There are also many references to miracles where Christ opens the eyes of the blind in the New Testament. All of these are considered to be metaphors about spiritual sight, reflecting Old Testament belief that all mortals have spiritual eyes though few are open. For example, consider the story of Hagar having her eyes opened and seeing a well (Gen 21:19) and Balaam having his eyes opened so that he could see the angel of the Lord (Num 22:31). There are also many Old Testament references where the prophets ask God to open their eyes so that they can see, feel, and then heal the people's afflictions.

Australian outback, where one can see all the cloudy milkiness of our galaxy spread overhead,[41] one can also see light from the Eagle Nebula that left there seven thousand years ago. If we developed the technology to read the detail of that light, we could see events that happened long ago as film on a giant video screen.

Even a moment's reflection on those ideas raises the question whether the Christian Godhead is beyond time and can thus hear and answer our individual prayers with or without other help as a kind of eternal tag-team. And that reflection leads to further questions—about prayer and answers to prayer: Are specific and unselfish personal prayers answered? Are they answered perhaps sometimes in the negative? When the answers are perceived and the will of heaven is communicated to the human intellect, are such prayers answered physically through the senses? Or are they answered from a transcendent space, as if we did not have physical bodies at all?

Strokes of intelligence do seem to come in flashes, and ideas can also come in folios that unfold if we reflect on them and turn the pages. And then there is the question, If God and Jesus Christ do answer our prayers, do they or do they not retain choice in the answers they give? That is, can they answer no, wait, or not yet?

Even these abbreviated reflections suggest that if time is taken out of the theological equation, matter does not matter! That is, matter does not limit God or his cocovenantors at all. Anthropomorphic members of the Godhead would be able to get around instantaneously.

Other Possibilities

This discussion in part 3 of this chapter has only scratched the surface of the consequences of Joseph Smith's theology. One subject that has to be grappled with if all spirit is matter and time is a mortal construct is the idea of ex nihilo creation. Stephen Webb says quite a bit about that:

> The Mormon Church stakes its whole theology on the coherence of the idea that God formed the world from a material substance that is not totally unlike his own divine nature. That makes Mormonism either a religious oddity in Western history or an utterly crucial metaphysical correction to our understanding of the role and value of matter in God's creation of the world. At the very

---

41. For example, at the Cosmos Centre in Charleville, Queensland, Australia.

least, Mormonism presents a prod to theological thought at the precise time when materiality is ... central to public awareness ... Matter has infinite folds and unbounded depths, for Smith, but it always evolves toward the form of Christ, which is our form too ... Smith does not pretend to know in exact detail where God is or what God looks like, but he is clear that the Father occupies space and the Son has a face not unlike our own. Moreover, there is a part of God that is able to pervade earthly matter, but that is what Smith calls the Holy Ghost ... The Holy Spirit is the most immaterial of the divine persons, and yet even the Holy Spirit takes a personal form.[42]

CONCLUSION

Raised as a Latter-day Saint, this author has taken Joseph Smith's theology for granted. But theological reflection occasioned by work in a Catholic university and reflection on Stephen Webb's analysis of ideas attributed to Joseph Smith have led to the conference presentation of which this chapter is a summary. The author's purpose is not to assert theological right and wrong, but to open minds to possibilities that may have been foreclosed through unrealized paradigms of thought. Thomas Kuhn coined the idea of the "paradigm shift" to explain how Newton and Einstein advanced understanding of theoretical physics.[43] The author believes that Joseph Smith's Christology presents as a similar paradigm shift for theologians.

BIBLIOGRAPHY

Balthasar, Hans Urs von. *Mysterium Pachale: The Mystery of Easter.* Translated by Aidan Nichols. Edinburgh: T. & T. Clark, 1990.

Blackwell, Ben. "Man as a God in Ruins: Theosis in the Christian tradition." *The Table* (blog), September 4, 2015. Biola Center for Christian Thought. https://cct.biola.edu/man-god-ruins-theosis-christian-tradition/.

Brown, S. Kent. *The Testimony of Luke.* Brigham Young Universaity New Testament Commentary. Provo: BYU Studies, 2014.

Church of Jesus Christ of Latter-day Saints. *The Book of Mormon, Another Testament of Christ.* Rev. ed. Salt Lake City: The Church of Jesus Christ of Latter-day Saints, 2013.

———. *The Doctrine and Covenants.* Salt Lake City: The Church of Jesus Christ of Latter-day Saints, 1981.

42. Webb, *Jesus Christ, Eternal God,* 253–55.

43. Kuhn, *Scientific Revolutions,* 4, 88.

———. *The Pearl of Great Price*. Salt Lake City: The Church of Jesus Christ of Latter-day Saints, 1979.

Givens, Terryl. *When Souls Had Wings: Pre-Mortal Existence in Western Thought*. Oxford: Oxford University Press, 2010.

Kuhn, Thomas. *The Structure of Scientific Revolutions*. 3rd ed. Chicago: University of Chicago Press, 1996.

Lefgren, John C., and John P. Pratt. "Oh, How Lovely Was the Morning: Sun 26 Mar 1820?" *Meridian Magazine* (9 October 2002). https://archive.bookofmormoncentral.org/content/oh-how-lovely-was-morning-sun-26-mar-1820/.

Lewis, C. S. *Mere Christianity*. C. S. Lewis Signature Classics ed. London: Collins, 2012.

———. *Surprised by Joy*. 1st American ed. New York: Harcourt Brace, 1956.

———. *The Weight of Glory*. San Francisco: HarperOne, 2001.

Origen. *On First Principles*. Edited and translated by John Behr. 2 vols. Oxford Early Christian Texts. New York: Oxford University Press, 2018.

Pitstick, Lyra. *Christ's Descent into Hell*. Grand Rapids: Eerdmans, 2014.

Russell, Norman. *The Doctrine of Deification in the Greek Patristic Tradition*. Oxford Early Christian Studies. Oxford: Oxford University Press, 2004.

Slick, Matt. "What Is Theosis?" *Christian Apologetics & Research Ministry* (website), April 22, 2014. https://carm.org/what-is-theosis/.

Smith, Joseph Feilding, comp. *Teachings of the Prophet Joseph Smith*. Salt Lake City: Deseret, 1938.

Webb, Stephen H. *Jesus Christ, Eternal God: Heavenly Flesh and the Metaphysics of Matter*. New York: Oxford University Press, 2012.

9

Engaging Jesus in Secular Australia

David Merritt

The reception of Jesus in contemporary Australian culture is more problematic now than at any time in our history. Anyone seeking to engage with Jesus today faces a double dilemma: widespread lack of religious literacy in an increasingly secular society, and the challenge to traditional understandings of Jesus in light of critical biblical scholarship. A progressive religious educator today needs to extend their professional skills using processes that explicitly recognize and affirm the lived experience of Australians.

A common approach has been to introduce Jesus by deconstructing texts in the New Testament Gospels in order to show their relevance to life today. An alternative approach is to identify issues in the lives of contemporary Australians and show that some texts in the New Testament Gospels present the wisdom of Jesus as relevant to enriched living today. The latter process provides an explicitly progressive perspective on Jesus for many Australians in a post-Christian world.

The two primary references are on one hand the findings of the scholars of the Jesus Seminar and the Westar Institute about what Jesus taught,[1] and on the other hand current understandings of the role of a learner's present experience and motivation to reflect and act on that experience as key factors in learning.[2]

The second educational approach is radically different from many traditional approaches to religious education about Jesus where the desired learning is prescribed by specified content such as a body of beliefs or church practices or privileged sacred texts.

In this chapter I am excluding addressing how to help people engage with beliefs about Jesus. That is an important issue for some scholars and some contemporary Christians but involves different—and more substantial—challenges in how to relate those beliefs to the experience of secular Australians.[3]

CONTEMPORARY AUSTRALIA

The distinction between the two broad approaches above is given added relevance by evidence of the increasing secularity of Australians and decreasing involvement of Australians with traditional religion.

One illustration of increasing secularity in Australia is the change in the percentage of people completing the national census who indicated their religion as "None." In the 1991 census the "Nones" represented 12.9 percent of the population; in 2006 this had risen to 18.75 percent; while in the latest census (2016) "No religion" was 30.1 percent.[4] Bouma and Halafoff report:

> We discuss three main categories of religion in contemporary Australia; the 'nones'; the spiritual but not religious; and the religious and spiritual. The data reveal a new context of superdiversity in Australia . . . The religious landscape is most definitely changing,

1. Funk and Hoover, eds., *Five Gospels*; and Funk and the Jesus Seminar, *Acts of Jesus*. For a convenient snapshot of the message of the historical Jesus, see Funk and the Jesus Seminar, *Gospel of Jesus*.

2. For a summary of current educational theory, including results of empirical studies of learning, see Kolb, *Experiential Learning*.

3. Consider, for example, the narratives about the birth of Jesus in Luke 1:4—2:40 and in Matt 1:1—2:27 where a series of complex beliefs have their origin in Jewish religious texts and, to a lesser extent, in Roman history.

4. Bouma and Halafoff, "Australia's Changing Religious Profile," 131.

away from a predominantly white, Christian society, to a much more multicultural, multifaith and non-religious one.[5]

As the gap grows between knowledge about Jesus in contemporary culture and knowledge about Jesus presented in contemporary biblical scholarship, the processes adopted to bridge that gap deserve careful consideration. That is precisely what this chapter seeks to address as it considers the potential advantages of an educational process that gives more attention to the lived experience of Australians than has been the case in much traditional religious education.

That so many people in the 2016 census identified as in some way "Christian" does not necessarily mean they are committed to being Christian. Dr. Philip Hughes of the Christian Research Association reports infrequent involvement of Australians with religious activities. "Eighty-four percent of Australians are not involved in religious activities on a regular basis (monthly or more often)."[6] The National Church Life Survey (NCLS) reports that the situation for religion in Australia is dire. Based on a 2016 survey, it found that only four in ten Australians agree that the Christian religion is good for society. A similar number are neutral or unsure, while two in ten disagree.[7]

The situation for traditional religion in Australia has changed dramatically. It is urgent for educators to recognize that the starting point when working with contemporary Australians is likely to be an increased focus on the life situation of Australians.[8]

A TWO-THOUSAND-YEAR DETOUR

Starting with the texts requires a two-thousand-year detour from life today to encounter Jesus in the New Testament Gospels and confronts people with formidable challenges to understanding. That journey is relatively easy for scholars, especially if they have pre-existing commitments to the significance of early Christian documents in the New Testament. However, it is a strange world far removed from life in Australia today.

5. Bouma and Halafoff, "Australia's Changing Religious Profile," 129, 133.

6. Hughes, "Some Notes about Religious Identification."

7. Pepper and Powell, *Australian Community Survey.*

8. One of my daughters posted a Facebook update to help her think about an upcoming trip to Finland and Latvia: "Anyone been to Riga in Latvia?" Among assorted responses was, "Latvians?"

Starting with the Gospels—even after critical deconstruction—also presents complex problems that arise from introducing first-century concepts and language into twenty-first century discussions of meaning. The list of cognitive and cultural hurdles includes at least the following: the status of Jewish scriptures within a Christian Bible; ancient social roles such as Priests and Levites, Pharisees and Sadducees, Herodians and Zealots, scribes and rabbis; anachronistic geopolitical labels such as Israel, Samaria, Judaea, Galilee, and the Decapolis; religious practices such as temple sacrifices and purity codes; and specific beliefs about God, Jesus, angels, and evil spirits (including a premodern view of the universe), divine causation of droughts and sickness, gender stereotypes, slavery, and sexuality and marriage. That list is incomplete, but its complexity hints at the challenges we face. Terms and concepts that have distinctive first-century meanings are not always easy to transfer across the two-thousand-year divide. To start with a need to explain such terms is a significant handicap for learners and a deterrent to educators.

There is a further problem of motivation for nonspecialists, who compose the vast majority of twenty-first-century Australians whether or not they are involved in a church community. In my experience, the most common concerns of people involved in progressive Christian groups—after a continuing diet of "deconstruction"—are requests for "something directly relevant to my life," "something enriching for my everyday life," and "something that helps me to be a more spiritual person." Relevance, personal transformation, and practical spirituality are major concerns for people likely to be in our groups.

None of this is to question the great gifts that progressive Christian scholars have given to many people involved in churches, especially freedom from unquestioning subservience to the Christianity that was expressed in fourth-century creeds. Scholars such as Marcus Borg and John Shelby Spong have pioneered the way. For example, they have shown how the writings, beliefs, and practices of the Christian movement developed from the first-century teachings and life of Jesus to become the complex and ever-changing array of scriptures, beliefs, and practices of later Christianity. Whether we are thinking about the first century or the fourth century, those beliefs and practices were the products of people and cultures whose worldviews were vastly different from ours. The insights of these scholars lifted from me and many others the intellectual and lifestyle burdens of "impossible beliefs."[9]

In retrospect, the catalogue of beliefs largely disconnected from living today is substantial. The heroes of deconstructing ancient beliefs for people today are justly celebrated. We no longer need to affirm that everything in the Bible is true or relevant, let alone divinely inspired. The suggestion that Jesus was born from a virgin can be seen as a devotional legend. The resurrection of Jesus need not involve a physical revival of the body that was killed on the cross. Doctrines which insist that humans are inherently sinful or that the purpose of Jesus' life was dying for sinners can be set aside. We can reject the idea that the purpose of our lives is preparation for the next life, or that we possess immortal souls. Many of us affirm that a statement of beliefs worked out by a gathering of church leaders under imperial patronage in the fourth century is neither definitive nor helpful.

A glimpse into the processes of change in how Jesus was understood in the contexts of ancient Jewish and Roman experiences has been liberating. It also invites people to a comparable process of finding meaning in the rapidly changing cultures of today. There is a clear need for us to do what each generation of Jesus' followers has had to do: work out as best we can a way to live while drawing on our heritage, our knowledge, and our own cultural circumstances. That is to do what the New Testament writers did. But the *content* of what they did, as distinct from the *process*, is often unhelpful in the very different cultural situations in which we live today.

Consider the radical differences in the area of sexuality and human relationships. The ancients had limited knowledge of human reproduction, genetics, and sexuality. For the most part there was little opportunity for travel and little understanding of differences across time or cultures. Today we have access to accurate information about sexuality in humans and animals, about the prevention of conception, about safe medical intervention in pregnancies, about diverse sexual practices, and about cultural differences across time and location. In a letter to the first-century residents of Corinth, Paul could describe sexual relations between males as "contrary to nature" and condemn sexuality outside marriage (1 Cor 6:9–10). Neither of Paul's views is likely to win wide acceptance in Australia today.

Another barrier to adapting the meaning of Jesus for today can be seen in the conserving function of liturgy. Adapting the ancient faith for the contemporary world has been shown to be beneficial to many individuals,

---

9. See Spong, *Unbelievable*.

but has often left them with institutional communities of faith dominated by what was supposed to be adapted but what has truly only partially been modified. I think our experience in progressive Christianity over the last fifteen years has shown that we are not likely to arrive at a faith for the contemporary world by starting from the faith developed in and for the ancient, predominantly prescientific, world. So, we choose between attending services—and putting up with strange language, irrelevant scriptures, pious homilies, and meaningless practices—or dropping out. As contemporary humans we can live only with great difficulty in this institutional world that does not breathe the same "atmosphere" or reflect the world we live in and the people with whom we share our daily lives.

CONSIDERING ALTERNATIVE EDUCATIONAL PROCESSES

Much of progressive Christianity in Australia is shaped by the deconstructive/adaptive approach (for example Marcus Borg and John Shelby Spong). This often has unforeseen consequences which are part of the reason progressive Christianity has little appeal to people under forty-five who have grown up in the contemporary world. These people naturally start from the world they know rather than looking for an adaptation of the tradition. On the other hand, people grounded in the tradition have an understandable, if not always helpful, bias towards adaptation of the writings of the first centuries of the Christian story.

To explore the two educational alternatives to engage the wisdom of Jesus, I will take selected teachings of Jesus. Historical Jesus scholars suggest that the characteristic original teachings of Jesus were parables—short, often dramatic stories, sometimes with unexpected endings that confront listeners with a choice of what to do—and aphorisms—short, pithy sayings that are memorable guides to behavior. I have therefore chosen a well-known parable from Luke[10] and an aphorism (found in both Luke and Matthew) that has entered our culture.[11]

---

10. See the Appendix for the text of Luke 15:1–22, known popularly, but probably inaccurately, as the parable of the prodigal son.

11. Luke 6:41 (and Matt 7:3) "Why do you see the speck in your neighbor's eye, but do not notice the log in your own eye?"

Engaging with the Parables of Jesus

Traditionally, educators and preachers alike start with the text. This may be thought to be well-known and straightforward. In fact, unless recent scholarship is disregarded and the text is taken out of context in the Gospel, it turns out to be a very demanding educational process for teachers and often quite complex for students. The work of scholars brings new assumptions and tools to the task. Consider, for example, the following statement about how to listen to those early texts:

> Everything in the Bible was written for someone else in another time and culture about something else. So we are listening through a keyhole to an ancient conversation not intended for us.[12]

In an educational program offering engagement with Jesus and taking contemporary scholarship seriously, considerably more is required. So in a gospel passage about a parable told by Jesus (in particular here, the parable of the prodigal son) a teacher may consider at least the following questions:

- The written text: Who wrote it? When? To whom? In what circumstances?

- What is in the text: What is the setting? What is the author's 'introduction'? What is it "about"?

- Who are the characters?

- What happens/what is said?

- What was the main meaning then? What action was required from those who heard the parable?

- "Listening in" to that text, what can we hear for us? What action by us could be affected?

This can be an informative experience for many people, but it is hard work. Repeated often it can induce something less than enthusiasm. More importantly, it starts with categories of thought that belong to the first century and then seeks to find meaning in them for people today. It can be a difficult journey to connect the ancient text with the world in which we live. It is common for people who start with enthusiasm for deconstruction of the biblical texts to want something different: "something that makes a difference to what is important for my life." Sallie McFague captures this dilemma well:

12. Westar Institute, *Westar on the Road* (video).

Entering the biblical world for many people is like going into a
time warp in which one is transported to a world two thousand
years in the past. We are aware of significant connections since
both worlds are inhabited by human beings, but the images, problems, issues, and assumptions are different.[13]

Before engaging with this parable of Jesus I encourage readers to re-
fresh their memory of the actual text from Luke that is reproduced in the
appendix. Memory can be deceptive. Readers are likely to be aware that
study of this parable, "The prodigal son," frequently ignores the setting in
Luke's Gospel, omits verses 1 to 10, and starts at verse 11. You may also
assume this is in some way the word of God to us. Understandably, people
will arrive at different conclusions about what Jesus is teaching. In my experience readers often understand it as a parable about a loving God forgiving
sinful humans. That process so clearly avoids attention to what Luke in-
tends as his Gospel that it is not considered here. However, the far-reaching
consequences of such an approach should be noted. Marcus Borg observes:

> In the last half century, probably more Christians have left the
> church because of the Bible than for any other single reason. More
> precisely, they left because the earlier paradigm's way of seeing the
> Bible ceased to make sense to them. Contemporary literalism—
> with its emphasis on biblical infallibility, historical factuality,
> and moral and doctrinal absolutes—is an obstacle for millions of
> people.[14]

Gretta Vosper is even more direct:

> As long as millions of people are still calling this book "the Au-
> thoritative Word of God for All Time (TAWOGFAT), as long as
> others continue to refer to it as wholly "inspired" by god, as long
> as anyone holds it up uncritically as the text that is relevant for
> everyone for ever, it will continue not only to declare a message of
> exclusive salvation for believers and sure condemnation for non-
> believers, but also, as it was in the Dark Ages, to deny freedoms
> that we have now established as right and good, many of which
> are not supported by its passages. It is time we who call ourselves
> moderate, liberal, or progressive Christians take responsibility for
> countering these harmful and dangerous messages.[15]

13. McFague, *Metaphorical Theology*, 8.

14. Borg, *Heart of Christianity*, 43–44.

15. Vosper, *With or Without God*, 135–36.

What at first seemed full of promise for introducing people of our time to the Jesus of the first century has proved difficult. This is at least partly because the cultural, conceptual, and language gaps have expanded exponentially while there has been a vast increase in scholarship about the biblical texts of the first century. There is another way

This alternative approach assumes a leader/teacher has been through a process similar to that outlined above. They have an understanding of the teachings of Jesus but present people with a more direct way to engage with those teachings based on issues in their own contemporary experience. There is no difference between the two processes in their regard for biblical scholarship. The differences are in the second approach's recognition of the relevance of today's culture when seeking engagement with the teaching of Jesus.

The setting in Luke 15:1–3 makes it clear that Luke saw the three parables, including the story of the father who had two sons, as about how to treat people who were regarded as sinners:

> Now all the tax-collectors and sinners were coming near to listen to him. And the Pharisees and the scribes were grumbling and saying, 'This fellow welcomes sinners and eats with them.' So he told them this parable.

There is no exact match in the contemporary world with the characters in this part of Luke's Gospel. The tax collectors were not staff of the Australian Tax Office, and the "sinners" were not necessarily immoral persons even if they were despised by the religious elite of the time. But moral judgments are a part of the contemporary world. There are people regarded as undeserving by some of those doing well in our society, or even by our own religious elites.

Consider a group of adults wanting to explore the relevance of Jesus' teaching for them. They could start with a discussion of choices about how we treat people who are different from us. For example:

- The leader might begin with a question: "Are there people in our society who suffer discrimination?"

- "Our society is divided about how to treat people who have not made a success of their lives. What about unemployment benefits?"

- "Some people say you have to earn respect and assistance, or that assistance should not be sufficient for decent living. Others say we should respond to need wherever it is. What do you think? How would you decide?"

- "Should treatment of someone who has been foolish and squandered their money but now urgently needs a job for income for basic living be treated differently than someone who has kept a steady job?"

- "What about someone who has contributed to their desperate need by using drugs that have messed up their life?"

Following is a possible link to the parable in Luke, which might be used by the leader:

> One of the strong criticisms of Jesus by religious and political leaders in his day was that he spent time with these kinds of people who were regarded then as sinners. These were people who were despised and marginalized because of poverty or disability or occupation (such as a tax collector who worked for the hated Roman Empire). We shall now listen to one situation included by Luke in his Gospel about Jesus."
>
> Luke and other Gospels wrote that Jesus often used stories to answer questions. His stories were called parables. These are stories that sound simple but have a surprise or challenge in them. Listen for the kind of story Jesus uses. We know today that recognizing the kind of story being told can alert you to what is coming. If an Australian says "An Australian, a New Zealander and an Englishman went into a pub . . ." you are alerted to listen for what happens to one of them; most likely the New Zealander or the Englishman. If a story starts "A father had two sons . . . ," you can be confident this is not a story about boys who played happily together and grew up as best friends. You are alerted to listen for something that is going to go wrong. So listen to what kind of story Jesus tells and what it is about."
>
> Read Luke 15:1–3 and 15:11–32

Some of the questions that could be used for discussion are

- Who are the main characters in the story about the father who had two sons?

- What is the story about?

- How can you know the story is not mainly about how the father acts?

- How does the story end? Does the ending complete the story? What would you like to know that the story doesn't tell you? For you, what would be a good ending to the story?

- What did Luke say the story was "about"?

- What could you suggest would be a good title for this story?
- What is Jesus teaching in this story?
- What could it mean for us to live this "Way of Jesus"? Where do we face situations about how we treat less fortunate people?

> The conversation between the father and the older brother is compelling. The brother protests that it is not fair for his waster (prodigal) brother to be treated so well when he, the older brother, has been dutiful all his life. The father reminds him that he has enjoyed a good life. The younger brother has wasted the benefits he had but now in desperate need asks for minimum support to live on. The older brother renounces the relationship" "This son of yours." The father asserts the relationship that requires generosity: "This brother of yours has come to life."
>
> The parable ends before the older brother responds. "What will he do?" is the question hanging over the end of the story. It is the question implicitly directed by Jesus to the judgmental religious leaders who had criticized his welcoming relationships with people they looked down on as sinners. It is a question posed by Jesus' teaching about a different way to live, and a question with potentially far-reaching consequences for followers of the Way of Jesus today.

The experiences of participants may include active concern about discrimination, about how individuals or our society treat people with special needs. They may have found themselves overlooked by a prosperous society. In such cases the parable can evoke deeply engaging consideration of how to live.

Before offering a learning opportunity that begins with the experience of the participants, the leader first needs to identify the "life concern" from the first century addressed by the parable. Such a preliminary step will assist the leader to identify contemporary experience that may serve as an entry point to the discussion. This may sound self-evident but it is not uncommon for such parables to be assumed to be about beliefs that are central in traditional Christianity. Biblical scholars have helped us understand that the first-century context may guide us to very different conclusions about what Jesus was teaching. Only after identifying what aspect of living a parable was addressing can we identify how it can relate to contemporary experiences of living that could motivate energy to engage with Jesus' teaching.

Engaging with the Aphorisms of Jesus

As noted earlier, while parables tend to vivid stories (sometimes very brief) that challenged the listener to see the world differently, the aphorisms of Jesus are constructed around a vivid turn of phrase, such as "Let those with ears listen!"[16]

For this case study, we shall use the aphorism about observing splinters in another person's eye while ignoring the log in our own eyes (Luke 6:41–42):

> Why do you see the speck in your neighbor's eye, but do not notice the log in your own eye? Or how can you say to your neighbor, "Friend let me take out the speck in your eye," when you yourself do not see the log in your own eye? You hypocrite, first take the log out of your own eye, and then you will see clearly to take the speck out of your neighbor's eye.

If starting with the text, this session could begin in various ways. One option would be to ask whether participants have heard of any saying of Jesus that has stuck in their memory. Why have they remembered it? Alternatively, the leader could ask whether there is a quotation or a famous saying from anyone that they find easy to remember. Again, why have they remembered it?

Introduce the idea of memorable sayings and the role they play in our lives before reading Luke 6:41–42. Explore the relevance of this aphorism with questions such as the following:

- Do you think this is relevant to people today?

- Do you think there is too much criticism of other people in our society?

- Do you think it is fair for this saying to call people hypocrites?

- Criticizing others while ignoring our own faults was frequently mentioned by Jesus as something to avoid. For example, just before this short parable in Luke's Gospel Jesus says, "Do not judge, and you will not be judged; do not condemn, and you will not be condemned. Forgive, and you will be forgiven" (d). One of the memorable lines from the Lord's Prayer is: "Forgive us our sins, for we ourselves forgive everyone indebted to us" (Luke 11:4).

- Discuss what difference the wisdom in this aphorism could make to our lives.

16. This example is found numerous times in the New Testament, including in Mark 4:9 || Matt 13:9 || Luke 8:8b and Rev 2:7, 11, 17, 29; 3:6, 13,22; 13:9.

Once again, an alternative to starting with the text is a process that begins with the lived experience of the participants. Some questions that could elicit discussion of participants' experiences are

- Do you think there is much hypocrisy today? Does it have bad effects on people?
- Can you think of any time when criticism of you or people you know has been unfair and hurtful?
- What could be practical ways to improve a family, a workplace, friendships, or politics?

Following this opening discussion, the conversation could move to consider some of the teachings of Jesus. Jesus gave a lot of attention in his teaching to our attitudes towards other people (Luke 6:41–42; Luke 6:37; Luke 11:4).

- Would this teaching be easy for us to follow in our lives?
- Do you know of examples of hypocrisy like this?
- Discuss how following this teaching of Jesus could make our lives better and improve how we relate to other people.

Comparing this example of an aphorism with the previous example of a parable makes us aware how difficult it can be for a first-century text to have genuine impact on twenty-first-century lives. There is a greater chance of Jesus' teaching being heard as relevant if it is approached from shared experience in our lives now so as to provide a connection point, than there is if it is approached primarily as writing from twenty centuries ago.

As previously noted, a preliminary step during the preparation phase would be to identify what scholars have established about the life setting of the text. It will then be clear which aspects of contemporary experience offer a launching pad for exploring the aphorism and the implications of Jesus' teaching for living today.

CONCLUSION

This chapter has explored educational processes used in group learning settings. It would be possible to apply similar processes when preparing a sermon or some other address where the speaker's intention is to show the relevance of the Way of Jesus for living today.

There is a well-known parody of a lecture as a process in which the notes of a lecturer are transferred from the notebook of the lecturer to the notebooks of students without passing through the minds of either. That we can recognize some element of truth in this caricature gives force to the search for more involving and potentially life-changing processes in assisting people to engage with Jesus.

The proposal in this chapter is that focusing on the contemporary life experience of a learner is directly relevant both to motivation to engage with Jesus' teaching and to the possible impact of that teaching on how a learner lives today. The movement from experience today through relevant text to implications for our experience now provides more motivation to invest energy in internalizing what can be learned. Moving from experience to text is more effective than attempting to move from an ancient text to life today, and such movement starting from life experience celebrates the nature of the gospel texts as about enriched living. For a progressive Christian understanding of Jesus as a teacher of wisdom for living, this is the heart of the educational process.

In our day, engaging with Jesus as the teacher of wisdom for living requires more than knowledge about what was written in the first century. It requires a connection between the experiences that shape who we are and that dynamic first-century teacher, Jesus, who presented a vision of a different world from everyday Jewish life under the oppression of an occupying power. Jesus spoke of the "kingdom of God" as an alternative way to live. To appreciate his radical message we require engagement that not only *connects* with our experience of living today, but also *confronts* and potentially *reshapes* that experience. Taking contemporary experience seriously in the educational process opens possibilities for a more dynamic engagement with Jesus the teacher of wisdom for living.

APPENDIX: LUKE 15:1–32[17]

Now all the tax collectors and sinners were coming near to listen to him. [2]And the Pharisees and the scribes were grumbling and saying, "This fellow welcomes sinners and eats with them."

---

17. Care has been taken not to title this passage from Luke "The Parable of the Prodigal Son" so that people can consider what the parable is about for Luke (why Luke included it in his Gospel) and therefore what an appropriate title might be for us.

[3]So he told them this parable: [4]"Which one of you, having a hundred sheep and losing one of them, does not leave the ninety-nine in the wilderness and go after the one that is lost until he finds it? [5]When he has found it, he lays it on his shoulders and rejoices. [6]And when he comes home, he calls together his friends and neighbors, saying to them, 'Rejoice with me, for I have found my sheep that was lost.' [7]Just so, I tell you, there will be more joy in heaven over one sinner who repents than over ninety-nine righteous people who need no repentance.

[8]"Or what woman having ten silver coins, if she loses one of them, does not light a lamp, sweep the house, and search carefully until she finds it? [9]When she has found it, she calls together her friends and neighbors, saying, 'Rejoice with me, for I have found the coin that I had lost.' [10]Just so, I tell you, there is joy in the presence of the angels of God over one sinner who repents."

[11]Then Jesus[*] said, "There was a man who had two sons. [12]The younger of them said to his father, 'Father, give me the share of the property that will belong to me.' So he divided his property between them. [13]A few days later the younger son gathered all he had and traveled to a distant country, and there he squandered his property in dissolute living. [14]When he had spent everything, a severe famine took place throughout that country, and he began to be in need. [15]So he went and hired himself out to one of the citizens of that country, who sent him to his fields to feed the pigs. [16]He would gladly have filled himself with the pods that the pigs were eating; and no one gave him anything. [17]But when he came to himself he said, 'How many of my father's hired hands have bread enough and to spare, but here I am dying of hunger! [18]I will get up and go to my father, and I will say to him, "Father, I have sinned against heaven and before you; [19]I am no longer worthy to be called your son; treat me like one of your hired hands."' [20]So he set off and went to his father. But while he was still far off, his father saw him and was filled with compassion; he ran and put his arms around him and kissed him. [21]Then the son said to him, 'Father, I have sinned against heaven and before you; I am no longer worthy to be called your son.' [22]But the father said to his slaves, 'Quickly, bring out a robe—the best one—and put it on him; put a ring on his finger and sandals on his feet. [23]And get the fatted calf and kill it, and let us eat and celebrate; [24]for this son of mine was dead and is alive again; he was lost and is found!' And they began to celebrate.

[25]"Now his elder son was in the field; and when he came and approached the house, he heard music and dancing. [26]He called

one of the slaves and asked what was going on. [27]He replied, 'Your brother has come, and your father has killed the fatted calf, because he has got him back safe and sound.' [28]Then he became angry and refused to go in. His father came out and began to plead with him. [29]But he answered his father, 'Listen! For all these years I have been working like a slave for you, and I have never disobeyed your command; yet you have never given me even a young goat so that I might celebrate with my friends. [30]But when this son of yours came back, who has devoured your property with prostitutes, you killed the fatted calf for him!' [31]Then the father said to him, 'Son, you are always with me, and all that is mine is yours. [32]But we had to celebrate and rejoice, because this brother of yours was dead and has come to life; he was lost and has been found.'"

BIBLIOGRAPHY

Borg, Marcus J. *The Heart of Christianity: Rediscovering a Life of Faith.* San Francisco: HarperSanFrancisco, 2003.

Bouma, Gary, and Anna Halafoff. "Australia's Changing Religious Profile—Rising Nones and Pentecostals, Declining British Protestants in Superdiversity: Views from the 2016 Census." *Journal for the Academic Study of Religion* 30 (2017) 129–43.

Funk, Robert W., and the Jesus Seminar. *The Gospel of Jesus according to the Jesus Seminar.* Santa Rosa, CA: Polebridge, 1999.

———. *The Acts of Jesus: The Search for the Authentic Deeds of Jesus.* San Francisco: HarperSanFrancisco, 1998.

Funk, Robert W., and Roy W. Hoover, eds. *The Five Gospels: The Search for the Authentic Words of Jesus.* New York: Macmillan, 1993.

Hughes, Philip. "Some Notes about Religious Identification in 2016 Census." Pointers: *Bulletin of the Christian Research Association* 27.3 (2017) 1–4.

Kolb, David A. *Experiential Learning: Experience as the Source of Learning and Development.* 2nd ed. Upper Saddle River, NJ: Pearson Education, 2015.

McFague, Sallie. *Metaphorical Theology: Models of God in Religious Language.* Philadelphia: Fortress, 1982.

Pepper M., and R. Powell. *2016 Australian Community Survey.* Sydney: NCLS Research, 2016. http://preview.ncls.org.au/research/2016-acs#results/.

Spong, John Shelby. *Unbelievable: Why neither Ancient Creeds nor the Reformation Can Produce a Living Faith Today.* San Francisco: HarperOne, 2018.

Vosper, Gretta. *With or Without God: Why the Way We Live Is More Important Than What We Believe.* Toronto: HarperCollins, 2008.

Westar Institute. *Westar on the Road: Who We Are, and What We Do.* 2017. https://www.youtube.com/watch?v=AbkvQcf6kJg/.

10

Jesus and the Transforming Influence of Friendship

John H. W. Smith

This chapter explores how our values-deficient Western culture might benefit from the values displayed in the life of the Galilean sage, Jesus of Nazareth, who was able to empower and transform the lives of those he met. The importance of friendships cannot be overestimated in the well-being and respect of others. Relationships are fundamental for our own personal sense of identity. We are who we are through the friendships we form.

Friends who value us as worthwhile human beings will bring us to a sense of wholeness. Living in community we discover that friendships grow when we invite each other into a process of intimacy. This affirms our need for belonging, particularly for those experiencing aloneness. Friendships invoke feelings. They also offer us the opportunity to experience empathy, which encourages us to respond with compassion for those we befriend.

FOLLOWERS AND FRIENDS

When examining the life of Jesus of Nazareth, we discover that ethical values are expressed not only in his personal relationships but also in his questioning of the authorities, be they political or religious. Those committed to a relationship with Jesus will have to challenge these same authorities if their actions or policies disregard the importance of caring and compassionate relationships. If we accept that the transforming power of Jesus comes from his ability to form close personal relationships, then we his followers must respond compassionately to those people with whom we engage.

The defining attribute of a faith community that embraces the values of their friend Jesus will be the ability of community members, Jesus-followers, to share and support the development of these personal values one person with another in their community. Within such a Jesus community, the role of each individual will include advocating on behalf of people who have been disadvantaged by the dominant values of the wider society. In this way we will be able to ensure that those who have been disadvantaged will receive the justice and inclusion to which they are entitled.

In the gospel narratives and other recently recovered sacred writings we see that Jesus had a belief in the inherent goodness of the people he encountered and befriended. The Jesus Seminar—in analyzing the "voice-print" of Jesus and placing his words and actions in their historical matrix—has given us a glimpse of this historical figure.[1] People were attracted to Jesus because he made them feel worthwhile, included, and valued.

Jesus' personal values are demonstrated in the Gospels through his treatment of women as equals to his male followers. Women are an integral component of Jesus' entourage, for example, in Luke 8:1–3: "The twelve were with him, as well as some women who had been cured of evil spirits and infirmities."

One such story in which we see Jesus' response to people seeking healing involves a woman who has been hemorrhaging for twelve years.[2] The story begins with Jesus walking with Jairus, one of the elders of the synagogue. They are heading to his house because his daughter is sick, and Jesus has been asked to heal her. On their journey they are surrounded by a large crowd. As these people begin to press in, Jesus experiences a special contact

---

1. See especially Funk and Hoover, eds., *Five Gospels*; and Hoover, ed., *Profiles of Jesus*.

2. This story can be found, with variations, in three Gospels: Matt 9:18–26, Mark 5:21–43, and Luke 8: 40–56.

by a woman who has been hemorrhaging for twelve years. As a result of this woman's touch, Jesus stops what he is doing to respond to her need. While he is speaking with the woman, he hears of the child's death. Undeterred, he continues to the house of Jairus and announces that the girl is not dead but sleeping. He recommends she be given food.

Jesus had a reputation for sharing meals and time with all comers, including unattached women. Thus, his direct response to this woman is not out of character. Jesus condemns the world of exclusion, because he does not condemn the woman for her actions. His acceptance of her is demonstrated by his use of the term "daughter." His words affirm that her blood flow did not make her unclean.

Another story tells of a woman who comes uninvited to the house of Simon the Pharisee, bringing with her an expensive jar of perfumed ointment (Luke 7:16–50). Jesus, in the custom of the day, is reclining on the cushions at the banquet. Approaching him from behind, she begins to anoint his feet with the ointment and her tears. Not only does she dry his feet with her hair, but she also kisses them.

Jesus understands the woman's need for acceptance: she is seeking recognition from a person she respects. In return she is welcomed with dignity as well as respect. Note Jesus' words: "She has shown great love" (Luke 7:47), or "She has done something beautiful" (Matt 28:10, author's translation). Jesus is able to accept what this woman offers as a way of seeking connection, without condemning her past behavior. He does not say, "Depart from me, you wicked temptress, because you are evil, and your soul shall rot in hell for the sins you have committed."

Another story is preserved in some ancient manuscripts of the Gospel of John (8:3–11) and sometimes in Luke (after 21:38). In this orphan tradition, which is not preserved in the oldest manuscripts of either Gospel, Jesus was urged both to judge a woman and also to approve of her public execution by stoning. The authorities are trying to trap Jesus based on his eventual response here to a poor woman caught in the act of adultery. The authorities saw it as their chance to stone a woman to death for adultery, and also to be able to charge Jesus with religious disloyalty.

Jesus' response is compassionate. He bends forward and begins to trace something on the ground for the woman's eyes only. Then he challenges those gathered regarding who has the moral right to cast the first stone. Those gathered are confronted by Jesus' challenge, which makes them realize that it is men who are largely responsible for sexual crimes. Slowly they all move away, leaving Jesus alone with the woman.

Jesus was offering a new understanding of God as one who is not judgmental but compassionate. This is a radical message. Jesus addresses the woman tenderly and respectfully by calling her "woman." Then he asks if there was anyone left to condemn her. She replies, "No one." Jesus realizes that this woman needs reassurance and not condemnation, so he responds to her, "Neither do I condemn you." In today's world where women are treated so violently, this is a radical message.

In John 13:34–35 Jesus is portrayed as giving a different kind of "Great Commission" than what we find in Matt 28:19–20. Here John has Jesus say, "I give you a new commandment that you love one another. Just as I have loved you, you also should love one another. By this everyone will recognize you as my followers if you love one another."[3] For the Johannine followers of Jesus, authentic friendship expressed in mutual affection is the hallmark of both their identity and their mission: the followers of Jesus are to love others in the same spirit as Jesus himself had practiced (". . . as I have loved you . . ."). We find similar exhortations to compassionate solidarity even with opponents and occupying military powers in the Sermon on the Mount (Matt 5:38–48), while the Two Great Commandments passage (Mark 12:29–31 and parallels) puts loving others on a par with devotion to God:

> Jesus answered, "The first is, 'Hear, O Israel: the Lord our God, the Lord is one; you shall love the Lord your God with all your heart, and with all your soul, and with all your mind, and with all your strength.' The second is this, 'You shall love your neighbor as yourself.' There is no other commandment greater than these."

In Luke 10:30–35 we have the classic story of a compassionate Samaritan. The attitudes and actions of this despised outsider illuminate the heart of the gospel message. The compassionate ("good") Samaritan helps us understand in practical terms the meaning of Jesus' message.

Elsewhere in the Gospels we see that the distinctive nature of the Jesus movement was to name the presence of the kingdom: to identify God's active presence and to invite everyone to collaborate with God's program of compassionate friendship. The story of the Samaritan—as told by Jesus— conveys his commitment to a compassionate multiculturalism.

---

3. This translation is from Taussig, *New Testament*, 208–209.

If Jesus of Nazareth proclaimed a positively inclusive and loving God, then how should we act when confronted with a situation similar to the one the Samaritan found himself in? The story of the Samaritan challenges us to think more deeply about the contours of compassionate friendship, even for those who discriminate against us. The story is presented as a response to the question, "Who is my neighbor?" While often seen as a model for compassionate action towards others in *their* need, it can also be heard as an invitation to rethink the range of people from whom *we ourselves* would accept compassionate friendship. As followers and friends of Jesus, we are called not just to offer friendship to others, but also to accept friendship even from people whose compassionate solidarity we might prefer to decline.

Note that the description given to the actions of the Samaritan is longer and more detailed than any other element of the story. Great care has been taken to describe the goodness of the Samaritan to the hearers because they would have been skeptical.[4] The greatest emphasis is on the doer, not what is done.

Jesus does not simply make compassion a means to earn the love of God. We have to love the other person for their own sake. In this story the Samaritan responds to the person who has been beaten and robbed, simply because that person was in need.

The Samaritan binds up the victim's wounds. He alleviates his pain. He sets the injured man on his beast and brings him to an inn. He leaves him in the care of the innkeeper. After paying for the initial expenses, he promises to make good any further expense when he comes back that way. Compassionate friendship without limits is on display.

Jesus reacts emotionally to the death of Lazarus in John 11:35–36. The story portrays Jesus standing at the tomb of his friend Lazarus, the brother of Mary and Martha. As Jesus weeps (11:35), the crowd watching him closely observes, "See how he loved him" (11:36). Crying at the death of a friend suggests that Jesus is resolving the grief he experienced with the loss of a loved one and also expressing his emotional attachment to friends. This story suggests that Jesus' friendships were not built purely on social and physical proximity, but also on deep emotional bonds. Jesus personally experienced the pain and suffering of his friends.

---

4. Within the cultural world of late Second Temple Judaism, Samaritans were disdained as a rival faction, with the enmity occasionally flaring into violence. Making a Samaritan the hero of his parable, in contrast to the pure temple functionaries (the priest and the Levite), was Jesus' deliberate and provocative rhetorical strategy. For many Jews at the time, the concept of a "good" Samaritan would have been an oxymoron.

In another classic episode, we see how close Jesus' personal relationships were with his friends and disciples. In Matt 12:46–50, while Jesus is speaking to the crowds with his disciples, his mother and brothers are standing outside waiting to speak with him. When someone comes to Jesus and tells him this, Jesus replies:

> "Who is my mother and who are my brothers?" And pointing to his disciples he said, "Here are my mother and brothers! For whoever does the will of my Father in heaven, is my brother sister and mother."

This response indicates the closeness of the relationship between Jesus and his disciples. They are his authentic family. Here we see Jesus in a form of kinship relationship with his friends.

Jesus' sense of solidarity with the poor and needy is seen even more vividly in the parable of the day of judgment (Matt 25:31–46). Jesus explains to his disciples that he identifies with all who are suffering—be it people without food or clothing, the sick or those in prison. To help them is to be compassionate towards Jesus; to ignore them is to overlook him.

Many values underpin positive friendships that promote personal growth, including compassion, integrity, empathy, perseverance, and humility. The core value of Jesus was compassion, a feeling of distress and pity for the suffering of others, and a desire to alleviate it. One way to understand the mission of Jesus is that he practiced an outlook of abundance as part of his kingdom of God message: "I came that they may have life, and have it abundantly" (John 10:10). Jesus' life was grounded in a commitment to freeing people to love wastefully, beyond their boundaries and their fears, regardless of race, ethnicity or gender.

Did the words and actions of Jesus convey his emotions? Yes, when he cried at the death of a friend and again when he reached out to touch people who were unclean, welcoming them with terms of endearment. Jesus made people aware of their worth, affirming the spirit of sacred energy within them. He empowered them recognize and draw on this power so they could accept themselves as whole in the eyes of God. Jesus offered a "brokerless realm,"[5] in which people did not require a broker to communicate with God. They were able to access this Sacred Spirit directly. As Jesus explained, the kingdom (*basileia*) was within them.

---

5. Crossan, *Jesus*, 101.

A distinctive Greek phrase—*basileia tou theou*—seems to have been at the heart of Jesus' own sense of what he was doing and what it might mean to his audience. However, the traditional English translation as "kingdom of God" may not properly reflect what Jesus meant. Rather than a spiritual empire with sacred authority coming from above, Jesus may have been reflecting an ancient Aramaic concept of kingship (*malkuta*) as mutual empowerment.[6] If those scholars who think that Jesus' native tongue was Aramaic are correct, then this core concept at the heart of his mission denoted mutual empowerment, a realm of radical inclusion, and a community of radical equality where each has the power to engage with the sacred spiritual energy we call God.

This understanding of *basileia* fits well with John Dominic Crossan's proposal that the kingdom promoted by Jesus was in reality a "companionship of empowerment."[7] When Jesus called people to "seek first the kingdom of God" (Matt 6:33), he was inviting them to share in that companionship of empowerment. In this community of friends, we find that it is relational activities that truly liberate us, nurture us, and lead us to wholeness.

We see the importance of the personal response to others not only in Jesus' words but also in his actions. The stranger was not simply tolerated, but respected and welcomed at the table. Perhaps it is time for us all to reclaim the message of Jesus as opposed to the message of "Churchianity."[8] This may require dispensing with the hierarchical images of the divine and substituting our human capacity for compassion to all. In doing that we reveal the spirit of God within all people, as Jesus did with his friends. Then the spirit of the sacred energy we call God will be revealed in the way we care for each other.

COMPASSIONATE FRIENDSHIP

How then did Jesus display the value of compassion? We need first to recognize that compassionate love is countercultural. It creates upheavals in the way we understand ourselves, others, and the world around us. Compassion does not alleviate suffering, but it does transform our engagement with suffering. It helps us experience what injustice really feels like.

---

6. See ÓMurchu, *Incarnation*, 114.

7. Crossan, *Birth of Christianity*, 337.

8. For the pedigree for this term, see Shine, "Why the Church Must Die."

Compassion signifies standing in solidarity with another's suffering, feeling within ourselves something of the other's pain and trauma. In everyday English, *compassion* often functions as a noun. It can also be understood as a verb. In the words of Karen Armstrong:

> Despite various nuances of the word *compassion*, it is the most outstanding unifying force among the world's religions. It is the active living out of the universal desire to love unconditionally.[9]

In her "Charter for Compassion" Armstrong concludes that compassion is essential to human relationships as it fulfils our humanity.[10] For Armstrong, compassion is the path to enlightenment. It is indispensable in the creation of a just economy and a peaceful global community. This understanding of compassion denotes a social power that underpins harmony, solidarity, and a nonviolent power for healing and peace.

This force is also a political value that can foster economic and structural justice. However, most importantly Armstrong's definition of *compassion* as a verb reinforces "inclusiveness." If this form of compassion were released freely into our world, then it would most likely remove or at least alleviate the majority of the social evils that we are currently experiencing.

Why has this not occurred? One reason is because we fail to translate compassion into practical action as in the life, words and actions of Jesus, the Galilean sage. In the Gospels, compassion denotes a great deal more than simply feelings or emotion. Compassion in the New Testament is, in reality, a bold, subversive claim for justice, liberation, and empowerment.

In gospel terms, compassion is not simply a feeling of mercy or pity, which can evoke a patronizing concern rather than a commitment to action. The Greek word used for "compassion" in the Gospels is *splangnezomai*, which literally means, "being moved from the depths of one's bowels."[11] This is about the quality of an active response to rectify the wrong being felt or perceived. It emerges as inner enlightenment, seeking empowerment to resolve human suffering. It is a passionate pursuit of justice.

---

9. Armstrong, *Twelve Steps*, 5–6.

10. Armstrong et al., *Charter for Compassion*.

11. Note the very literal translation of this term in the older translation of Phil 2:1–3 "If there be therefore any consolation in Christ, if any comfort of love, if any fellowship of the Spirit, if any bowels and mercies, Fulfil ye my joy, that ye be likeminded, having the same love, being of one accord, of one mind. Let nothing be done through strife or vainglory; but in lowliness of mind let each esteem [the] other better than themselves" (KJV).

In the New Testament, "compassion" occurs seventeen times and is applied to Jesus on eight occasions. For Jesus compassion is always as a verb, never a noun. In other words, for Jesus compassion was not simply a feeling of pity but action to address a wrong. Compassion is what a person is compelled to do, and not only the concern they may feel.

Jesus' understanding is summarized in Luke 6:36. "Be compassionate as your Father God is compassionate." This call from Jesus goes beyond the priestly exhortation in Lev 19:2: "You shall be holy for I the Lord your God am holy." For Jesus, compassion is more important than purity. A similar point is implicit in the parable of the Samaritan as well as in the many instances of Jesus violating the Sabbath.

Jesus' emphasis on compassion rather than on purity was a radical development from the focus on ritual purity, which was such a feature of Second Temple Judaism. We saw this earlier in the graphic episode of the woman who washes Jesus feet with her tears. That story in one form or another is recorded in the four canonical Gospels (Matt 26:6–13; Mark 14:3–9; Luke 7:16–50; John 12:1–8). Each version of this story has its own particular emphasis regarding the place, the people present, and the particular moment in Jesus' ministry. Whether the woman is a local prostitute or Mary (the sister of Lazarus), the act of kindness is the same, and the response from Jesus is the same. To some extent so is the reaction of the observers, as they dismiss this act of love. The values of Jesus encourage us to accept and embrace each other and to share in open commensality not only our food but also our very selves.

A WORLD WITHOUT REAL FRIENDS

In our world there are many issues that demonstrate the value of genuine friendships and authentic social connection. The world is currently facing a major humanitarian crisis according to the "Global Report on Food Crises 2020."[12] There are now around 183 million people in forty-seven countries, classified as being in stressed conditions and at risk of slipping into crisis. These food insecurity forecasts for 2020 were produced before COVD-19 became a pandemic. They do not take into account its likely impact on countries facing food crises.

Further, personal violence and especially violence against women is a major concern in many societies. Family, domestic, and sexual violence

12 ReliefWeb, "Global Report."

is a major health and welfare issue. It affects people of all ages and from all backgrounds, but mainly women and children. A June 2019 report by the Australian Institute of Health and Welfare exploring the impact of family, domestic, and sexual violence among vulnerable groups found that one woman was killed every nine days, and one man every twenty-nine days by a partner between 2014 and 2016. The Australian Bureau of Statistics also reported personal safety findings in 2016 and estimated that 2.2 million adults have been victims of physical and/or sexual violence from a partner.[13] Further, one in two women and one in four men have been sexually harassed, and one in six women have experienced stalking.

During the twelve months of 2018, on average, a current or former partner killed one woman each week in Australia.[14] These statistics have much wider implications. Domestic and family violence is the principal cause of homelessness for women and their children. It also contributes significantly to high levels of psychological stress. Violence against women is even higher among indigenous women, who are thirty-five times more likely to be hospitalized for family violence than the wider female population.[15]

Another social evil that creates real concern in Australia and globally is economic inequality. At a time when wages have not increased for the longest period on record and the cost of living continues to increase, the gap between the rich and the poor is growing. In some cases, staff have not been paid the legal rate of wages.

As a result of this income inequality, many families are struggling to cope with rising energy prices. To manage their living costs, families are going without food in order to pay their energy bills. Foodbank Australia is Australia's largest food relief organization, supporting the frontline charities who are feeding vulnerable Australians. It provides more than 70 percent of the food rescued for hunger relief. In October each year, Foodbank releases the "Food Hunger Report," which examines food poverty around Australia over the previous twelve months. Their 2017 study reported that more than one in five children in Australia live in a food-insecure household, and that one in three parents (32 percent) say that their children do not have enough to eat.[16] Most parents (nine out of ten) in this study are going without meals to feed their children, and this is occurring on a weekly basis.

13. Australian Bureau of Statistics, "Personal Safety, Australia."

14. Australian Institute of Health and Welfare, "Family, Domestic and Sexual Violence."

15. Better Health Channel (Victoria). "Family Violence."

16. Foodbank Australia, "Hunger Report 2017."

In addition to alleviating the physical health implications of a diet imbalance, food security reduces psychological stress in families. It also encourages positive, healthy, growth-promoting social relationships. People who feel secure are more likely to reach out with love to others.

Inequality in the distribution of wealth has also led to a rising problem of homelessness. Data from the Australian Bureau of Statistics indicate that more than 116,000 people were experiencing homelessness in Australia on the census night in 2016.[17] That is fifty homeless persons per ten thousand people.

Another social evil on the rise is racial hatred. Racism takes many forms and can happen anywhere. It includes prejudice, discrimination, or hatred directed at someone because of the color of their skin, their ethnicity, or their national origin. One of the most significant factors in the rise of racism is fear based on ignorance. Fear of the unknown can cause anxiety, which leads to defensive reactions. This was recognized even in ancient times: "Ignorance dissolves when one gains knowledge of another."[18] Through personal involvement, attitudes can change.

Research by the Australian Human Rights Commission indicates that as many as twenty percent of Australia's population experienced racial discrimination in 2019.[19] Aboriginal and Torres Strait Islanders, and those from culturally diverse backgrounds, experience racial abuse more frequently than others. We need to realize that we share a common humanity with all people.

Another concern is the support by some politicians for people who propagate hate speech—such as British journalist Milo Yiannopoulos—with the argument that as Australians we must support "free speech." Yiannopoulos's extreme and at times irrational views are deliberately designed to incite neo-Nazis and misogynists to violence, through his tirades against women, indigenous people and Muslims. Moira Rayner, barrister and writer, has stated:

> The people of 'Australasia' are at a crossroads. If we sow the seeds of hate, through dog whistling and hate speech, we will reap the consequences. It's time to rebuild our society, otherwise we will tear ourselves apart.[20]

17. Homelessness NSW.org/ (website), "NSW Census Data."
18. Gospel of Truth 10:12.
19. Australian Human Rights Commission. "Let's Talk Race."
20. Rayner, "Hubris and Hate Speech."

These social evils stem from the very values we hold individually and jointly. We need to consider the importance of encouraging a different set of values, such as those we find in the words and actions of the sage Jesus of Nazareth. These values that underpin supportive personal relationships. They need to be affirmed if we are to reduce the impact of the many social evils in our society today.

A SOCIETY OF FRIENDS

The message of Jesus, portrayed by his words and actions, could resolve and prevent the social evils currently plaguing our society. How can those who identify as friends of Jesus communicate this message more widely?

In Australia and New Zealand over the last two decades people describing themselves as Progressive Christians have gained some prominence. They are seeking contact with people with similar interests to explore the relevance of emerging scholarship for faith and practice. Many of these people continue as members of their traditional faith communities, but they are seeking a deeper understanding of the Jesus message through relationships within a society of friends.

In 2012 I conducted a grassroots research into these groups in Australia and New Zealand.[21] I concluded that the "principal strength of these groups is that they are vibrant discussion groups, exploring contemporary scholarship in a safe open and inclusive environment." These groups were providing an atmosphere where nothing is taboo, where hostility and ridicule is not tolerated, and where open and frank exchange of ideas is encouraged. Many members of these groups developed personal support for each other, which in many cases evolved into close friendships.

Through this research we discovered that the majority of the groups had been informally established, with no agreed structure and, of course, with no formal national or state registration. People who were familiar with the new biblical scholarship surrounding the historical Jesus usually organized these groups. In most cases there was no defined leader. It was left to participants in the group to take turns conducting the meetings. Do these groups provide us with an example of how a future network committed to transforming the world with the compassionate values of Jesus can be formed and activated?

21. The title of that research project was "Living the Progressive Dream," and its findings were published in Hunt and Smith, eds., *Why Weren't We Told?*, 203–27.

Regarding the religious beliefs of Australians, Australian Bureau of Statistics shows that regular participation in the life of Christianity had been reduced to approximately 5 percent of the total population. In a presentation to the Progressive Christian Network of Victoria, Professor Gary Bouma reported that 52 percent of teenagers claim no religion, while—most importantly—83 percent claim that they lived ethically without religion.[22] It can be concluded that the average Australian has written off the church and religion in general. The hangover of a religious past—of a stage in Australian and Western religious history when little attention was paid to evidence-based knowledge of the world and of the way human beings interact—this legacy appears to have no relevance twenty-first-century Australians.

It is possible that small groups such as those developed by people who call themselves Progressive Christians can be a way ahead for the followers of this Galilean sage. Such communities of people who identify as "friends of the historical Jesus" will need to prioritize the importance of sharing time together in conversation over meals. They will also need to acknowledge that the spirituality with which they were born is the ultimate force that binds them to their world, and that encourages them to love not only all human beings but all of creation.

These new Jesus communities will need to gather and share with each other, because they are yearning to connect and draw upon the sacred source of energy which surrounds us. Most importantly, the members of these groups must be prepared at times to practice compassionate friendship for one another, particularly in times of distress. This will also require an ability to be openly honest with each other.

These groups will be communities where everyone is welcomed, accepted, and supported. They will encourage their members to be actively involved in the needs of the wider community. This may at times include standing in solidarity with those seeking justice, freedom, and healing. At times it will require the leaders of these groups to challenge the authorities, be they religious, political, or cultural.

CONCLUSION

My research indicates that resolving the damaging worldwide social problems—whether violence towards women, racism, cultural extremism, or

---

22. This presentation was based on the research published in Bouma and Halafoff, "Australia's Changing Religious Profile."

endemic economic inequality—cannot simply be achieved by our political systems or by the dominant forms of contemporary Christianity. Further, it is apparent that the root cause of oppression, violence, and domination is primarily the lack of compassion. The way forward is for each and every one of us to be more compassionate. It is only when we commit ourselves to the values of loving care—authentic friendship—that we can heal the world.

This can be achieved when we embrace the example of the historical Jesus of Nazareth. He showed us through his words and actions that there are many things more important than fame, money, power, and ideology. What matters most are the personal values of compassion, love, and respect that we find in our genuine friendships. Jesus embodied a more compassionate way of responding to the reality of life. The way of Jesus requires us to be humane as we to strive together to alleviate human suffering. This is to live the abundant life that Jesus envisaged, and this requires us to live by the values which Jesus espoused.

It is appropriate to conclude that significant social change can be wrought through the empowering nature of friendship. It is also important to realize that this need not initially require a major systemic restructuring; because it is within the power of small groups to effect significant social change.

Since personal relationships are a transforming influence, then as companions of Jesus, the sage of Nazareth, we can use our personal relationship skills to create a more inclusive and caring community. To be successful there will be times when we need to operate subversively. This may also require us to be bold in challenging the current expressions of normative Christianity, as well as engaging in nonviolent civil disobedience to secure political action to redress social injustice.

Small groups committed to the ethical values and the way of life of the historical, compassionate Jesus can be catalysts for the renewing of our world. The evidence as presented here is clear: Today's world is in desperate need of healing and will only be transformed through acts of kindness and through compassionate friendship.

BIBLIOGRAPHY

Armstrong, Karen. *Twelve Steps to a Compassionate Life*. London: Bodley Head, 2011.
Armstrong, Karen, et al. *The Charter for Compassion*. https://charterforcompassion.org/charter/charter/.

Australian Bureau of Statistics. "Personal Safety, Australia." https://www.abs.gov.au/statistics/people/crime-and-justice/personal-safety-australia/latest-release/.

Australian Human Rights Commission. "Let's Talk Race: A Guide on How to Conduct Conversations about Racism (2019)." https://humanrights.gov.au/our-work/race-discrimination/publications/lets-talk-race-guide-how-conduct-conversations-about/.

Australian Institute of Health and Welfare. "Family, Domestic and Sexual Violence in Australia: Continuing the National Story 2019." https://www.aihw.gov.au/reports/domestic-violence/family-domestic-sexual-violence-australia-2019/contents/table-of-contents/.

Better Health Channel (Victoria). "Family Violence and Aboriginal and Torres Strait Islander Women." https://www.betterhealth.vic.gov.au/health/healthyliving/Family-violence-and-aboriginal-and-torres-strait-islander-women/.

Bouma, Gary, and Anna Halafoff. "Australia's Changing Religious Profile—Rising Nones and Pentecostals, Declining British Protestants in Superdiversity: Views from the 2016 Census." *Journal for the Academic Study of Religion* 30 (2017) 129–43.

Crossan, John Dominic. *The Birth of Christianity: Discovering What Happened in the Years Immediately after the Execution of Jesus.* San Francisco: HarperSanFrancisco, 1998.

———. *The Historical Jesus: The Life of a Mediterranean Jewish Peasant.* San Francisco: HarperSanFrancisco, 1991.

———. *Jesus: A Revolutionary Biography.* San Francisco: HarperSanFrancisco 1995.

Foodbank Australia. "Foodbank Hunger Report 2017." https://www.foodbank.org.au/wp-content/uploads/2019/05/2017-Foodbank-Hunger-Report.pdf/.

Funk, Robert W., and Roy W. Hoover, eds. *The Five Gospels: The Search for the Authentic Words of Jesus.* New York: Macmillan, 1993.

Homelessness NSW.org/ (website). "NSW Census Data and HNSW Factsheets." https://homelessnessnsw.org.au/resource/nsw-census-data-and-hnsw-factsheets/.

Hoover, Roy W., ed. *Profiles of Jesus.* Santa Rosa, CA: Polebridge, 2002.

Hunt, Rex A. E., and John W. H. Smith, eds. *Why Weren't We Told? A Handbook on "Progressive" Christianity.* Salem, OR: Polebridge, 2013.

Ó Murchú, Diarmuid. *Incarnation: A New Evolutionary Threshold.* Maryknoll, NY: Orbis, 2017.

———. *Inclusivity: A Gospel Mandate.* Maryknoll, NY: Orbis, 2015.

Rayner, Moira. "Hubris and Hate Speech in Mark Latham's Nation." *Eureka Street* 29 no. 6 (2019). https://www.eurekastreet.com.au/article/hubris-and-hate-speech-in-mark-latham-s-nation/.

ReliefWeb. "Global Report on Food Crises 2020—September 2020 Update, in Times of COVID-19." https://reliefweb.int/report/world/global-report-food-crises-2020-september-2020-update-times-covid-19/.

Shine, Jessica. "Why the Church Must Die—Part 1." *Progressing Spirit* (blog), October 24, 2019. https://progressingspirit.com/2019/10/24/why-the-church-must-die-part-1/.

Spong, John Shelby. *Unbelievable: Why Neither Ancient Creeds Nor the Reformation Can Produce a Living Faith Today.* San Francisco: Harper One, 2018.

Taussig, Hal, ed. *A New Testament: A Reinvented Bible for the 21st Century combining Traditional and Newly Discovered Texts.* Boston: Houghton Mifflin Harcourt, 2013.

II

In Celebration of a "Wild" Faith
Jesus in the Australian Landscape

Rex A. E. Hunt

Study the wild lilies and how they grow. They neither work nor spin; yet I tell you that even Solomon in all his splendor was not robed like one of these.[1]

For the last twelve years I have lived on the New South Wales Central Coast (Darkinjung Country), near a large coastal wetland. In addition to flocks of pelicans—always a personal plus—and an abundance of mosquitoes (with or without Ross River virus)—always a personal negative, two hundred meters further along in the Cockle Bay Nature Reserve is a remnant patch of Swamp Mahogany (*Eucalyptus Robusta*) trees, one of the largest forest clusters in the district.

Such clusters have a very high interrelationship with the local fauna. As the only major winter flowering community in the area, the Swamp

1. Matt 6:28b, from Taussig, ed., *New Testament*, 32.

Mahogany is considered essential to the survival of many nectar-seeking species—Yellow Bellied Glider and Regent Honeyeater—that flock to these clusters to feed. To enter such a cluster is to be struck by wonder and awe, and to feel one is in the presence of something vast that transcends our understanding of the world.

Awe and wonder are two self-transcending natural responses many have when they engage "the bush." Scottish American naturalist and co-founder of the American Sierra Club, John Muir (1838–1914) said the two greatest moments of his life were when he camped at Yosemite in California USA, and when he found the rare orchid calypso blooming alone in a Canadian swamp.

Awe experiences shift our attention away from ourselves, make us feel we are part of something greater than ourselves, and, as research indicates, make us more connected to and generous toward others. While there are several "flavors of awe,"[2] my concern is beauty-based awe, which may be elicited by a natural scene (e.g., a waterfall, a rainforest, a Manta Ray) or artwork (e.g., Albert Namatjira's *Ghost Gums* or Claude Monet's *Water Lilies*).

For the most part our southern hemisphere religious responses have tended to ignore the awe-inspiring landscape—or seasons. One exception—in part only—is the work done by some liturgists (often Catholic, mainly prayer book traditions) in recent efforts to enculturate the liturgy.[3]

Important as these liturgical efforts are, and I will return to these later, I want to argue there is a need to push additional boundaries. Thus my three-part thesis:

1. Nature and naturalism are the main game for any progressive spirituality. We not only *depend* on nature and are a *part* of nature, we also profoundly influence the natural world of which we are a part;

2. The natural world has the capacity to engender a response called religious or spiritual from humans;

3. The context and nature attentiveness of the storytelling Jewish sage Jesus was formative then, and similar attention and empathy can help shape a progressive, natural, wild faith now.

2. The flavors of awe include five experiences: threat, beauty, ability, virtue, and supernatural causality (Keltner and Haidt, "Approaching Awe").

3. See Pilcher, "Poinsettia."

As natural beings among diverse other natural beings, we humans are at home in nature. But as we spend a lot more time inside human constructions—in workplaces, in vehicles commuting to work, or at home captured in a reality TV trance—we spend less time outside exploring nature. We have lost touch with our wildness. As others have observed, when we are outside, often our gaze is fixed on our smartphones: we're taking selfies to post on YouTube for others to appreciate instead of being in the moment and appreciating for ourselves the wonders and beauty of the natural world and how amazing it is.

NATURE, NATURALISM, AND DESERT/WILDERNESS

There is something deeply *human-izing* about being in a garden. Listening to the rustle of eucalyptus leaves in a light spring wind overhead. Watching a bee flirt with a yellow daisy bush. Kneeling on a patch of garden soil planting a newly purchased seedling, while gently moving aside a startled reddish-purple Squirter earthworm or two . . . Biophilia—the love of nature and living things.

Earthlings have a special connection to the planet. Out of the stars have we come, says the poet. The human story and the universe story are the same story, says the geologian. We are not encapsulated, separated, isolated beings, says the cosmologist. Earth's climate—warm and stable—allows for life to thrive in a bewildering diversity. As the Brazilian physicist Marcelo Gleiser writes,

> A short stroll through a jungle or a coral reef and we are overcome by the ecological wealth, plants and animals that fight for survival, searching for food, struggling to preserve their genetic imprint from generation to generation. Life uses the present to create the future.[4]

Earth—a pale blue dot—is our home within the universe. Responsibility for the future of the planet rests with us. So how we picture the world and ourselves is important. Instead of being rulers of the universe, we need to see ourselves as part of an interconnected web. As the golden wattle is the universe in the form of a tree, so we are the universe in the form of a human, with or without arthritic fingers!

4. Gleiser, "Unruly children of earth," 2.

Catholic feminist theologian Elizabeth Johnson explains it this way.

> Out of the Big Bang the stars; out of the stardust the Earth; out of the molecules of the Earth, life. They were single-celled creatures at first, for millions of years. Then out of their life and death an advancing tide, fragile but unstoppable: creatures that live in shells, fish, amphibians, insects, flowers, birds, reptiles, and mammals . . . In the human species, nature becomes conscious of itself and open to fulfillment in grace and glory. As Rabbi Abraham Heschel (1907–1972) noted, this makes human beings the cantors of the universe.[5]

"Cantors of the universe" . . . I love that phrase! The capacity of the natural world to inspire a religious response from humans has long been recognized. In several essays religious naturalist Jerome Stone has said that taking nature to heart does not leave a person with any fewer spiritual benefits than taking to heart the teachings of *super*naturalist traditions. Stone's language becomes direct:

> If we can go to special places, built by humans, which are designated as sacred, surely we can go to special places, shaped naturally, which are recognized as sacred . . . What we need is to realize that to have a sense of sacred place is not tree worship, in the sense of confusing the one Creator with a plant, but is rather the acknowledgement of the awesome, of the overriding and overwhelming.[6]

But as Lynn Townsend White Jr. pointed out in his 1966 lecture,[7] there is a strong monotheistic tradition of cutting down the sacred groves, which stripped the natural world of any spiritual meaning.

Citing the biblical Genesis creation story, White argued that the Bible asserts humanity's dominion over nature and establishes a trend of anthropocentrism, and also that Christianity makes a distinction between humanity (formed in G-o-d's image) and the rest of creation, which has no soul or reason and is thus inferior.

By destroying pagan religions, White claimed, Christianity made it possible to exploit nature in a mood of indifference to the feelings of natural objects. For White the ecological crisis—global warming, irreversible ozone depletion, massive deforestation, higher than acceptable methane gas concentrations—was fundamentally a spiritual crisis, for "Christianity

5. Johnson, "Deep incarnation."

6. Stone, *Sacred Nature,* 116.

7. White, "Historical Roots."

bears a huge burden of guilt." But warnings by White and others since have failed to generate widespread action on climate change.

What greater gift can there be than to be a species with an ability

> to wrap one's mind around the immensities of space and time is to feel awe, wonder, and humility . . . To rest our eyes upon the landscapes of our lives and to understand how they have enabled the formation of creatures such as us is to sense a surging loyalty to the sustained vitality of these life-giving ecosystems.[8]

Australia is an ancient and distinctive land, with animals and plant life that are quite remarkable in their own right—"the colours have an almost savage intensity, which accords with the primeval quality of the Australian bush."[9] During a visit to the MacDonald Ranges in Central Australia ethnographer Deborah Bird Rose wrote of the surrounding landscape:

> These rocks were ancient, and their colours suggested that instead of fading with age, geological eons had intensified them . . . Below us the riverbed was pale, pebbly sand, above us the sky was bluer than blue, and here and there we met eucalypts—most spectacularly, the white-barked ghost gums that articulate themselves so definitely against the red earth and blue sky.[10]

Ancient indeed! The oldest rocks in Western Australia, for example, are 4.3 billion years old—almost twice that of the rocks in South Australia, and seven times older than the oldest rocks on the east coast.[11] Yet those desert soils produce the planet's greatest diversity of flowering plants, with up to twelve thousand species.

Australia has ten named deserts, the largest being the Great Victoria Desert, which sits astride the Western Australia and South Australia border. It is over eight hundred kilometers wide with an area of 348,750 square kilometers. In total the ten deserts cover nearly 1.4 million square kilometers or 18 percent of the Australian mainland. Result? Australia has been called the driest continent on earth. A desert surrounded by a coastal fringe.

---

8. Braxton, "Religious Naturalism," 332.

9. These words are from an anonymous review article, "Australian flowers: Six splendid panes. Margaret Preston's work." in the *Sydney Morning Herald*, November 11, 1938.

10. Rose, "On the Spot," 221.

11. Thomas, "Western Australian Wildflowers Bloom."

Perception of what is a desert or wilderness area varies greatly. It depends on the different exposures people have to nature and the great outdoors. To a person living on the coast, the desert is often dry, arid, and dusty. A place without life. Empty. Expendable wasteland. Sites for the detonation of nuclear weapons, often by foreign powers!

For desert dwellers the "outback" has a compelling fascination as a place vibrant with life. The spinifex is blue grey with amber glints. They look soft but are prickly and hard. They survive tenaciously because no grazing animal can eat them out or destroy their roots. It may look as if nothing can live in the desert, but underneath the spinifex, the desert creatures leave their tracks in the red sand. No life stirs all day, but come night lizards, mice, and the rare animals of the desert live their delicate but vastly tough lives in this harsh habitat.

A desert's emptiness is also regarded in positive terms. In the heart of the Australian "red center" is a massive sandstone monolith: *Uluru* or "The Rock." As the tourist pamphlets declare, *Uluru* is more than just a rock. It is a living cultural landscape considered sacred to the Yankunytjatjara and Pitjantjatjara people. The spirits of the ancestral beings continue to reside in these sacred places, making the land a deeply important part of Aboriginal cultural identity and Dreaming stories. It symbolizes the spirit and heart of an ancient land . . .

The three major Abrahamic religions—Judaism, Christianity, and Islam—are all desert-born faiths. The desert is seen as a place where a person can more readily commune with the divine. According to a proverb of the nomadic Berbers, "The desert is the Garden of Allah, from which the Lord of the faithful removed all superfluous human and animal life, so that there might be one place where He can walk in peace."[12] Likewise, Christianity has a tradition of desert fathers (*abbas*) and mothers (*ammas*). They were early Christian ascetics and monks who lived mainly in the Scetes desert of Egypt from around the third century CE.

The challenge is to see deserts as they really are: the interrelationship of humans, rocks, plants, and animals, which for many forms a sacred and healing story. And to intentionally incorporate such a required attention into liturgies and festivals. As the Brazilian poet Rubem Alves writes,

12. Campbell, *Face of the Earth*, 238.

The desert is beautiful because it hides, somewhere, a garden. We are beautiful because inside us there is a garden which, once in a while, lets itself to be seen through our gestures.[13]

LITURGY, LANDSCAPE AND NATURE

The cry of the psalmist has now become commonplace in Australia: how can we sing the Lord's song in a strange land? Being in the Southern Hemisphere makes all major traditional Christian liturgical festivals foreign. There is a ritual discomfort when, shaped by northern seasons and inspired by theological imagery, they are simply imported wholesale. To encourage a greater awareness of being local, Catholic priest David Ranson suggested that by limiting ourselves to a cultural colonialism with Northern/European origins, "we risk missing seeing what actually 'Is.'"[14]

What 'actually Is' is what I discovered living in country New South Wales. From early November the grasses are changing color for a second time. The bush has begun to dry out. The smell of drying earth and blossom fills our nostrils with bursts of Jacaranda purple. Advent is beginning its local celebration. Then there are the wild cards of drought, bushfire, and flood affecting and altering the seasons! I chuckled at the description from poet Les Murray (1938–2019) of the seasons as comprising

> essentially summer and non-summer. A reign of heat, flies, snakes, beach culture and burgeoning growth is followed by a cooler time in which the discomforts disappear and both beach going and burgeoning tail off. And there is that bit of sniffling cold in the middle.[15]

Poets, musicians, and lyricists need to be encouraged to collaborate on new, more explicitly nature poems, reflections, laments, and songs, supported by a broadening of the biblical lectionary tradition to include contemporary readings of nature and landscape. (There is a religiosity beyond Christianity's narrow closed canon!) Where there is a lectionary shaping of a liturgy this be more a Commoners' (local) rather than a Common (international). Such a lectionary would also include the challenge of a list

---

13. Alves, *Poet,* 130.

14. Ranson, "Fire in Water," 1.

15. Ranson, "Fire in Water," 2.

of "life events, rituals and celebrations which local communities could use according to their seasons and struggles."[16]

However, I recall science writer Chet Raymo's comment that bacteria and viruses are also our "kith and kin,"[17] so what of SARS and COVID-19 epidemics? Or natural "disasters" such as the 2019 White Island volcanic eruption (in New Zealand) when forty-seven people were trapped on the island, with many killed? The moral ambiguity of nature—essentially neutral—can be a significant challenge for neo-orthodox lectionary liturgists and their worldview of *super*naturalism!

Two congregational songs associated with nature/landscape are Elizabeth Smith's "Celebrate Your Landscape" (also known as "Where Wide Sky Rolls Down")[18] and American Peter Mayer's "Blue Boat Home."[19]

Smith says the text of her hymn echoes Ps 148—the whole cosmos praising the name of the Lord, with an emphasis on the Australian landscape. While Australian theologians and sociologists argue that nearly all Australians live in big cities and near the coast, and seldom go anywhere near a desert, Smith asserts that "Australian Christians still like to sing about our unique landscape, and my text allows them to do so."[20]

Mayer's "Blue Boat Home" is a favorite with many progressives and religious naturalists. The lyrics rejoice in the blue boat of earth plying the ocean of the wide universe. It is universal in breadth. It brings to mind the famous 1990 "Pale Blue Dot" photograph of Earth from space. Both songs while similar, are also different from each other. Mayer's expresses a more horizontal transcendence (cosmic, nature, here/homecoming[21]) whereas Smith's song offers a more vertical transcendence (G-o-d language, doctrine, out there).

New Zealander Shirley Erena Murray, MNZM (1931–2020) was a lyricist who shaped more than five hundred progressive songs with a distinctive Southern Hemisphere voice, most with new words, new music, or both. Reflecting on her writing, Murray said the reason she wrote such songs was connected to the ethos of being a New Zealander.

> It seemed to me that the hymns we sang had no resonance with the world I lived in. There was no imagery that evoked a particular

16. Havea, "Local Lectionary Sites," 125.

17. Raymo, "My very distant cousin."

18. *Together in Song,* #188.

19. Unitarian Universalist Association, *Singing the Journey,* #1064.

20. Smith, "Crafting and Singing Hymns," 191.

21. Goodenough, "Vertical and Horizontal Transcendence," 28.

environment, no landscape of thought to accommodate the southern hemisphere, no connection with the Maori culture of our society, which is officially bicultural, nothing to articulate our own hopes and visions.[22]

Her hymns have been translated into numerous languages and are represented in more than 140 hymn collections. Titles that feature nature and landscapes include "Look in Wonder," "Touch the Earth Lightly," "When All the Good Is Gathered Up," and "As the Wind Song through the Trees."

An extensive collection of progressive songs, many reflecting the diversity of landscape and seasons, is *Singing the Living Tradition*—frequently used in Unitarian churches and fellowships in Australia and New Zealand. The songbook has more than four hundred songs, and titles include "Dark of Winter" (Shelley Denham), "Lady of the Seasons' Laughter" (Kendyl Gibbons), "Earth Is Our Homeland" (Mark Belletini), "Colour and Fragrance" (Norbert Capek, 1870–1942), "Earth Was Given as a Garden" (Roberta Ruby), "We Celebrate the Web of Life" (Alicia Carpenter), and "Seek Not Afar for Beauty" (Minot Savage, 1841–1918).

All these songs and song collections are great resources, I agree. But also needed is a more radical crafting of liturgical and festival rites, freed from restrictive creeds and dogmas and supernatural, neo-orthodox theology. The goal of such crafting is to arrive at a rich tapestry of language, metaphors, poetry, and design that firstly celebrates life in the present, but that also enriches such expressions of naturalistic beliefs and reflects that we are people of the earth rather than people on the earth![23]

Importantly, such liturgical events should be less like worship and more-like celebration—a celebration of life. Worship essentially moves from symbol to a transcendent "other" source—persons, word, places, Holy or G-o-d—perceived as present in the ordinary. Celebration, on the other hand, consists of rejoicing in the presence of things rather than going beyond them. Worship seeks to transcend the object. Celebration seeks to penetrate to its depth. Worship is only possible where there is a distinction or dualism between the sacred and the ordinary. Celebration seeks to dissolve such distinctions and dualisms.[24]

---

22. Methodist Church of the United Kingdom, "A jolt of reality: The hymns of Shirley Erena Murray." (www.methodist.org.uk/our-faith/worship/singing-the-faith-plus/posts/a-jolt-of-reality-the-hymns-of-shirley-erena-murray/) (Accessed 18 August 2020)

23. Hunt and Cranmer, *Seasons & Self,* 24–25.

24. Keen, *Apology for Wonder,* 209.

In addition to these resources and the necessary liturgical recrafting, a variety of nature practices—both group and individual—celebrating the grandeur of existence outside the Sunday morning experience could be explored. These include turning off our smartphones and getting outside, appreciating a particular piece of local nature by taking a walk along a beach or at sunrise or in a bushland, journaling observations and felt experiences, and acknowledging the nonhuman coinhabitants of the place. Another nature practice is to participate in ecowilderness multiday retreats, celebrating the four cardinal directions (north, south, east, and west). We could also craft and stage the Stations of the Universe—a ritual that depicts the story of the emerging universe in fourteen or twenty-five stations.

It is time to reimagine our religious traditions and sense of sacred just as it is time to begin rereading the landscape—a particular landscape. The sacred is not a separate, supernatural sphere of life driven by blinding-light revelations.

Positing an incomprehensible, invisible Other does nothing to explain the incomprehensible other that is palpably present, and which we actually encounter every second within and around us.[25]

A NATURAL HUMAN BEING

A naturalist sense of being human differs in many important ways from traditional views: changing our view of what it means to be human involves moving from a dualist view of body and eternal soul to a sense of ourselves as biological beings. Thus any naturalist view of the sage called Jesus will reflect that difference. The contemporary Catholic theologian Elizabeth Johnson writes:

> Born of a woman . . . and the Hebrew gene pool, [Jesus] was a creature of earth, a complex unit of minerals and fluids, an item in the carbon, oxygen, and nitrogen cycles, a moment in the biological evolution of this planet. Like all human beings, he carried within himself the signature of the supernovas and the geology and life history of the Earth.[26]

The earliest sources about Jesus known to biblical scholars suggest that he was an impoverished Palestinian situated in his historical

25. Fleischman, *Wonder*, 188.
26. Johnson, "Deep incarnation," 4–5.

circumstances—in the northwest corner of the Galilee, in the early Roman Empire sometime between the years 26 and 36 CE,

> who did things and said things that a real person could have rea-
> sonably believed or done at that time. An incredible Jesus is the
> one who came from the sky, who performed miracles by fiat, and
> who was as dead as a doornail only to magically return to life.[27]

We are the heirs of several ways of interpreting Jesus. One leads to a *super*natural understanding—the fully G-o-d and fully human "God-Man" mediator between human beings and G-o-d. This understanding has been advocated by mainline churches, both Protestant and Catholic, as orthodox: "the only proper way to think of Jesus."[28] The other leads to a naturalistic-humanistic understanding that supports Jesus' radical emphasis on love "as the overarching posture within which humans should live out their lives."[29]

With a scenario spinner's imagination—the tradition portrays him as one who speaks rather than as one who writes, although a literary form was given later—Jesus invited others to reimagine the world. His tools-of-trade were parables, short stories, and aphorisms. Most of his stories feature characters from the peasant class in an agrarian village society. All were part and parcel of first-century Judaism.

While some scholars suggest Jesus was not primarily interested in the processes of nature, the Sea of Galilee (the Kinneret)—the area where his brief public activity was mostly concentrated—"was critical to the physical and social dynamics of this region."[30] Hence several sayings and stories are set within nature and extol appreciating lilies and their natural beauty; involve sowing seed; center on the germination and growth of a mustard seed; and take for granted seeds and the fertility of the earth, fishing on turbulent Kinneret waters, foxes and birds, sheep, sun, and rain. Jesus was acutely aware of the natural world and embraced it in his recast vision of life, just as he was acutely aware that humans need stories—compelling stories.

Not only did Jesus gain important insights about himself from a locust-eating wilderness-frequenter known as John the Dipper, later—so the tradition says—he withdrew into the wilderness prior to commencing his public activities. The desert or wilderness was deemed important

---

27. Galston, *Embracing the Human Jesus,* 50.

28. Kaufman, *Jesus and Creativity,* 27.

29. Kaufman, *Jesus and Creativity,* 21.

30. Jenks, *Jesus Then and Jesus Now,* 17.

in establishing Jesus' credentials, even if some aspects of that tradition are now considered legend. Rabbi Mike Comins suggests wilderness (*eretz b'reisheeth*) stories and Judaism "are joined at the hip."[31] In Jewish mysticism G-o-d is not so much above us (vertical transcendence) but around us and with us (horizontal transcendence)—*Emmanuel*. As Nigel Savage affirms, the beauty, rhythm, and wisdom of Jewish tradition "arose in an encounter with the majesty and awe of the physical world around us."[32]

So, I return to the epigraph of this essay . . . "Study—get to know intimately—the wild lilies and how they grow . . ." These words appear in a collection of Jesus' teaching scenarios that has often been given the sectional title "On Anxieties"—all within a larger cluster called the Sermon on the Mount in the Christian scriptures. When scholars from the Jesus Seminar considered the authenticity of the "lilies" aphorism, they ranked it pink— signifying that Jesus probably said something like this.[33]

The congruence between nature and beauty in the Galilean sage's scenario prompts me to ask something more radical than "Did he say it?" I want to ask what role, if any, beauty played in Jesus' teachings. What are we to make of beauty? I suggest this is more radical than the historical question because theology has historically been big on truth, goodness, and holiness, but not so concerned with beauty.

The lilies scenario is not just a throwaway line about some unnamed wildflowers in a desert, which Jesus just happened to see. Whatever else the sage is suggesting in this teaching—teachings that are more ambiguous than they appear on the surface—he also seems to bring to his listeners' attention that everywhere they look—from the ground under their feet to the stars in the sky, to sunsets and sunrises, mountains and valleys . . . and wildflowers—the universe appears to be saturated with beauty.[34]

We may be impressed by "beneficial" beauty—beauty that improves the chances of survival for an organism. But we also need to acknowledge "intrinsic" beauty—beauty that serves no evident purpose "other than to make the natural world inexhaustibly interesting."[35] The German priest and physician Angelus Silesius (1624–1677)—a follower of Meister Eckhart

31. Comins, *Wild Faith*, 7.

32. Savage, foreword, xii.

33. Funk and Hoover, eds., *Five Gospels*, 36.

34. I note in passing that flowering plants are the dominant plants of the earth and are the reason the surface of the planet is not lifeless.

35. Sanders, "Useless Beauty," 3.

(1260–1328)—wrote a short mystical poem "Without Why" that captures this intrinsic sentiment: "The rose is without why / She blooms because she blooms / She does not care for herself / Asks not if she is seen."[36]

To appreciate the dynamics of the wild places, both attentiveness and empathy are needed—overlapping, together—because attention without feeling is only a report. Poet Mary Oliver (1935–2019), in a rare radio interview, said "reporting is for field guides. And they're great. But they're not thought provokers . . . Attention is the beginning of devotion."[37] Could this be an unspoken gift from the itinerant sage, Jesus? Provoking hearers to remember that beauty is the guiding lure in every becoming moment? Because "when we awaken to the call of beauty, we become aware of new ways of being in the world."[38] Could this also be for us the "afterlife" of that same Jesus "as it inspires in us an ethic of ecological care"[39] to make us passionate supporters of actions and regulations aimed at protecting air, water, soil, endangered species, and wilderness?

To ignore the nature hints and habits—events of grace—of the sage Jesus is to misunderstand this Palestinian Jew and to underestimate our potential role—appreciative awareness—in shaping a twenty-first-century "afterlife" of that same Jesus.

WONDER, AWE, AND REVERENCE

Religious naturalist Donald Crosby has a story of a brown pelican,[40] wings outstretched in flight.

> Scarcely a flicker of those magnificent wings is required for it to soar further and further aloft. Finally reaching an apogee of the spiral, it gently banks and slowly descends, only to be uplifted again in its circling flight . . . For me, at that moment, this pelican's flight is a compelling symbol of the numinous powers, presences, and wonders of the natural order to which we both miraculously belong.[41]

---

36. Quoted in O'Donohue and Quinn, *Walking in Wonder*, 40.

37. Oliver, "I was saved by the beauty of the world," 2.

38. O'Donohue, *Divine Beauty*, 7.

39. Sanders, "Useless Beauty," 6.

40. The Australian pelican (*Pelecanus conspicillatus*) is predominantly a white bird with black wings and a pink bill. It has the longest bill of any living bird.

41. Crosby, *More Than Discourse*, 3.

Living on the Central Coast there can always be an encounter with a pelican. At the Fisherman's Co-Op. Down by the local boat ramp. Spiraling high above the township. I reckon the pelican has become my person totem!

Crosby teases out how this natural event was religiously meaningful to him. First of all, it was a reminder that the self, the pelican, and all other living beings, human and nonhuman, share in a universe that has enabled us to come into being and to live in accordance with the distinctive traits and capabilities nature has conferred on our respective species. Secondly, the pelican's effortless flight brought into vivid awareness the evolutionary processes that formed the universe over billions of years. It spoke of the exuberance and joy of life. An image of hope, aspiration, and freedom.

But, as Crosby observed, the pelican's flight also symbolized a more precarious side of life, especially of nonhuman life forms that can be adversely affected by the choices, actions, and enterprises of human beings and human institutions.

> None of these statements or others can do justice to the firsthand experience itself and all that it meant to me at that time and continues to mean. The experience and what occasioned it are a powerful evocation, expression, and refining of my faith as a religious naturalist, and the meanings, associations, and ramifications of that faith outstrip verbal descriptions.[42]

Similar sentiments were phrased by empirical theologian Bernard Meland (1899–1993) nearly ninety years ago. Just home from postgraduate studies in Marburg, Germany (in 1931)—his professor was Rudolf Otto—and still shaping his "mystical naturalism," Meland wrote:

> Have you ever communed in the first person with this total wealth of living life about you? Have you ever stood with awe and wonder before the unbounded totality of all reality—this ongoing process we call the universe, feeling your own intimacy with all its life, thrilling with the realization of the magnitude of that relationship, relating you to all the world's life, past, present and future? If you have, you have experienced first-hand religion.[43]

Meland is upfront: the natural world has the capacity to inspire a response—an expression of our wonder and awe of nature, of our attraction to the mystery of existence, and to something intangible called religious or

---

42. Crosby, *More Than Discourse*, 6.
43. Meland, "Worship Mood," 665.

spiritual from humans. He was highly critical of religion that fostered "a sense of strangeness toward the natural world."[44]

All religious traditions need to appreciate that the primary sacred community is the universe itself. Every other community becomes sacred by participation in this primary community. In moments of wonder we delight in what is. Wonder invites a larger sense of life. It requires the language of reverence. When we lose our sense of awe, wonder, and beauty, we objectivize the Earth as a commodity that can be used and abused at our consumeristic whim.

AN UNCONCLUDING WORD . . .

Nature is the thread that completes the tapestry of life. We are curious creatures with a capacity for wonder. Or as philosopher Sam Keen suggests, each moment awaits our sensual "wonderosity." In a recent collection, Donald Crosby and Jerome Stone suggest:

> Thinking deeply about nature and our place as human beings in nature is an urgent and salutary activity for each of us and for the institutions of our societies, no matter what our personal religious or secular outlooks may be in this time of rampant species endangerment, global climate change, and looming ecological crisis.[45]

Hosanna! Not in the highest, but right here. Right now. This.[46] A Newer Testament. The gospel of the natural present moment. A natural wild spirituality . . . released from the captivity of *super*natural religion—as an expression of our awe of nature, of our attraction to the mystery of existence, and to something intangible.

Because . . . to celebrat a naturalistic *wild* faith is to move away from tradition towards heresy (another opinion)—often with radically new approaches and in provocative ways. If the potential of such a wild faith can be adopted, within posttheistic thinking, and shaped into progressive liturgies, events, and social/ethical action that both supports and summons us, then, to borrow Walter Wink's comment in another context, we are freed to go on the journey that Jesus *charted* rather than to *worship* the journey of Jesus.[47]

---

44. Meland, "Kinsmen of the Wild," 1.

45. Crosby and Stone, eds., *Handbook of Religious Naturalism,* 2.

46. Goodenough, *Sacred Depths,* 169.

47. Wink, "Son of Man," 177.

Because . . . celebrating a naturalistic wild '*faith*' is a body energized by wonder and awe and beauty. Paying attention to our experiences and thoughts and emotions and letting them be, is life affirming, even if they are hard. A surplusage of experience. A breathing and acting and encountering that throws life into a new frame as it makes its creative way in the real landscape world.

So, practice noticing! Inhale and absorb nature's elixir! For such is the twenty-first-century afterlife of the Palestinian sage Jesus, naturally.

BIBLIOGRAPHY

Alves, Rubem A. *The Poet, the Warrior, the Prophet.* The Edward Cadbury Lectures 1990. London: SCM, 1990.

Braxton, Donald M. "Religious Naturalism and the Future of Christianity." *Zygon* 42 (2007) 317–42.

Campbell, SueEllen, et al. *The Face of the Earth: Natural landscapes, Science, and Culture.* Berkeley: University of California Press, 2011.

Comins, Mike. *A Wild Faith: Jewish Ways into Wilderness, Wilderness Ways into Judaism.* 2007. 2nd printing. Woodstock, VT: Jewish Lights, 2014.

Crosby, Donald A. *More Than Discourse: Symbolic Expressions of Naturalistic Faith.* Albany: SUNY Pess, 2014.

Crosby, Donald A., and Jerome A. Stone, eds. *The Routledge Handbook of Religious Naturalism.* Routledge Handbooks in Religion. Abingdon, UK: Routledge, 2018.

Fleischman, Paul R. *Wonder: When and Why the World Appears Radiant.* Amherst, MA: Small Batch Books, 2013.

Funk, Robert W., and Roy W. Hoover, eds. *The Five Gospels: The Search for the Authentic Words of Jesus.* New York: Macmillan, 1993.

Galston, David. *Embracing the Human Jesus: A Wisdom Path for Contemporary Christianity.* Salem, OR: Polebridge, 2012.

Gleiser, Marcelo. "Unruly Children of Earth: Grow Up." 13.7: Cosmos & Culture: Commentary on Science and Society, Opinion, *National Public Radio* (website), May 18, 2014. https://www.npr.org/sections/13.7/2014/05/18/312170238/unruly-children -of-earth-grow-up/.

Goodenough, Ursula. *The Sacred Depths of Nature.* New York: Oxford University Press, 1998.

———. "Vertical and Horizontal Transcendence." *Zygon* 36 (March 2001) 21–31.

Havea, Jione. "Local Lectionary Sites." In *Christian Worship in Australia: Inculturating the Liturgical Tradition,* edited by Stephen Burns and Anita Monro, 117–28. Strathfield, NSW: St. Pauls, 2009.

Hunt, Rex A. E. *Seasons & Self: Discourses on Being 'At Home' in Nature.* Bayswater, VIC: Coventry, 2018.

Jenks, Gregory C. *Jesus Then and Jesus Now: Looking for Jesus, Finding Ourselves.* Preston, VIC: Mosaic, 2014.

Johnson, Elizabeth A., CSJ. "Deep incarnation: Prepare to be astonished." UNIFAS Conference, Rio de Janeiro. https://sgfp.wordpress.com/2011/02/15/deep-incarnation-prepare-to-be-astonished/.

Kaufman, Gordon D. *Jesus and Creativity*. Minneapolis: Fortress, 2006.

Keen, Sam. *Apology for Wonder*. New York: Harper & Row, 1969.

Keltner, Dacher J., and Jonathan Haidt. "Approaching Awe, a Moral, Spiritual, and Aesthetic Emotion." *Cognition and Emotion* 17 (2003) 297–314.

Meland, Bernard E. "Kinsmen of the Wild: Religious Moods in Modern American Poetry." *Sewanee Review* 41 (1933) 443–53.

———. "The Worship Mood." *Religious Education* 26 (1931) 661–65.

O'Donohue, John. *Divine Beauty: The Invisible Embrace*. London: Bantam, 2003.

O'Donohue, John, and John Quinn. *Walking in Wonder: Eternal Wisdom for a Modern World*. New York: Convergent, 2018.

Oliver, Mary. "I got saved by the beauty of the world." Interview by Krista Tippett. *On Being*, National Public Radio February 5, 2015. https://onbeing.org/programs/mary-oliver-i-got-saved-by-the-beauty-of-the-world/.

Pilcher, Carmel. "Poinsettia: Christmas or Pentecost—Celebrating Liturgy in the Great South Land That Is Australia." *Worship* 81 (2007) 508–20.

Ranson, David. "Fire in Water: The Liturgical Cycle in the Experience of South East Australian Seasonal Patterns." *Compass Theological Review* 26 (1992) 9–12.

Raymo, Chet. "My very distant cousin, the turnip." *Science Musings* (blog), Tuesday, August 6, 2019. https://www.sciencemusings.com/my-very-distant-cousin-the-turnip/. Originally published October 14, 1985.

Rose, Deborah B. "On the Spot: In the Red Centre." In *The Face of the Earth: Natural Landscapes, Science, and Culture*, by SueEllen Campbell et al, 219–23. Berkeley: University of California Press, 2011.

Sanders, Scott R. "Useless Beauty: A Canticle for the Cosmos." 2012. Republished in *Notre Dame Magazine*, 2020. https://magazine.nd.edu/stories/useless-beauty/.

Savage, Nigel. Foreword to *A Wild Faith: Jewish Ways into Wilderness, Wilderness Ways into Judaism*, by Mike Comins, xi–xiv. 2007. 2nd printing. Woodstock, VT: Jewish Lights, 2014.

Smith, Elizabeth. "Crafting and Singing Hymns in Australia." In *Christian Worship in Australia. Inculturating the Liturgical Tradition,* edited by Stephen Burns and Anita Monro, 183–93. Strathfield: St. Pauls, 2009.

Stone, Jerome A. *Sacred Nature: The Environmental Potential of Religious Naturalism*. Abingdon, UK: Routledge, 2017.

Taussig, Hal, ed. *A New Testament. A Reinvented Bible for the 21st Century combining Traditional and Newly Discovered Texts*. Boston: Houghton Mifflin Harcourt, 2013.

Thomas, Abbie. "Western Australian Wildflowers Bloom." *ABC Science* (blog), August 2, 2002. https://www.abc.net.au/science/articles/2002/08/02/2588185.htm/.

Together in Song: Australian Hymn Book II. East Melbourne, VIC: HarperCollins Religious, 1999.

Unitarian Universalist Association. *Singing the Journey: A Supplement to "Singing the Living Tradition."* Boston: Unitarian Universalist Association, 2005.

———. *Singing the Living Tradition*. Boston: Unitarian Universalist Association, 1993.

White, Lynn, Jr. "The Historical Roots of Our Ecological Crisis." *Science* 155 (1967) 1203–7.

Wink, Walter. "The Son of Man: The Stone That Builders Rejected." In *The Once and Future Jesus,* by the Jesus Seminar, 161–80. Santa Rosa, CA: Polebridge, 2000.

www.ingramcontent.com/pod-product-compliance
Lightning Source LLC
Chambersburg PA
CBHW030305100426
42812CB00002B/569